O9-BUA-230

A TEACHER SPEAKS

A TEACHER SPEAKS

by

PHILIP MARSON

DAVID McKAY COMPANY, INC.
New York

LIBRARY OF CONGRESS CATALOGUE CARD NUMBER: 59-12268

MANUFACTURED IN THE UNITED STATES OF AMERICA

VAN REES PRESS • NEW YORK

To my wife Rose Ulin Marson

whose courage has sustained me,

whose self-sacrifice has made
the luxury of teaching possible,

whose sense of beauty has expressed
itself in our home,

whose gentility and generosity
reach out to others.

FOREWORD

by LEONARD BERNSTEIN

On pages 227–228 of this remarkable book, Mr. Marson has seen fit to quote a few lines from a letter I wrote him some years ago. On rereading these words I find them not only immensely true and sincere, but far below the level of praise to which he is justly entitled. In everyone's young life there is always a key teacher, one who emerges from the crowded lists of instructors we have all endured. I am luckier than most in being able to point with gratitude and pride to several such key teachers, in and out of music. These have been minds and personalities that went far beyond merely relaying information, or even opinion; these were spirits that overleapt the discourse, that transcended the given material in such a way as to score a direct hit, mind to mind, heart to heart. This of course happened only intermittently; it would have been unbearable to suffer a constant stream of direct hits. But those hit moments burst like rockets, and illuminated all the grayer moments between. If I say that Philip Marson's name, lo, led all the rest, it is not to make value judgments or comparisons with my other teachers. It is only to say that he taught me something unique, incomparable, invaluable in education, far beyond the teaching of tetrameter or dangling participles or even the glories of English verse: he taught me how to learn. And for this I shall bless him always.

March 15, 1960
New York City

CONTENTS

1. Decision 3
2. Tradition 27
3. Routine 47
4. Contact 71
5. Freedom 91
6. Turning Point 118
7. Decline 134
8. Unity 150
9. Defeat 169
10. Resolution 191
11. Crusade 206
12. Appraisal 221

A TEACHER SPEAKS

1. DECISION

SURVIVAL OF WESTERN INDIVIDUALISM WILL DEPEND UPON trained minds rather than trained missiles. Education, therefore, becomes our greatest concern. Unless the youth of our nation can be induced to gain knowledge and an understanding of the complexities of the world, our way of life will disappear. The most effective instrument to prevent such a disaster is the public school. But schools are only as strong as their faculties. At this critical moment of our history we find ourselves without sufficient personnel, and what personnel we have is unable to function effectively. Convinced that our present weakness can be overcome only if properly understood, I am—for purposes of diagnosis—subjecting myself to autobiographical exposure.

My story covers precisely the period that brought about our present illness. By specifying how one classroom teacher—at the height of his effectiveness—was prevented from performing his essential function, I hope to reveal some of the causes as well as the potential cures for a very sick educational system. The details of my experience can be significant only if they are applicable to all teachers in their present dilemma, and I hope to restrict myself to those details that suggest a solution.

The key to the learning problems of the young is the teacher.

Buildings, facilities, audio-visual aids, and other contemporary advantages are undoubtedly desirable; but we must have, above all else, the capable teacher, and we must make it possible for him to teach. The success of any teacher is dependent on three fundamental conditions: (1) the possession of certain innate characteristics and qualifications; (2) the application of the most important of these characteristics—will power, energy, and patience; and (3) the proper educational climate for teaching and learning. Should any one of the three be lacking, the teacher will be a pedagogical misfit or cripple.

If the gods who preside at birth are kind to the future teacher, they will provide him with the essential characteristics and conditions or give him the ability to develop them. He might be able to get along without some of them; but if he is to be effective and happy, he must have an ample supply. To overcome the natural resistance of most children to irksome and sometimes difficult processes of learning, he needs a sympathy for their pain; for he must realize that they are in the unnatural situation of stationary mental activity instead of mobile physical exuberance. Not only sympathy for their discomfiture, but understanding of the obstacles they are encountering on their rough journey must be inherent in the born teacher. To resist his eagerness for speeding the voyage, he must have patience compounded of the best elements in Job and Hillel. He will also need the judgment of another biblical hero, Solomon, to deal with the thousands of deviations from the norms listed by Gesell and Ilg. And yet, despite the discouragement and mystification that will inevitably be his, he will have to appear at all times cheerfully enthusiastic to the boys and girls in his classes. Obviously, if such an image is to be created, he must have limitless energy and boundless humor. From this characterization, it is clear that if the gods included all these qualities in one person, we should see not only an ideal teacher but a peerless human being. Let us assume, nevertheless, that to whatever degree or in whatever quantity a man might be endowed with these characteristics, his success in dealing with children—and, above all, with adolescents—would be directly proportional to the amplitude of his natural endowment.

Inborn gifts are strictly providential, but so are environmental factors that will largely dominate his life. An educational revolution would certainly affect one's pedagogical career; but less apparent influences can obstruct, color, distort, thwart, and defeat. Whether a lad finds himself growing up in a humming Northern metropolis or a sleepy town in Georgia makes a difference in his outlook, his ambitions, his opportunities; but where his family happens to be living at the time of his birth, he can do nothing about. The accident of birth may make him black or white, rich or poor, Jew or Gentile; and, although he did not select his parents and was not consulted as to his preference, he will soon find that the ones who happen to be his will have a direct bearing on his career as a teacher, or even the possibility of becoming one.

Up to the time I arrived at Boston Latin School, I had spent my life in becoming a thoroughly qualified master of my trade. Trained in four good schools, I felt ready for the challenging assignment. Now I could devote myself, with a clear mind and a free spirit, to my profession. So I thought as on a brisk day in April, 1926, I passed the imposing Harvard Medical School quadrangle. It was not only the weather that quickened my steps. An interview was about to take place with the headmaster, genial and respected Patrick A. Campbell. I was to learn whether or not he looked favorably on my appointment as a member of his English department. To a young teacher the prospect would have been awe-inspiring or at least frightening; but I was no neophyte, nor did I lack confidence. As I approached the building with its massive pillars and its two huge bronze plaques lettered in the Latin vernacular of the school, I turned over in my mind its past achievements and its present reputation. Surely to become part of this great institution would be an incomparable opportunity.

The interview was not difficult. The fact that everybody spoke of the dignified headmaster as "Pat" was a measure of the man. Warmth, interest, and understanding were immediately conveyed in his greeting, his glowing smile, and his informal speech. He told me with simple candor that a place on his faculty was available, that I was entitled to it by virtue of my having earned top spot on the candidates' list, and that he would be delighted to recommend my appointment. He knew, however, that many considerations would have to enter into my decision and advised me in fatherly tones to think about all aspects of it before giving him an answer.

Naturally, as I departed jubilant and lighthearted, my mind leaped to the possibilities of the future. But as Francis Bacon—a much more worldly man than I—once advised, one should "weigh and consider." Many questions loomed and demanded answers. At the time, I was completing my third highly successful year at a good private school. As head of the English Department and director of student activities, I was on the policy-making executive committee of the Rivers Country Day School. My work involved almost all aspects of life at the school: the teaching of classes; supervision of the English faculty from Grade I through the high school; direction of the magazine, which I had established; coaching of the football and baseball teams; putting on plays; and running a student forum. I was a big man in a small school. I had also to take into account the important matter of salary. The year before, when I had been offered a considerable increase by a leading boarding school (Deerfield), Chairman Roland G. Hopkins, of the Board of Trustees, had induced me to stay by means of a one-way three-year contract. It provided an annual income nine hundred dollars more than the maximum that I was to receive in Boston. Certainly a young husband and father could not disregard financial considerations.

To complicate matters even more, I was at that moment invited by Headmaster Samuel Tower to join his South Boston High School faculty. In addition to teaching English, I was to coach teams in the three major sports, for which service I should receive twelve hundred dollars. Thus, a substantial sacrifice in income would be imperative if Boston Latin School was my choice.

My decision, however, had to be determined on other grounds as well. I found myself at an educational crossroad. One clear conclusion disposed of several murky doubts that had been troubling me: To be a true and complete teacher, I should have to give up the joys and advantages of being a coach. Logical and simple as this idea seems to me now, carrying it out at that time was extremely difficult. The activities of the playing field revive, stimulate, and satisfy both player and coach. Informality, honesty, and clarity establish a bond beween man and boy impossible to attain in the classroom. In spite of the knowledge that I was giving up an irreplaceable privilege, I was convinced that my most valuable contribution to the growth of my students was intellectual rather than physical and recreational.

I faced still another set of alternatives: private or public school, small or large classes? Philosophical, pedagogical, and social judgments were involved. Finally, after much mental wrestling with questions that were partly resolved and partly unanswerable, I decided that I must cast my lot with Boston Latin School and leave the wisdom of my choice to the revelations of future events and circumstances. My reasons (or rationalizations) appeared to be sound: (1) a chance in a big public school to teach the many rather than the few; (2) classes based on homogeneous mentality instead of small groups of individuals with widely varying intellectual ability and unified only by their parents' wealth; and (3) the opportunity to help in training local and national leaders. One last complication served to make me more uncertain than ever about the wisdom of my final decision. When I formally resigned from Rivers, I suddenly found myself confronted with an opportunity that a schoolmaster dreams about but does not dare to hope for—the offer of a headmastership of an independent school with the prospect of putting my ideas into action. The Rivers trustees offered it, hoping that I might thus be tempted to stay, but I refused the offer. I had resolved to cast my academic lot with the oldest and most widely respected public school in the nation, Boston Latin School.

I confess, however, that conflicting philosophies and prejudices continued to disturb me as I faced my future at the Boston Latin School. It was difficult to foresee how my personal views and training, which were decidedly on the modern side, would prepare me for life in a school dominated by a three-hundred-year-old classical tradition and a consequent rigid pattern of instruction implicit in the inflexible curriculum. Not only had I attended a comprehensive high school and taken advantage of the elective system by selecting my own easy course of study; but I had continued my wayward educational journey in a very liberal Universalist college, Tufts, where my degree of bachelor of science was mandatory because, like Shakespeare, I knew little Latin and less Greek.

Notwithstanding this temporary uncertainty, my self-assurance was restored as I reviewed my long and carefully planned training and experience as a master craftsman in my chosen field. As an undergraduate at Tufts, I had, after all, concentrated in English composition and literature; and, with teaching definitely chosen as a career, I had selected as supplementary courses only those that I deemed helpful—German literature, with a climactic study during one year of Goethe, Lessing, and Schiller; French, ending in similar fashion with Racine, Corneille, and Molière; several in history and economics (including sociology); and one called theoretical biology, which required the reading of works by Darwin, Huxley, Spencer, Wallace, Tyndall, *et al.*

In addition to this grounding in liberal arts, my educational preparation had included a year of pedagogical studies in a special course given for college graduates at Boston Normal School (later renamed Teachers College). There I had become acquainted with such subjects as the history of education and educational psychology (with emphasis on the progressive principles and theories of Dewey, Kilpatrick, and Thorndike), plus courses in methods and techniques to be applied in the several subjects taught in high schools. As a result of this well-spent year, I must express my gratitude for what I gained in a type of institution which has been much maligned in recent days. Particularly important was the emphasis placed on the presentation of subject matter. I discovered that each teaching unit had to be organized from two points of view: the logical approach, which took into account the information the teacher planned to impart; and the psychological, which was aimed to consider the problems of the learner. These principles had become so thoroughly ingrained in my teaching by the time I was ready for my Latin School appointment that they were unconsciously applied to each lesson.

Was this background and training enough? And even if it was, my inclinations, convictions, and temperament might well prevent success in a hide-bound atmosphere such as I was about to enter.

Would my tendencies make me a maverick, or could I make the adjustments necessary to fit into the traditional scheme of things? But as these doubts continued, I realized that beyond all philosophical considerations, the most important element in my decision to establish myself permanently at Boston Latin School was the desire for complete identification. I could feel comfortably at home only when the past feelings of insecurity were laid at rest. These feelings had deep roots.

Why, in the first place, should anyone—particularly a man—become a teacher? Now that I have completed forty-one years of teaching, I have reached the proper level for perspective. Boys, I have observed, are puzzled by the strange persistence of a man who, they believe, might have succeeded in a world far more challenging than that enclosed by the confining walls of a high school. But they are not the only ones who have wondered: grown-ups, too, have been mystified. Very early in my career, Henry Bellows, then editor of an excellent magazine *The Bellman,* had tried to discourage me with the warning that I was attempting the impossible in trying to teach people how to read and write. Low opinions of the profession had been expressed perennially. Bernard Shaw says somewhere, "Those who can, do; those who cannot, teach." H. L. Mencken has made teachers squirm by stereotyping them as chief breeders of the "great booboisie."

In many ways the belittling of teachers has from time to time led to self-examination; but nothing has broken or even bent my resolution to teach. More potent than insinuations of clowns or cynics, was the remark once made by a respected fellow-teacher: "What I can't stand about this profession is its hypocrisy." It took me many years to understand its full meaning. Not until I had found it necessary to be careful where I was seen, to hide unorthodox views, or to hedge on controversial issues, did I get the full meaning of his observation. With the passing of the years, it became increasingly clear that the American public does not look upon teachers as a group to be admired, respected, or rewarded.

Why, then, should a young man—with a world beckoning—choose teaching as a life career? If he does, he abandons many hopes, dreams, ambitions; for he is asked to give up any chance of wealth, power, and what Milton called "the last infirmity of noble mind"—fame. What can this work possibly offer in place of rewards that motivate millions? In truth, the rewards are few and intangible, but they are strong, vital, and permanent. Often they are not discernible to the one making the decision. I hope, though, when the last words of this account are written, that it will be apparent why, despite bitter and disillusioning experiences, I should—if given a second chance—follow the example of the characters in Barrie's *Dear Brutus* and gladly teach once more.

The choice of a vocation is always difficult. When the selection is tempered by handicaps, it becomes infinitely more complex. When I was born sixty-seven years ago, it seemed to "proper" Bostonians that only the well-born (that is, those of white Protestant ancestry) should be permitted to teach. For many years I was not aware of this unwritten law. Certainly my parents, when they recorded my birth at City Hall, had no inkling of how great a part their origins were to play in their son's professional life. Little did they know that their family name, Marzynski, would sound too foreign to Back Bay ears and that their religious faith would exclude him from consideration for most school positions.

Yankee prejudices would, of course, have no influence on family judgments. Thus, when my mother pictured her favorite brother's life as a well-known and loved teacher in Frankfurt-am-Main, the image became indelibly fixed. This suggestion and others helped to make my parents' German background a prime factor in molding the boy as father to the man. Constant use of *echt-Deutsch* as the household tongue made me not only bilingual, but more sympathetic to people with linguistic problems. I was being prepared indirectly for my vocation.

Happily adjusted though I was at home, strong influences soon began to work at school. It became clear that the foreign roots of the past would have to be buried and that the future demanded complete surrender to American folkways. Both school and playground conveyed vital messages. The most important was that acceptance demanded conformity. Gradually, cultured speech gave way to slurred syllables, glib profanity, and incorrect syntax. Proficiency in sports became an increasingly important goal. To become a star athlete, I devoted hours to practice of such techniques as catching bounding baseballs with irregular "hops," perfecting lay-up shots under a basketball backboard, or developing a spin in spiraling a football. In school, which I found easy enough, I learned to hide carefully any interest in books and to become "one of the boys" by clowning and misbehaving. By the time I was graduated from the Mather School (founded in 1639 and named later for the famous theologian) I had become thoroughly integrated and could now be called a completely American boy.

So thoroughly had I been indoctrinated, that I neglected my studies in order to become an all-around athlete. After gaining prominence as a high school basketball player, becoming captain of the Tufts College freshman football team, and making the varsity baseball line-up, I had become convinced that winning a college letter was more desirable than election to Phi Beta Kappa. Along with these dubious notions, I had come to believe that Americanization assured social acceptance.

My ingenuous assumption made me painfully vulnerable to disillusioning experiences. Perhaps I should have been more aware of the facts of life. In my early teens traumatic incidents should have forewarned even an optimist. Once our entire baseball team—the Arcadias, at the time fourteen-year-old champions of Massachusetts—decided, after a strenuous practice session under the hot sun of Mount Ida, to go for a cooling swim at Savin Hill Beach. In the one-room bathhouse, we quickly stripped. Suddenly an observant pal discovered that I was circumcised and laughingly pointed out the oddity to our teammates. Struck mute with embarrassment, I dawdled until everybody had gone out, slipped quickly into my clothes, and dashed for home. From that day on, I always dressed and undressed in locker rooms with my back to others.

Another incident that should have served as a warning signpost occurred during a summer vacation. I decided to get a job and began the round of Boston employment offices by bounding confidently up the steep steps of a Bromfield Street agency. At the head of the stairs stood a bespectacled, pink-faced Yankee who drawled pleasantly, "What can I do for you today, boy?"

When I replied clearly and firmly, "I'd like to get a job, sir!"

he reassured me by saying, "That's fine; we've got lots of 'em for good lads willing to work. Just fill out this application blank, and I'll be right with you."

When he scanned the completed questionnaire, however, his expression changed, and his words floored me: "Jew-boy, eh? Sorry, nothing today." Walking disconsolately down the long flight of stairs, I decided to forget about summer employment and return to the Dorchester Town Field for more baseball.

With the easy comradeship that athletic success had given me with Christian schoolmates, I soon forgot unpleasant experiences and assumed that all was well. In fact, the first instance of collegiate prejudice seemed amusing rather than prophetic. At Tufts the 1911 freshman football squad, on which I was the starting quarterback, had evidently assumed that my long name was Polish and elected me captain. Immediately fraternities, with their customary speed in corralling athletes, began to rush me. Invited here and there, I, the green neophyte—unacquainted with pledging routines—became confused. Despite my bewilderment, however, I could not help observing that not a single Jew, Catholic, or Negro was a member of any chapter I had visited. Imagine the confusion of the Zeta Psi emissary who was about to pledge me when I asked, innocently enough, if a Jewish boy would be acceptable to his fraters. Needless to say, after his awkward explanation and embarrassed withdrawal, I ceased to be either a desirable prospect or a bewildered innocent.

The incident served a useful purpose; for finally, I was forced to accept the fact that intolerance was to be a permanent factor in my life. Now I would have to combat it; if possible, conquer it; at the very least, recognize it and make adjustments. As a result, I have never been startled since whenever intolerance has reared its ugly head.

Awareness of my handicap produced interesting by-products. Besides making me more introspective, self-reliant, and wary, it also forced me to realize that success depended upon my being much better equipped than my fair-haired colleagues. The result: I changed my academic ways and exerted greater intellectual pressure. Up to this point, I had been satisfied with gentlemanly grades in sufficient number to assure eligibility for scheduled games; but now, as I entered my junior year at college, I became as serious a student as I had been an athlete.

Scholastic interest had been sparked long before by a succession of outstanding teachers. Miss J. Annie Bense, by her emphasis in the ninth grade on the structural niceties of language and her appreciation of the fine arts, had awakened interests that are still with me. William B. Snow, a sharp-witted and perceptive man, by his insistence on absolute accuracy and precision as a teacher of French during my three years with him at Boston English High School, had left ineradicable marks. On the college level, unpretentious but hard-working Albert Hatton Gilmer was an excellent teacher of composition, an eloquent lecturer in literature, and an enthusiastic expert on the theatre. As a former varsity athlete, he knew healthy young men well enough to lead them into the world of poetry through the virilities of Masefield's *The Everlasting Mercy* and Whitman's *Leaves of Grass*. His qualities as a man and as a teacher transmuted learning into a natural process and a delight.

One other teaching genius I encountered as a post-graduate at the Boston Normal School. Scholarly and yet imaginative, Miss Katharine Shute had completely mastered her art—and with her, teaching was just that. Under her direction, a class became a symphony orchestra, each member playing his instrument with his utmost skill. Every lesson was a complete composition, every phrase and grace note distinct and yet related to the whole. She planned each movement with such care that when the piece came to completion, it was so perfectly timed that the dismissal bell rang just a moment later. Never have I seen greater skill in establishing unity of design, relationship of parts, and a mood.

To any professor of liberal arts who scoffs at pedagogy, I need only point to this exemplar of technical perfection as effective refutation. These four great teachers made me wish to go forth and do likewise. Nothing at that time seemed to stand in the way of my resolution—not even love and marriage. Often, I am sure, pedagogical recruits have been discouraged by dreary vistas of poor pay and obscurity. Even greater numbers who themselves might have been willing to take the vows of poverty and work have not been willing to take that of celibacy; and their more worldly wives have pushed them into more lucrative careers. Fortunately I have never been confronted with the problem of having an ambitious woman on my hands. Not only has Rose, my hardy partner of more than forty years, shared my views and been willing to live modestly through a prolonged period of frugality until a profitable summer camp removed financial worries; but she has always encouraged me—through fair weather and foul—to continue the work I have wanted to do.

For ten years, in four well-established teaching laboratories, I put theories to the test, crystallized ideas and convictions acquired during and after student days, and perfected classroom practices. As a fledgling, I tried my wings; and finding in early excursions that they had sufficient native strength and adaptability, I gained confidence enough to fly independently and yet purposefully.

My first workshop was in a middle-income suburban community —Needham, Massachusetts—whose high school in 1917 had an enrollment of some 250 representative boys and girls. When interviewed by the superintendent and the principal, they informed me that as I looked like a man who could handle a troublesome disciplinary situation, they would recommend to the School Committee my appointment as head of the English Department at a salary of $800 per annum. As only one other member of the faculty taught English, the title was somewhat dubious; but I was grateful for the opportunity to teach the upper classes (three of them college preparatory), to plan the course of study, and to select the texts.

The last-named function introduced me to a sordid side of school administration. When requested to examine and recommend the purchase of new copies of Burke's *Speech on Conciliation,* Washington's *Farewell Address,* and Webster's *Bunker Hill Oration,* I proceeded in logical but what proved later to be ingenuous fashion to make a comparative study of every extant edition for its annotations, typography, and cost. When I found that one publisher had included all three speeches in one satisfactory volume at far the lowest price, I made out a requisition for that. The books arrived under the imprint of another company in two volumes at approximately six times the cost. I soon learned that I had been unceremoniously introduced to what some irreverent members of the profession call the "textbook racket."

From the beginning I was aware that students of composition could learn to write only by writing continuously and, for improvement of their product, by helpful corrections and comments on the part of the instructor. With this principle in mind, I assigned weekly themes to be submitted on Mondays and to be returned seven days later. No sooner had I corrected and returned the first few sets of compositions, than I was confronted with a major problem.

Fully as conscientious and eager as the busiest of beavers, I had covered the margins of my students' papers with proofreaders' hieroglyphics and my own considered comments to convey to them why they had received the grades inscribed above the title. A painstaking and time-consuming job it had been; for no matter how fast I read and wrote, each theme took from five to fifteen minutes and thus an average class of some thirty would eat up at least three hours of my precious week-end. At the time, I had five classes, the usual assignment for a beginner—and, may I add, back-breaking for any one.

On Mondays, in accord with my promise, I returned the compositions just before the close of the period. My amazement and dismay are hard to describe as I watched each boy and girl on their way out glance quickly at the marginal notes and corrections and then at the grade before dropping the papers in the waste basket. Realizing that my efforts had been futile and their learning negligible, I resolved to search for a way to remove the first serious roadblock I had encountered to teaching.

During the next few weeks I spent many hours in the Teachers' Room of the Boston Public Library searching through the back files of professional journals. I hoped that they might reveal a successful method of overcoming student inertia, indifference, or resistance. My job was to penetrate the rocky surface and reach the metal below. Finally, I found the tool I was looking for—a fool-proof method of theme correction. This instrument was invented by an instructor of composition at Rice Institute; but as I examined it in detail, I found that it would have to be modified and perfected.

This adaptation, the brain-child of two collaborators at Saint Paul Academy—where I was to spend almost four years after my baptism of fire at Needham—turned out to be a beautiful device. I was aided in setting this trap to ensnare unsuspecting schoolboys by Sherman Cawley, who spent all the rest of his professional life at Taft School and, like me, continued to use our contraption to the last classes that he taught. To the best of my knowledge, he and I were not only the originators but the sole users of our innovation.

Although the workings of a teaching device belong more appropriately in a pedagogical journal, a rough outline may show why we were unable to induce fellow practitioners to adopt it. Most teachers, like other mortals, have an aversion to labor-increasing gadgets; but both Sherm and I were atypical and preferred the extra work load to the producing of an inferior product. Our scheme involved a student's looseleaf notebook, which was divided into three sections: (1) for his returned and corrected themes, which by the end of the year became a sizable volume of his original manuscripts (in some cases, at least, invaluable to posterity); (2) for the correction of all errors in the mechanics of composition (separated into compartments for spelling, capitals, punctuation, grammar, sentence structure, and other sins of omission or commission); and (3) for his notes, lists of books for collateral reading, and teacher's hints and suggestions. It is easy to see that the plan requires careful proofreading and thoughtful criticism on the part of the instructor for each theme and book review, the recording and correcting by the student of every last error, and the careful checking at least twice a year of the notebooks. Obviously the plan calls for work, sweat, and perhaps a few tears for everybody involved; but the results are worth the effort.

During my first year in harness at Boston Latin School, as soon as the authorities became aware of The Method and its effectiveness, they arranged to have the theory explained and its application demonstrated at a meeting of the English Department. Although embarrassed by thus forcing my colleagues to attend a special unscheduled powwow, I had to obey the official request. I knew that a new man could scarcely win friends or even influence people by such procedure. My instincts proved true; for although my captive audience unanimously agreed that it was an admirable scheme, a triumph of efficiency, and a sound technique, I won nary a convert. Despite my failure to proselyte, however, I myself continued to use with great success the Cawley-Marson Method for thirty years.

In each successive school I had become more and more impressed with the importance of the work of the teacher. At the two public schools and at the two private, not only were we influencing youngsters at the most impressionable period of their lives, but for the majority preparing them for college and possibly for positions of leadership.

At that time and until about 1940, one governing influence dominated all preparatory schools. This unifying force was national in scope and reached into rural districts and small towns as well as into big cities. It shaped every curriculum and the course of study in each subject. Even if pupils were not heading for colleges demanding examinations, their studies were dictated by it. This co-ordinating factor, which created cohesive ties among the secondary schools throughout the land, was the agreement among the colleges on what should be taught, how intensively each study should be pursued, and how results should be measured.

The most powerful body in establishing this unity was the College Entrance Examination Board, with offices at Columbia University. Its organization at the turn of the century brought about uniformity in requirements for admission and consequently guided secondary schools in preparing students for both examinations and undergraduate studies. The prestige and widespread influence of the Board may be understood by listing some of the institutions represented by its officers and members: Harvard, M.I.T., Yale, Princeton, Pennsylvania, Bryn Mawr, Wellesley, Andover, Columbia, Mount Holyoke, Radcliffe, Smith, Hamilton, Dartmouth, Cornell, Vassar, Tufts, Williams, New York University,

Wesleyan, Headmasters Association, Head Mistresses Association, Private School Association, Secondary Education Board, and many public school systems.

Clearly numerous benefits would stem from so reputable an educational organization. Its greatest contribution was the establishment of order, unity, standards, and system. Every school and college, every teacher and admissions officer knew exactly what was demanded; and if changes were found desirable from time to time, they were notified in due course so that the necessary adjustments could be made. If such directive power seems to promote too much interference with local authority or tyrannical domination by colleges over secondary schools, I must insist that the order created was infinitely preferable to the chaos which followed its abolition.

To meet the specific requirements set by the Board, the teacher of English had to become a highly qualified specialist. His duties required both a mastery of general knowledge in the fields of grammar, composition, and literature and a thorough understanding of the precise nature of the problems that would confront his students when they entered the examination room. His immediate task was to prepare them for all contingencies; and his success as a teacher of college preparatory English would depend largely on his ability to inspire confidence and to assure satisfactory results.

Until I was forced to take this aspect of my job seriously, I had devoted myself more to understanding and reaching my students than to the technicalities of questions and answers on C.E.E.B. papers. My first trial flight at Needham began my ten-year apprenticeship. It served to acquaint me with the broader problems of approach, organization of subject matter, and division into units of work to complete the projected course of study. My next stint at Saint Paul Academy from 1917 to 1921 proved helpful because I served in a dual capacity as junior master of English and director of athletics. The headmaster—John deQuedville Briggs, son of the illustrious dean at Harvard, LeBaron R. Briggs—like most private school men, even to the present day, viewed with skepticism any exponent of scientific teaching. Always willing, at that time as at this, to discuss any subject—however controversial—I engaged him in many a conversation on advanced teaching techniques just then emerging from Columbia and Chicago *via* the disciples of Dewey, Kilpatrick, and Thorndike. Although I was interested in both philosophical and practical aspects of secondary education, I had not yet been called upon to face the intricacies of the specialized preparation for the Board examinations in the graduating class. As my top section at the Academy was in the eleventh grade, I could afford the luxury of theorizing about instruction while devoting much of my energy to other channels of interest like sports and sundry extracurricular activities.

What I learned as an athletic coach about establishing contact with my students was of great value in the classroom. Before teenagers will either listen or become articulate, they must have complete confidence in the adults they meet. During my first ten years of alternating between public and private schools, I learned the most effective formula in the educational laboratory. To form a compound called student-teacher solidarity, one must use—to bring about the proper synthesis—four elements: ability + time + willingness + enthusiasm. The resultant reaction is worth the effort, for an indissoluble bond is created by the natural affinity between boys and men engaged in any constructive activity.

My predilection for sports now paid off. Fresh out of college and still in excellent condition, I first turned to coaching those branches of athletics in which I had acquired sufficient proficiency and information—football, basketball, and baseball. At that time we as a nation—despite a healthy emphasis on competitive sports—had not yet developed the highly commercial attitudes which have ruined most of our games. I could, therefore, with a clear conscience, encourage every boy to play and thus become happily adjusted to his world. I am still convinced that the independent schools (whether day or boarding) have the right answers to the problems of physical education in their athletics-for-all program.

As director of athletics and coach of football and baseball, I had ample opportunity to test theories and observe results. My duties covered all aspects of the school program, academic and extracurricular. One father, whose boy was on the football squad and also in one of my English classes, expressed his approbation of my dual activity: "I get a terrific bang out of seeing a man who at two o'clock has been pointing out to these bruisers the beauties of Browning and just one hour later is running up and down the field drilling them in line play and backfield strategy." Aside from advantages such circumstances afforded me over the classroom drudge or the strictly professional coach, they opened doors for the study of adolescent behavior inaccessible to psychiatrists, social workers, or school administrators. Furthermore, the trust instilled in boys when they see their English master earnestly engaged with them in producing good teams—and enjoying every minute of action—is, of course, invaluable as an asset when back in the classroom.

Football, above all other games, can impress the most self-centered individualist with the importance of co-operation and with his dependence on others. Ed Sommers, one of the most likable lads I have ever known, was also one of the greatest enigmas to his headmaster and to other members of the faculty. Aside from his refusal to be cudgeled into energetic cerebration, he could not be induced to arrive at school on schedule or to leave it before he was good and ready. Sometimes our Swedish janitor, reluctantly departing at supper time, left Ed still contemplating his navel in the shower room, where he sat for hours on a bench posed like Rodin's *Thinker*. I spotted him more than once at the transfer point on his way home by streetcar at eight in the evening. But slow and maddeningly deliberate as he was on such occasions, just as fast and alert did he become on the gridiron. He was naturally shifty, catlike, and ferocious—clearly the answer to a coach's dream of an ideal halfback. He did everything just right. But could his talent be co-ordinated with his teammates' mediocrity? It could, and it was.

In the same way, Ed Sommers' superlative quality as a pitcher was utilized by the baseball team; for while he was occupied in holding the opposition to a scant run or at most two, he and his fellows always produced enough power to win as a result of special team-play which they had perfected. By means of this device, the high point of my career as a coach was reached when, in my final year at the Academy, we climaxed an unbeaten season by winning the private school championship of the Northwest in beating Shattuck School at Faribault, Minnesota, 5-2. The score shows graphically how the individualistic Ed Sommers, by virtue of his almost perfect control and fast-breaking curve, had prevented Shattuck from scoring more than twice and had thus made it possible for his mates to use their indispensable team strategy. The co-operative effort depended on the perfection of one play, which we had developed by persistent practice. As in most small schools, we could count on very little power-hitting, or, as in this case, not much of any type. Therefore, we spent almost the entire batting drill in perfecting the technique of bunting. The results were gratifying, for even my poorest batters could always be depended upon for sacrifices or, if we were lucky, an occasional infield hit on a perfectly placed dribbler. In the final show-down with Shattuck, our long practice sessions paid off: four of our five runs had been scored on squeeze plays. So memorable did this day become in the annals of the Academy, that when I returned—like Rip Van Winkle—some twenty-five years later to visit, the still active headmaster, John Briggs, looked up from a sheaf of papers on his desk and, after the first shock of recognition, came out with this question: "Tell me, Phil, have you worked the squeeze play lately?"

My teaching had evidently left faint imprint on his mind as compared with my coaching exploits. Honesty demands at this point that I admit some doubt as to the relative merits of classroom and playing field in the complete education of a boy. It is rare indeed that any one in adolescence can experience from any academic situation the uninhibited exhilaration, the practical application of unified group action, or the personal satisfaction possible in sports. I have often wondered since if enthusiasm aroused for efforts of the mind can ever attain the heights reached for those of the body.

Important as extracurricular activities are in the all-around growth of youngsters, they must still be considered as only supplementary to the primary function of a secondary school—that is, intellectual preparation for later life. In the case of a preparatory school, the mastery of academic subjects becomes all-important and must take precedence over all other considerations. In the period I am discussing we had not yet lost our perspective; and the colleges continued to consider scholastic achievement of candidates for admission the paramount qualification. Consequently, their requirements were sufficiently exacting to call for highly skilled teachers at the secondary level. When, therefore, I was given (in 1921) senior classes at Newton composed exclusively of boys and girls preparing for the entrance examinations in English, I realized the seriousness of my assignment and the importance to my students of my competence. From that time on, I became much more concerned with my class work than with extracurricular activities.

Both at Newton and at Rivers I concentrated on perfecting a complete technique to serve a double purpose: first and foremost, to prepare my students thoroughly for the specific examinations they were about to take; and secondly, to give them an extensive course in reading and sufficient practice in writing so that they could later cope with studies on a university level.

But successful as I was during my first ten years, I felt the need to remove an unpleasant obstruction to composure—bigotry. Very early in my life as a teacher, an old hand (I have forgotton who) advised caution in making educational moves. Much like a chess player, a schoolmaster should carefully consider his position, avoid haste, and weigh consequences. After having jumped successively from a small public high school to an excellent academy, from there to large and reputable Newton High School, and then to a semi-administrative post in a country day school, I decided to make my final move to Boston Latin School.

It was final for many reasons. One was a feeling of freedom and identity which came with the removal of the strongest shackle in a chain of prejudice which had bound me. Each move had served to impress upon me an inexorable condition of my life. I had long before learned to accept obstructive circumstances without whimpering and with adequate grace, but I had never submitted to anti-Semitism without self-conscious shame and a desire to find a spot where it would not affect my teaching. Not until I reached Boston Latin School did I gain what should be everyone's birthright—the possibility of carrying on my work without being made to feel like a Hindu untouchable.

One humiliating experience had followed another in my search for complete identity. Each encounter had left its indelible mark. In 1918, after Headmaster John deQ. Briggs of Saint Paul Academy (Minnesota) had examined my papers and interviewed me at the Fisk Teachers Agency in Boston, he said to me: "I'm going to be frank. Never before have I felt the need to consult with my Trustees about a candidate; but in your case I must get approval, for I am not sure that they will accept a man with your religious background. As far as I am concerned personally, I have no prejudices and I am eager to have you with us. If they are agreeable, will you take the position?" I accepted of course; for I should be associated with a leading preparatory school, I should be increasing my salary by six hundred dollars (over sixty per cent), and I could marry the girl to whom I had been engaged for three years. Nevertheless, the provisional nature of John Briggs's decision had made me feel the insecurity which for many years continued to haunt me. Overcome though it was by the unequivocal success which followed in this instance, I found that the same fundamental problems would arise whenever I decided to change positions.

Each year at Saint Paul Academy was a happy one; for I enjoyed my work in the classroom, on the playing fields, and wherever else my several extracurricular activities took me. Socially, too, my wife and I had an exhilarating whirl greater than any since. We were entertained lavishly by parents of my pupils, among whom were sons and heirs of the "Empire Builder" James J. Hill, lumber king Weyerhauser, plumbing magnate Ordway (of Crane and Ordway), Supreme Court Justice Pierce Butler, railroader Ralph Budd, Solicitor-General William Mitchell, and other equally prominent Saint Paulites. Yes, we were wined and dined, invited to spend vacations at country estates located near such spots as White Bear Lake and the Saint Croix River, and asked to join interesting groups on many levels—social, economic, artistic, and political. But, after three years of interesting activity, we wished to return home—and for sentimental, almost foolish reasons. The most important one was strictly emotional; for I could not remove from my mind's eye the vision of my father's expression the last time he said "Good-bye and good luck" to us as we boarded the West-bound train at the end of the summer. I decided then that, despite great professional success and almost complete social adjustment, I would look for a position in the East.

Oddly enough, I had still not realized the full impact of the forces of bigotry. I continued to be ingenuous enough to believe that character, personality, and deeds were sufficient assurance of the opportunity to teach anywhere; and, after all, I had certainly written a brilliant record at the Academy. It took only a short time, however, to make me realize that I was receiving very few replies to letters of application—and those few were politely worded rejections. After many more perfunctory "brush-offs" without a single interview, I was forced to the conclusion that I must rid myself of my foreign-sounding name. Despite inner rebellion at what seemed like surrender, I went to court to Americanize a highly individualistic family symbol and to lose part of the valuable identity I had already established. Although ostensibly easy for actors, musicians, and writers to shed this outer mark of personal identification, it seemed to me a serious defeat.

Its practicality, however, was quickly proved. I had no sooner changed my name than numerous cordial replies including invitations to confer and later to join faculties poured in. It was not until I returned to Boston in 1921, with a new-born daughter to support but without a position, that I got what I wanted. When I was notified of an opening at Newton Classical High School, I was happy to apply. As soon as I entered the office of my interviewer, Samuel Thurber—nationally known teacher of English, son of an equally famous educator of the same name—I was welcomed with open arms. The reason for his enthusiasm was revealing: he had just returned from a trip through New England in a fruitless search for a suitable man to fill the vacancy and had interviewed twenty-seven candidates, all of whom looked, talked, and acted as though they should be wearing lace panties. As I was the first one with visible signs of masculinity, he was more than glad to find that I also had the qualifications and hired me on the spot. As he had asked me no questions concerning race or religion, I assumed that these factors did not matter. But this was the first time I had effectively used my abbreviated name and therefore had misgivings about my assumption. Later I was to learn that I had been accused of having come to Newton under false colors. Naturally I had some consciousness of guilt for not having volunteered the unrequested information. I was uncomfortable for the rest of my stay.

When Robert W. Rivers, founder and headmaster of the Rivers Country Day School, came along with an offer of a more challenging job with a big increase in salary, I was glad to rid myself of these self-conscious apprehensions. Again, however, I was confronted with my undemocratic bête noire. This time it took a new form. During the inevitable interview, Mr. Rivers explained smilingly that he, of course, had no feelings about engaging a man of Hebrew antecedents; but his clientèle might well object, and he wondered if it would be possible for me to avoid revealing this well-hidden fact. My reply was short but explicit: I did not make a practice of wearing on my sweatshirt a sign proclaiming "I am a Jew"; but I should have to reserve the right to be truthful if any boy or his parents asked me a question calling for a direct answer. Although he offered me the job and I accepted, this conversation could hardly reassure an already battered young man. Thus, when I saw a chance to throw off this unjust and unnecessary handicap, I jumped at it.

The chance was hatched out of the hard shell of bigotry which had surrounded me for so long. Even though my position as a teacher and as a policy-shaping administrator at Rivers was secure, I was worried about the future—partly because the financial structure of the school was precarious, but mostly because a shake-up in the Board of Trustees and a new headmaster could produce antagonistic forces strong enough to unseat me. With such misgivings and no assurance of permanent tenure, I began to give more and more thought to the advantages of a big city school system like Boston, where iron-clad examinations seemed to decide standings on lists for appointment, where tenure and pension plans were firmly established, and where a merit system determined promotions. I thought a sense of security would permit me to function as a teacher at the top of my form. The competitive tests—administered under the chairmanship of an incorruptible and able veteran of many academic wars, Joel Hathaway—were fair, though exhaustive and searching. Teachers of English were subjected to four major sets of examinations: (1) English and American literature; (2) English history; (3) composition and rhetoric; and (4) pedagogy. When the results were published in 1926, I was happy to find that I was placed at the head of a list of some twenty-eight candidates, far ahead of my nearest rival.

Consequently, by virtue of the School Committee rules and regulations, any Boston headmaster having vacancies in his English faculty would be required to offer me the first position available. This system persists to the present time; and, despite some weaknesses, guarantees every man and woman a fair chance and an equal opportunity. Such a plan—if adopted on a wider scale for county, state, or nation—would assure at the very least fundamental standards of scholarly achievement as well as the observance of fair play in the selection of the fit and qualified.

2.

TRADITION

ENTERING BOSTON LATIN SCHOOL—EITHER AS A MASTER OR AS A student—was a significant event. From that moment one became part of American history-in-the-making. The very halls and walls were saturated with a dominant atmosphere created by a sacred tradition, an exciting heritage, and a dynamic life. It was felt at once, and it remained as a permanent and pervasive force.

In the school catalogue, a quotation from the colonial *Town Records* revealed to the newcomer that "on the 13th of the second month, 1635 . . . att a Generall meeting upon publique notice . . . it was . . . generally agreed upon that our brother Philemon Pormort shall be intreated to become schoolmaster for the teaching and nourtering of children with us." This action to establish the first public school in America was due in large measure to the efforts of the Reverend John Cotton, who wished to produce a replica of the Free Grammar School of Boston, England, in which Latin and Greek were taught.

Beginning on that day in 1635, only five years after the founding of Governor Winthrop's Massachusetts Bay Colony, the school has taken in boys and turned out men who have made history. A new master is awed and almost staggered by the responsibility he has assumed; but at the same time he is also impressed with the importance of his task and the significance of the school in the life of the community and the nation. With the years my knowledge of and respect for this ancient institution continued to increase as I came to realize its close relationship to the birth and development of American democracy and the astounding number of its "boys" who had become not only founding fathers but national leaders in almost every conceivable field of activity. In some circles, particularly in recent times, claims have been continually made that the narrow and rigid classical curriculum and the insistence on behavioral conformity stunted intellectual growth and creative impulse. Genius was smothered and individuality stamped out. The argument impresses with its surface logic, but it is not borne out by the facts.

A mere listing of significant alumni names is sufficient to demolish theoretical suggestions, but consideration of what they mean leads us into many areas where men have exercised free minds and bold spirits. Above all, the men named below exemplify originality, rebellion, independence, courage, eccentricity, and creative genius. To accentuate not only their individualism but their influence on their fellows and their times, I am placing them chronologically in the several periods of our history:

COLONIAL TIMES (1635-1775)

Among the boys enrolled during the school's first year (1635), just before Harvard College was founded to take care, as some wag has suggested, of the first Boston Latin School graduates:

JOHN HULL—Mint Master
JOHN LEVERETT—Governor of the Province of Massachusetts Bay

The first of four alumni who have served as presidents of Harvard:

A second JOHN LEVERETT, who administered the College from 1707 to 1724
COTTON MATHER—theologian, scholar, witch-baiter, scientist

Prominent Revolutionists

HENRY KNOX—General, Continental Army; later Secretary of War in Washington's Cabinet

Five Signers of the Declaration of Independence:

SAMUEL ADAMS—firebrand of the Revolution
BENJAMIN FRANKLIN—free thinker and one of the most versatile Americans of all time
JOHN HANCOCK—President of the Continental Congress
WILLIAM HOOPER—Member of the Continental Congress from North Carolina
ROBERT TREAT PAINE—prosecutor of British troops indicted for murder in the Boston Massacre trial

Other prominent citizens, Loyalists as well as Patriots:

JOSIAH QUINCY—defender of Captain Preston and his Royal troops in the Boston Massacre trial
JAMES BOWDOIN—benefactor to the college named for him and founded in 1802 under a charter for the benefit of boys "not rich enough to go to Harvard."
GOVERNOR THOMAS HUTCHINSON—author of a history of Massachusetts which reflects his loyalty to the Crown
SIR WILLIAM PEPPERELL—son of the first American-born baronet
ISAAC COFFIN—Admiral in the Royal Navy

FROM REVOLUTIONARY DAYS TO THE END OF THE CIVIL WAR (1776–1865)

EDWARD EVERETT—orator, statesman, educator
RALPH WALDO EMERSON—philosopher, essayist, poet
CHARLES BULFINCH—architect of State House (Boston) and Capitol (Washington)
THOMAS BULFINCH—author of famous *Mythology*

Many famous Abolitionists, among them these leaders:

CHARLES SUMNER—United States Senator who threw Congress into a frenzy in 1856 with a powerful speech, "The Crime Against Kansas"
WENDELL PHILLIPS—orator against slavery, capitalism, and exploitation of workers and immigrants
HENRY WARD BEECHER—a great minister and inflammatory orator

FROM 1866 TO 1926

EDWARD EVERETT HALE—minister, orator, author
CHARLES W. ELIOT—educational reformer and president of Harvard
SAMUEL P. LANGLEY—physicist and pioneer in aeronautics, who in 1896 had constructed a plane which flew 3,000 feet five years before the Wright brothers had finished their first glider
PHILLIPS BROOKS—orator, Episcopal Bishop of Boston
HENRY LEE HIGGINSON—banker, founder of Boston Symphony Orchestra
DARIUS COBB—artist
CHARLES FRANCIS ADAMS—minister to Great Britain
GEORGE SANTAYANA—philosopher, poet, essayist
BERNARD BERENSON—critic and collector of fine arts

The record of Boston Latin School is history; but as a new master, I was concerned with the present. In 1926 the school was a teacher's paradise. Security and opportunity stimulated effort. The basic ideology was simple and clear: willing and able boys, by means of a traditional classical curriculum, were to be thoroughly prepared to meet the requirements of the most exacting colleges. As a result, the success of a teacher was measured almost exclusively by the effects of his instruction as shown by the final gauge—examinations set by the College Entrance Examination Board. To achieve the goals of the school, the headmaster and his kitchen cabinet established policies that became unwritten laws.

Probably the most important of these was that the master was absolute ruler of his domain—the classroom. No one questioned his authority, interfered with his methods, or criticized his procedures. Boys or parents (even if they were officials in the Boston political hierarchy or members of the School Committee) would not presume to question grades or the application of discipline. If anyone attempted to argue about a decision, he was arbitrarily brushed aside. No appeal for mercy, charity, or even justice could alter the circumstances. This situation was often painful and unreasonable for the boys; but for the teacher, strong or weak, it was ideal. The feeble and incompetent masters were buttressed, if only temporarily and partially; the sturdy and capable were inspired to produce almost incredible results, as evidenced by school morale and the quality of the students turned out.

From the beginning, I had no desire for a position more challenging or gratifying than that of classroom master at the Boston Latin School. Here I could attain my ultimate objectives. Exercising my skill as a teacher, I could create conditions favorable to the learning process of my students. What more could a man want?

Percy Marks once entitled an essay on education "Under Glass" to suggest that a school was really a greenhouse in which the best possible conditions should be provided for the nurture of young plants. Boston Latin School, during my first fifteen years there, was just such a greenhouse. It was an inspiring workshop for the interested horticulturalist, for conditions had been created prior to his arrival favorable to intellectual health and growth.

A tradition of scholarship had been firmly established. The wisdom of antiquity was emphasized even before one entered the building. Carved in the granite of the terrace railing was a Latin inscription composed by a devoted alumnus and renowned classicist—Dr. Robert Montreville Green, '98, professor of anatomy at the neighboring Harvard Medical School. Translated, it read: "This new and enlarged building, devoted to the old-time salutary learning and to the study of the humanities, for the prosperous years to come, with the greatest confidence, hope, and love, to our boys reverently and to our America most gratefully we dedicate." On the great bronze plaques facing the street on each wing of the façade and flanking the main entrance on Avenue Louis Pasteur, were reminders also in the ancient tongue. On the right Cicero stated, "These studies nourish youth, delight old age, adorn prosperity, and offer a refuge and solace for adversity"; while on the left Juvenal admonished, "The greatest respect is due a boy. It is pleasing that you have given to the country and to the people a citizen if you are making him a citizen fit for his country."

As one became increasingly part of this tradition, the atmosphere of the school stimulated effort, created respect for learning, and instilled admiration of intellectual achievement. The student with the keen mind and the will to apply it was in high repute.

He was in no danger of being considered odd, obnoxious, or traitorous by the less studious; for there were too many others like him, and the faculty gave no quarter to those who preferred to devote their energies more to the athletic and recreational side of school life than to the academic. The aims of those in charge had always been specifically and strictly scholastic, and any student activities carried on outside the classroom would perforce be voluntary and supplementary. Therefore, if grades suffered by virtue of time used for play instead of for study, the boy accepted the verdict of his masters as final, irrevocable, and just.

The specific objective of the school—preparation for Harvard—was always kept in mind and governed all matters of policy as well as of personal procedure. It dominated every action of the classroom master; for his standing with his superiors and with his colleagues depended on his ability to ready his boys for admission to the university. As the requirements were until about 1940 well defined and strictly academic, the individual teacher knew exactly what was expected of him. His reputation would depend on the examination grades achieved by his boys in the "Boards." "Examination grades," I say; for whatever the teacher's original estimates of the boys' ability might have been—accurate or not, fair or unreasonable—they were ignored as long as everybody in the class passed and a goodly number received honors as judged by the Board readers. Thus, the student's grades became the final gauge of the teacher's ability. The methods he employed were neither observed nor questioned, provided only that good results were obtained in the examinations. But should his boys fail to pass in sufficient numbers—say, 90 per cent of them—he was quietly and unceremoniously relegated to the limbo of lower classes, out of harm's way, and permanently tagged as a pleasant (or unpleasant) fellow but unfit for the work at hand. Thus, juniors and seniors were assured that they would be conditioned for the big game by the most effective coaches available. These men might not always be the most congenial on the faculty; but they had the ability, by whatever methods, to impart information essential to their students' entering the college of their choice. The boys recognized their competence and, if they could not always love them, respected them.

This respect for their masters was accompanied by a pride in the school and its academic achievements. The school was known throughout the land, but it was admired and cherished by the residents of the city. In fact, it was so highly esteemed that parents considered graduation from Latin School a mark of distinction for their sons. Public officials not only called attention to the school in speeches but also took visitors from all over the world to this showplace of scholarship. Such admiration and acclaim caused many boys to submit to the rigors of its curriculum and the absolutism of its standards. As a result, masters could impose with impunity whatever labors they deemed most efficacious for their purposes. This great asset gave them immeasurable power and innumerable opportunities for both greatness and meanness.

For almost three centuries the dedication of successive faculties to the primary objectives of the school had been a prime factor in establishing the right climate for growth. Each headmaster had felt the influence of the past and the necessities of the present as he assumed his duties. The great names among the alumni, the excellent reputation of the school, and the quality of the student body all reminded the headmaster that he had to instill in all members of the faculty a feeling of respect for what had been done in the past and a determination to carry on. Upon my arrival in 1926 and for about fifteen years thereafter, I was confident that the atmospheric conditions were fixed and would continue. Surely the policies of both headmasters during that period (Campbell and Powers) were aimed to assure permanence.

What they conceived to be the purposes of the school and their part in furthering them was clear enough. Both loyal graduates, they were imbued with enthusiasm for its traditional principles and practices. Pat Campbell, '89, often recalled, for the benefit of outlanders like me, incidents and personalities that would convey to us the spirit and glory of the school. Usually he spoke of the giants among the masters he revered as a young man. Among others, he singled out particularly the famous teacher of classical languages, "Cudjo" Capen, who, like the Colonial academician Ezekiel Cheever, taught until he was eighty-five and was a law unto himself. His method of grading, for instance, was peculiar; and on one occasion, as a result of a system devised to give extra credit for voluntary recitations, he awarded a student—William Calley, later an admiral—a monthly mark of 110 per cent.

Often, however, Pat Campbell spoke with admiration of his immediate predecessors. Dr. Moses Merrill he called the "rock upon which the success, the scholarship, the integrity, and the growth of the school was founded." His favorite reminiscence concerned Arthur Fiske, who had achieved distinction as a Greek scholar and classicist. Although seemingly delicate and physically unimpressive, he proved to be one of the strongest headmasters in the history of the school. An example of his uncompromising standards and courageous resistance to political pressures was occasionally cited by Pat to impress upon us the need for independence when meting out justice to students. When the School Committee voted to issue diplomas to boys whom Fiske had refused to graduate, he addressed the committee in his peculiar nasal drawl: "Yes, I thought you might; but I can't bring myself to sign them." The boys in question were not graduated. Such integrity, which had been accepted by every headmaster up to that time, was expressed also on the matter of curriculum: "I shall never give an order which, to my mind, is the first step toward making Boston Latin School second rate."

Just prior to Pat Campbell's ascendancy, Henry Pennypacker, who had also been a renowned teacher of Greek, continued the strong rule and firm adherence to principle established by previous administrators. In a booming voice and with a flashing wit, he taught his classes and addressed assemblies. Of him an alumnus said, "He is one of the great men of old whose portraits you see hanging in the hall, but him you can call back to plod with you, if only for an hour, the weary march of the Ten Thousand or camp with you on the Trojan plain." The reference applied to the fact that at the time (1932) our former head was accessible to us in his post of Director of Admissions at Harvard. Both Pat

Campbell and Joe Powers, colleagues of Henry Pennypacker at Latin School, often prevailed upon him to return to the school. In this way, and in many others, we were constantly reminded of our indebtedness to its past and of our duty to preserve its well-earned reputation.

When Joe Powers, a teacher of mathematics for twenty-three years, succeeded Pat in 1929, he voiced his profound belief in all aspects of Latin School tradition, theory, and practice. When interviewed, he made clear that no diminution of zeal in maintaining the ideals of the past would be countenanced. A reporter put the question directly to him: "An objection has been made that the school holds too many of its traditions and ancient customs, thus making it old-fashioned. What is your attitude on this objection?" The reporter was answered at once: "As long as my administration continues," said Powers, "the traditions will be upheld. . . . They are really the backbone of the school. . . . To remove them would lower its high standards and destroy its individuality. . . ."

With such assurances from men in command, I was certain that the work of the teacher would be respected and guarded. No forces within the school could or would disturb the continuity of the practices of the past. The members of the faculty, I found, were in complete accord. The masters, almost without exception, believed in the basic theory and the established procedures. Nearly all of them—particularly those entrusted with the upper classes—were veterans of long standing. At least twelve masters had begun their service in the school at the turn of the century. Not until 1935 did any one of these men retire, and then only at the compulsory retirement age of seventy, after having taught for not less than thirty-four years, with one master (Jeff Winslow) having completed forty-four years of continuous work in the classroom. Stability of staff made for uniformity of practice, excellence of performance, and harmony of spirit. Typical of this nucleus which formed a thoroughly unified organization, the two who retired first—Norton in 1935 and Henderson a year later—will serve to illustrate the quality of the faculty when I came to the school.

Both William Kimball Norton and William Pride Henderson entered the Boston Latin School as students in the same year and were graduated from Harvard in the same class in 1888. In the *Liber Actorum,* the yearbook of 1935, the Dedication reads: "To William Kimball Norton, who has so ardently cherished the ideals and traditions of the Latin School, who has so carefully guided our faltering steps towards the very top; who has been to us the symbol of Latin School perseverance." In his Benediction on the opposite page, the master remarks, "Fifty-six years cover the associations and recollections of the old school." Considering that this span represents over one-sixth of the life of the Latin School, one can understand the significance and influence of such a generation of masters in the matter of continuity of a tradition. But Billy Norton did not represent age and rigidity; he was to his last day in the classroom youthful, exuberant, and genial. His classes were happy, carefree, and occasionally even hilarious. Discipline rarely intruded on freedom. Only when things got really out of hand, did "Uncle Billy" invoke what had become his well-known battle-cry: "I mark you severely—*one mark!*" This outburst symbolized the limit of his impatience; for his genial personality permitted nothing worse. When interviewed, he revealed his interests: horticulture, puzzles (he was Puzzle Editor for several national publications), and bowling. Although Billy Norton's approach to teaching was highly unorthodox, his adherence to Latin School dogmas was unswerving and unquestioned.

Much more traditional in manner and method was Bill Henderson, described in the 1936 annual as the "embodiment of that quality called the Latin School spirit." At Harvard he was an outstanding student—winning second-year honors in classics, final honors in modern literature, and election to Phi Beta Kappa. After serving his apprenticeship in New Jersey, he returned to Latin School in 1897, where he was promptly installed as the master of "Botany Bay," a section named for the famous penal colony in Australia and made up of pupils described as "terribly stupid or stupendously terrible." In 1905 he became head of the French department, which he administered for thirty-one years. On his departure, he said:

Fortunate indeed is the man who leaves his work with happier impressions than mine. It is the teacher's lot to grow fond each year of a group in his own room only to bid them farewell in the early summer. Last September I wondered what fortune would deal me for roommates in my final year. Let me assure the boys of 303 that I was not unmindful of the little kindnesses that my partial helplessness of the early fall [caused by a damaged arm] made welcome, though those who showed them to me have forgotten them. . . . They will carry away with them, those boys of the strong lungs and friendly faces, my very good wishes. . . . Five headmasters have reigned in my time; each has been my friend; each has made for me days of pleasantness and a path of peace. To the present Head I owe many courtesies, and, notably on the occasion of one of my major errors, a fine forbearance. . . . In my own department I have been surrounded for twenty-seven years with a personal loyalty that has been my wonder and my joy. My colleagues I count my friends. . . . By them my mistakes have been lightly passed over; my days have been brightened by genial fellowship. I shall miss them. . . .

These words express well the spirit of co-operation, camaraderie, and purpose felt by all members of the faculty in those happy years before World War II. Alumni and student body bolstered the *esprit-de-corps,* both by words and deeds. In the very year when Messrs. Norton and Henderson were getting ready to retire, George Santayana, '82, wrote on the occasion of the Latin School Tercentenary:

In spite of all revolutions and all the pressure of business and all the powerful influences inclining America to live in contemptuous ignorance of the rest of the world, . . . the Latin School, supported by the people of Boston, has kept the embers of traditional learning alive, at which the humblest rushlight might always be lighted; has kept the highway clear for every boy to the professions of theology, law, medicine, and teaching, and a window open to his mind from these times to all other times and from this place to all other places. . . .

The merely modern man never knows what he is about. A Latin education, far from alienating us from our own world, teaches us to discern the amiable traits in it, and the genuine achievements; helping us, amid so many distracting problems, to preserve a certain balance and dignity of mind, together with a sane confidence in the future.

. . . New ideas in their violence and new needs in their urgency pass like a storm; and the old earth, scarred and enriched by those trials, finds itself still under the same sky, unscarred and pure as before.

The proof of a plan and procedure, educational or any other, is in the results. Records bear out philosophers like Santayana and the supporters of orthodoxy at the Latin School. Some great names from the alumni roster were listed early in the chapter; but the achievements of our graduates during the years under scrutiny (1926-1940) will serve further to justify confidence in the ideology and the system and explain the reluctance to modify it. Miscellaneous items from the columns of the school magazine, the *Register,* speak for themselves:

Item:

Harvard College was founded in 1636. For the past 296 years, Boston Latin School has been sending a steady stream of scholars through the portals of the University. Over fifty years ago, a well-known graduate of both schools remarked that "the Latin School dandled Harvard College on her knees." Since then, the situation is unchanged. That the calibre of the students whom we send . . . in these days is up to standard is well attested to by the fact that we have gained permanent possession of the Phi Beta Kappa Trophy donated by the Harvard chapter. [NOTE: The award was made to the school for having obtained the highest average in the nation in the College Board examinations during a seven-year period—1925 to 1931.]

Item:

Shades of '28 . . . The four young men named below have merely strengthened the opinion of Harvard that Latin produces the best. Phi Beta Kappa choices—Isenberg, Kozodoy, Sawyer, and Zoll (in his junior year) who leads the class. . . . At Yale, Bernard A. Herman, '29, won a Yale Club Charm as one of the first ten in the Freshman Class. . . . John J. Hessian, '31, has received five A's for his first year's work at Harvard. He is ranked in Group I on the Dean's list. . . . Boston Latin School ranked second in the list of schools with men on the Dean's list. Of 81 Latin boys, 25 (or 30.9 per cent) made it.

Item:

Teddy White, '31, and Harvard, '35 (*summa cum laude*), has a fellowship in China. . . . Bowdoin College recently announced (1940) that Latin School has won the cup awarded annually to the secondary school whose representatives in the freshman class maintain the highest scholastic grades. . . . Dean B. A. Thresher of M.I.T. presented to Mr. Powers, for the Library, a prize volume—*The History of Mathematics*—in recognition of the work of Arthur Vershbow, '39, who earned the award for his school by ranking first in a particular subject and among the first five in all studies in the class of six hundred.

The continuous flow of honors and the persistent reminders of past performance had the desired effect on contemporary students. When a reporter from a national magazine visited the school and interviewed seniors who hade been subjected to the rugged curriculum and strict discipline of the six-year course, he was surprised at the replies. "I'll tell you why we come here," said one. "It's to train the old thinking apparatus, the same as a football player trains his muscles. After a boy gets out of here, he can apply himself to almost anything." "You learn to work here," said another. "You learn that you don't get anything for nothing." A third boy summed up what his classmates had been repeating: "There's no short cut to education. It's hard work—but that's what we come here for."

The same reporter related an incident which illustrates the adherence of Latin School to the practices which had established its character, its individuality, and its reputation. A few years after the tercentenary, the director-general of schools in Tasmania (Australia) visited the school. The headmaster, Joe Powers, accompanied the visitor on a tour of the building; and as they walked, they conversed.

"Do you give Greek?" asked the director-general.

"Certainly. What year do you wish to see?"

"What year?" asked the visitor incredulously.

"We teach three years of Greek," explained the headmaster.

The director-general sighed. "I'm in heaven." Then he told of his visits to other American public schools. In California, a high school principal had told him. "We're the last word," and led him into a gymnasium full of card tables and chairs. Across each table a boy and a girl faced each other.

"What's this?" the director-general had asked.

"This is our class in social contacts," the principal proudly explained.

"What for?"

"It's hard for boys and girls to meet one another. Here they develop social skills."

"And you give *credits* for this?"

"Why, certainly!" replied the principal somewhat miffed. Small wonder, then, that the Tasmanian, after such experiences, found Boston Latin School an intellectual heaven.

For the schoolmaster who wished to teach, it could be termed just that. With the wholehearted support of the community, the backing of influential alumni, and the co-operation of the selected student body, the fortunate masters who taught the upper classes worked under ideal conditions. The unfit or the unwilling among the boys had left the school before they had to face the formidable college entrance examinations. The 35 per cent who had survived the rigors of the course were highly intelligent, studious, and eager. Pride in the school, unity of purpose, and complete efficiency in meeting the academic demands of the colleges combined to make Boston Latin School an ideal workshop.

Almost perfect conditions made teaching fruitful and learning inevitable. Whatever the temperament or the methodology of the individual master, he became easily adjusted to the over-all academic pattern. He might be a precisionist like Joe Hobbs, a purist like Mark Russo, or a paternal guide like Bill Pierce. One could find as many varieties of teachers as there were members of the faculty, which numbered about eighty to care for the 2,500 boys. Martinets or inspired performers, rigid disciplinarians or free-wheeling liberals, tempestuous firebrands or mild tranquillizers—we had them all; but they were unconsciously absorbed in the amalgam that was the Latin School.

After only one year in the school I had sensed the power and influence of tradition and system. I was, therefore, certain when I faced my first senior division in 1927, that I had found my niche in the world of education. This confidence stemmed not only from ten years of unbroken success, but from the knowledge that the boys in my classes were equal to any tasks I might set for them, would carry out all assignments unquestioningly, and, most important, were eager to learn. Thus, all I had to do was to plan the work and to individualize the instruction so that each lad would realize his greatest potential.

Such objectives are, of course, commendable, but are they attainable? Certainly they are under such conditions; but even then, attainment requires planning, insight, and back-breaking labor. Although the classes that faced me were more homogeneous in ability and aims than in any other American school, individual differences were still great enough to pose the usual pedagogical dilemma of shooting at a mythical norm. In one situation I was verbally assailed by slower students who protested the length of a reading assignment. The complaint justified investigation, and I therefore conducted a simple but reasonably accurate experiment. In this ninth-grade class I had the boys read and briefly summarize in writing a seven-page chapter of Jack London's *The Call of the Wild,* surely a fair sample of simple narrative prose. The fastest boy in the room finished in 7 minutes flat; the slowest, in 28. Obviously, if it took the one youngster four times as long to perform the task as it did the other, the problem of home assignments could not be lightly resolved. To be just and at the same time cover the minimum ground is not a simple or easy act.

What does the reasonable teacher do? He must not be guided by the rapid reader with the photographic mind. Macaulay startled adults when, as a child, he recited from memory long poems after only one reading. In that first senior division Arnold Isenberg emphasized the point I am making. When a book report of nonfiction came due, he came to my desk with a list of some twenty titles of long and difficult works to ask which one I should prefer to have him discuss. Among them I remember Renan's *Life of Christ,* the Beards' *Rise of American Civilization,* Wells' *Outline of History,* and Durant's *Story of Philosophy.* This type of student

I have met only once or twice in four decades; and I should not, of course, cite him as representative. In the same class, in fact, were boys looking for the thinnest acceptable book. From experiences such as these and from reading and observation, the conclusion is inescapable that in assigning class study or in suggesting books for collateral reading, a teacher must acknowledge and act upon wide differences of ability, taste, and will.

This knowledge led me to definite procedures in pursuit of my first great aim: to develop in my students the habit of reading good books. For the best results, my methods had to be many-sided and flexible. In a school which has a demanding curriculum with long hours of outside preparation, additional pursuits, whatever they may be, must be strictly limited. Reading of any kind, whether volitional or compulsory, becomes a problem even for the habitual or rapid reader. Thus, I had to make sure that my approach was psychologically sound.

My first concern, not only for the best results in reading but in writing and speaking, was to create a natural and friendly atmosphere. The essential rapport would then be established with every boy in the class, whatever his tastes, temperament, or endowment. How can this be done? Although not a simple or quick process, the teacher can from the first meeting project, by means of spraying with an efficient mental shotgun, pellets of sympathy and understanding that may reach the most unpromising and resistant teenager. He will have to employ a mixture of humor and seriousness, candor and subtlety, simplicity and challenge in his effort to stimulate the interest and sustain the attention of the athlete, the intellectual, the love-sick, the politically awakened, the musician, the mechanically minded, the shy introvert—in short, everybody. A man-sized task, but it can be done.

The bond must be cemented, no matter how. The miracle may be wrought by incidental mention of an infield fly which spelled defeat for the Red Sox the day before or the breaking of an interscholastic track record. Passing reference to a popular song or a Beethoven symphony might trap the music-lovers. Well-placed and not-too-obvious comments or even serious discussions of teen-age problems, in school or out, may crystallize the essential relationship.

The fact that an adult, and a teacher at that, can be interested in things that really matter to the boy and goes out of his way to establish contact makes an immediate and lasting impression. When, after sufficient time has passed and he has given every one of his boys the feeling that he is personally involved in their future well-being—social, athletic, artistic, or intellectual—the real work of education can begin.

The boy then feels that his teacher knows what he is talking about, is sympathetic to youthful tastes and desires, and understands adolescent problems and difficulties. Now suggestions will be heeded, and action will follow. Not until this meeting of the minds takes place, can the educational process begin; but when it does, the sparks ignite the fuel and may even start a full-scale blaze. When the brightness and all-consuming intensity of the fire increases, the satisfactions of the arsonist, who knows that the combustion was not entirely spontaneous, are as deep as they are boundless.

The trick is not magic performed with mirrors or with the help of props, but it is nevertheless the work of a magician, and it is startling—even to the performer. Whenever the act is successful, it is reassuring and encourages the teacher to work with every student, no matter how unpromising have been his previous efforts.

Every craftsman has his own techniques, and I had mine. To induce a non-reader to begin his first good book, I had to become acquainted with him first. What manner of boy was he? Athlete or nature-bug? Curious or sensitive? Gregarious or shy? Worker or shirker? Any facts or valid impressions gleaned from apparent or hidden sources would help an effective approach. To gain such data, I had to observe my students constantly for personal clues, to frame questionnaires, to study themes for subjective hints, to listen carefully when they conversed with me or others, and to catch overtones of their personality by means of their dress or speech or manner. The initial step was dependent on my knowledge of their individual backgrounds, interests, and tastes.

Once I had obtained the necessary information and had gained their confidence, I could suggest with greater assurance books to be read by each boy. If the first study unit was drama, the collateral reading assignment called for three plays by a single dramatist, preferably a contemporary one. To heighten interest, I usually read to the class an exciting or amusing one-acter. A favorite was O'Neill's "Ile," which would satisfy almost any seventeen-year-older with its suspense, its egocentric and ambitious sea captain with his pathetic wife, and the Arctic setting for the whalers. After the reading, when I listed the playwrights who would be acceptable, with quick but suggestive synopses of their works, even skeptical non-readers assumed that my recommendations were beyond suspicion. Sometimes, of course, I misfired and sometimes I failed to gain my ends; but usually the trick worked, and my boys were introduced to a new land inhabited by such interesting people as Galsworthy, Shaw, Anderson, Maeterlinck, and other playwrights of stature.

Such treatment may sound a bit highbrow or even stuffy, and if applied unremittingly and without relief, it might not reach the less susceptible or more playful members of the class. Humor, of whatever sort, is an irreplaceable ingredient in the recipe for rapport with this age group. Whether one uses an off-beat quip or a tried-and-true monologue, it works. Even in teaching Milton, for purposes of keeping alert the dreamy-eyed or the inert, I have found helpful a reference to "Diana forever chaste (or chased)," to the "watery bier (beer)" of Lycidas, or to the College Board boner when the candidate referred to the "pie-eyed daisies" instead of to "fields with daisies pied." Although one must be careful not to insert such spurs to attention with too great frequency, they serve to make boys understand that the master has not lost his perspective and prevent his soaring into the poetic empyrean far above the earthy atmosphere in which they live.

The prolonged type of serio-comic dissertation might come with the paragraph in Macaulay's *Johnson* when the clever stylist—carried away with some of his more obvious devices—tries to make out that the eccentric subject of his essay was nothing short of insane. Superficial readers are convinced by the concentrated details that the truth has been stated. Facts they surely are, but they are not the truth. As proof of Johnson's "madness," Macaulay refers to incidents such as the lexicographer's touching every post on a street and retracing his steps if he missed one, looking at a clock and a moment later not recalling the time, twitching off a lady's slipper at a party, and others of similar nature. When I asked if the class thought Johnson was "off his rocker," the affirmative vote was unanimous. At that point I went to work to explain that Macaulay, by clever manipulation of precise trivia, had distorted the portrait and had produced a caricature.

To prove the point that the essayist had been more interested in captivating his reader than in telling the truth, I proceeded to make out a similar case against their own schoolmaster, Phil Marson. On the basis of it, he could have been put away. Actually, I explained, I should have to plead guilty to most of the charges leveled against Johnson, to wit: (1) I had many times, in walking along a concrete sidewalk, attempted to touch each dividing groove and had felt frustrated if I missed one; (2) On occasion I had continually kicked a pebble ahead of me on a dirt path and had even gone out of my way to kick it back when it swerved; (3) I had left my study to find out the correct time, and on my return found that I had forgotten it; and (4) I had not, as far as I could recall, pulled off a lady's shoe, but I remembered comparable playful and silly pleasantries perpetrated in high moods at parties. Yes, all of us might be adjudged mad on occasion, especially if all our aberrations were concentrated in one paragraph. This routine was always a sure-fire hit.

Dangers there surely are in the too frequent use of humor, excellent device though it be. Some boys might listen for the next witticism rather than absorb the serious subject matter. The teacher might be carried away by too receptive an audience. It was not necessary, however, to go out of one's way to entertain, to sustain interest, or to fight for the attention of boys who had already proved their mettle. Of those who had entered in either the seventh or the ninth grade, only one-third had both the skill and the will to survive the course and become seniors.

Students came from all sections of the city, largely from Jewish and Italian or Irish Catholic homes; but almost every element in the population made up the school roster—Negro, Chinese, Syrian, Lebanese, and just plain Yankee. For these typical American boys the school offered, as it had for more than three hundred years, the opportunity to prepare for the greatest universities in the land fully as effectively as the best academies and independent schools. Among these fortunate lads were sons of lowly artisans, municipal employes, and even recipients of welfare funds as well as sons of doctors, lawyers, preachers, and businessmen. After school hours many of them sold papers, shined shoes, or delivered bundles, while their more affluent classmates engaged in sports or other activities. Whatever their circumstances, they were all Latin School boys and were all treated alike. It was truly democracy in action.

3. ROUTINE

SECONDARY SCHOOLS IN 1926, PUBLIC AS WELL AS PRIVATE, generally followed a national pattern. Originally designed in Europe, it had been adapted to American use by Puritan settlers working from British grammar school models and had been utilized continuously for almost three centuries. Although city and suburban systems later provided various types of vocational and commercial courses to supplement strictly college preparatory studies, most high schools based their curricula on the long-standing college admission requirements of English, Latin and other foreign languages—ancient and modern, history, mathematics, and science. Boston Latin School, which specialized in preparing its boys to meet the exacting demands of the College Board, felt an even greater responsibility to retain this program; but, in addition, its long history as upholder of the classical tradition imposed upon it an almost sacred duty to be true to its name. At the very first faculty meeting that I attended, Headmaster Pat Campbell went to great lengths to impress upon every one, particularly the new members, that we were at the *Latin* School, not to be confused under any circumstances with a high school.

His definition was then expanded to include curriculum, tests and measurements, disciplinary procedures, and personal relationships. The shock of his remarks still lingers; for I found them almost incomprehensible. Fresh from the congenial informality of a small country day school, where the individuality of each boy and master was taken into account and respected, I was not prepared for his comments and was startled and alarmed. Up to that moment I had been led to believe, both by study and practice, that success in teaching depended primarily on the establishment of a friendly relationship between teacher and pupil. Yet I heard the man say distinctly and forcefully that under no circumstances were members of the faculty to break down the formal and established barrier against too much familiarity with students, that deviation from this deportment could lead only to unfortunate results, and that he hoped that we all took his words seriously.

Mentally I reserved the right to continue my own conversationally easy ways both in and out of the classroom. I was glad that I did, for later I learned that Pat Campbell himself was proud of his reputation as an informal, easy-going, and approachable man, a devil's advocate, and a true friend to hundreds of boys. Why he felt called upon to deliver himself of these grim dicta, I do not know; but I have suspected that as he was the first Irishman and Roman Catholic to hold his exalted office, he wished to reassure his predominantly Yankee faculty that no radical departures would be made from the strict Puritanical customs and traditions of the past.

The other implications of his remarks, however, I found to be only too true. Scholastic rigidity was so great that it amounted to medieval ossification. The narrow curriculum was inflexible. No escape was possible for the occasional youngster who, because of either native tendencies toward art or science or a desire to escape the rigors of time-consuming and disproportionate emphasis on linguistic studies, attempted rebellion or resistance.

I should not have been surprised by the fixed nature of the curriculum, the Spartan indifference to the psychology of its boys, or the resistance to change. After all, the man chiefly responsible for the establishment of the school in 1635 was John Cotton, of whom Cotton Mather (an alumnus) said, "Twelve hours in a day he commonly studied and would call that a scholar's day."

His successors in setting the policies of the school had withstood every assault upon the famous cleric's original plan, and the curriculum had been changed little since those early days.

When my tenure began in September of 1926, every boy entering the school for the six-year course beginning with the seventh grade (only about one-third of the student body preferred starting in the ninth) faced the following undeviating academic ordeal: six years of English, five or six years of Latin, three or four years of French, two or three years of Greek or German, five or six years of mathematics, four years of history (two of American, one of English, and one of ancient), and three years of science (two of general science and one of physics). This unbalanced diet of sixteen to nineteen parts linguistic studies to only six parts social studies (history and geography), and eight or nine parts mathematical-scientific studies, proved to be sufficiently indigestible, unpalatable, or distasteful to force at least two-thirds of the boys to leave the school. During my thirty-one years as a master, I observed that only 250 of the 750 lads who usually were enrolled in the entering classes were graduated. Of the five hundred who left for less exacting institutions, I estimate that about 80 per cent could have met the requirements if they had been willing to submit to the inflexibility and unceasing labor required to survive. Nobody could escape the continuous grind of daily recitations, weekly tests, and monthly grades.

The graduates (and even many of those who had left us en route) carried with them invaluable byproducts of the mill that was Latin School. The system was undeviating, efficient, and permanent. Every one who became part of it—master or pupil—felt the effects for the rest of his life. By virtue of the work done, the cold evaluation of results, and the habits established, the practices of the school had proved through the centuries their effectiveness.

Inexorable routine produced permanent mutations. No matter how brilliant a boy might be, he was forced into action. Five major subjects (with only one study period during each school day) required at least three hours of study at home. He could not avoid it; for he had to face a formidable battery of daily recitations, weekly tests, and monthly reports. With the day of reckoning inevitable and nauseatingly repetitious every four weeks, when he had to face his parents with the record, the boy worked incessantly. But the master was just as great a slave to the gods of learning; for he was smothered under endless reams of detail. To meet deadlines essential to smooth operation of the assembly line of scholastic production, he had to map out the year's work on a day-to-day schedule, be ready for each challenging recitation and be sure to cover the ground, prepare tests and individual assignments, grade all papers, keep accurate records, and submit for every student a precise monthly mark (figured to the exact percentage point). The work was hard, but the effects were gratifying. We were all repaid when the records of the College Entrance Examination Board attested, year in and year out, to the efficacy of the system. As our boys continued to make brilliant records at college and to become leaders in the nation, our labors were more than justified.

With so much to be done in so short a time, most boys were too busy for the customary adolescent aberrations. Even so, a sufficient number of irrepressible, incorrigible, and rebellious teenagers appeared each year to keep masters alert and to make permanent a unique disciplinary scheme originated by an ingenious headmaster (Francis Gardner) in the early nineteenth century. It has proved highly effective in restraining most of those whose natural enthusiasm conquers discretion. Other schools, notably the Service academies, have somewhat similar systems; but Latin School has its own particular refinements. All offenses against decorum or authority are punishable by the imposition of misdemeanor marks by the master. In addition, for severe infractions he may recommend to the headmaster that the miscreant be given the ultimate penalty—the censure of the school. Three censures, it has been generally understood, would automatically result in the request to the boy's parents that he be withdrawn from the school. (Actually, no boy could be expelled, for public education is compulsory until age sixteen; but usually these boys have been transferred to other secondary schools in the city.)

Misdemeanor marks were given for many reasons. They might be inflicted for trivia like failure to bring a note on the day following absence or tardiness, turning around during a recitation, or gazing out the window; or for more serious offenses like calling attention to Simmons girls playing hockey in scanty shorts on the adjoining field or to doctors and nurses assisting in the birth of a baby in the delivery room of the Lying-In Hospital next door. Censures were reserved for the most heinous crimes: persistent misbehavior, as evidenced by the accumulation of seven or more misdemeanor marks within the short space of a week; fist-fighting in the corridors; truancy; or insolence to a master, either overt or implied by gesture and expression. While the school was still maintaining its highest academic standards, comparatively few marks or censures were given, for most boys were too busy for mischief. After World War II, however, when deterioration both in quantity and quality of work set in, these punishments became so frequent and so severe that they lost much of their effectiveness. With the loss of scholastic standards, came a breakdown in behavior and a diminished respect for the school.

The administration of such a system of work and discipline would necessarily depend for its success on the judgment, ability, and discretion of the men who administered it. As a result, when one talks with alumni of the school, stories of individuals and incidents—some amusing, others grim—often appear to be characteristic but just as often incredible or apocryphal. Boston Latin School had its proportionate share of unusual personalities on its faculty. The lives of boys in their classes were unpredictable, sometimes tense, at other times hilarious, and in some extreme instances nightmarish. George Orwell, in an essay dealing with horrible boyhood experiences in a British private school, describes the unscrupulous and cruel couple who conducted it in more villainous fashion than any Dickensian academic scoundrels; but, according to some of our own alumni, we might be able to reproduce their counterparts.

Only recently I received a letter from a former student, Bill Callaghan, now a professor of philosophy at Michigan State

University, in which he loosed long-pent-up anger at some of his tormentors. A short passage will suffice to indicate what many boys must have felt but never expressed:

> . . . Perhaps you never fully appreciated how dreadful it was for a pupil under the old régime. Do you remember big, red-headed Frank Riley? If you do, you'll recall him as, among other things, a tough and competitive type. Frank told me that every day as a boy, streetcar-riding to Latin School, his fear and hatred of the place would increase as he got closer to it. He estimated that there were hundreds of mornings when he vomited away his breakfast at Park Street before making the transfer to his final trolley. So it was not really sensitive plants only that found the place dreadful. As for me, I remember a nearly universal contempt and dislike for students by masters, an attitude so pervasive that it filled the school like a smell.
>
> Of course it ought never to come down to this. It should be—it is—possible to have good schools and good teaching without concentration-camp attitudes or techniques. And at present surely the big trouble is woolly-headed unconcern for core subjects.
>
> . . . Perhaps I shall never have so good a chance again, so I shall say here that I have remembered you and your teaching vividly, with gratitude and affection.

The last sentence prompts me to say that any teacher who showed a modicum of sympathy and understanding became a savior to boys like Bill Callaghan and Frank Riley. It was not always easy to reach such lads; but the unimaginative pedants and the rigid disciplinarians made contact less difficult for the rest. The lives of their victims were often fearful and tense. Many a graduate has repeated the legend that a certain master who was blind in one eye reflected his only glint of kindness from the acrylic optic. Hundreds have recalled their mortal fear of entering the classroom of Bob Drummey, whose fits of temper and booming voice echoed through corridors; of John Cray, whose cold stare, stinging tongue, and precise manner froze them into monolithic attention; and of Bill Roche, a Ph.D. in philosophy from Harvard, whose eloquent grades and vocal opinion of his pupils led them to wonder whether they should heed his advice to stop their futile struggle with Latin and Greek and to turn to important work like ditchdigging and lumbering. Too many masters belonged in this category to make the school a pleasurable refuge for indolent or easygoing normal adolescents.

At the beginning of each school year boys entered new homerooms with fear in their eyes and dread in their hearts in anticipation of what the front blackboard might reveal. The telltale program, showing only room numbers to which the section was assigned for its five subjects, was usually enough in itself to implant terror in the bravest of them. Wild shouts of enthusiasm or groans of dismay came with the identification of each master in the "set," as the quintet was called in the lingo of Latin School. It was a matter of pure chance as to whether a boy was to have an almost unbearable year or whether it was to be reasonably pleasant. Whichever it turned out to be, he knew that he would have to work only three times as hard as his friends who attended one of the neighborhood high schools. Is it any wonder, then, that at least 65 per cent of those who entered the school did not survive the course? And is it not clear that any master who made his students feel somewhat more worthy than galley slaves and instilled in them self-respect beyond that of an untouchable would win their approval and even their affection?

Beyond the Darwinian doctrines of survival of the fittest and of natural selection which separated the men from the boys—whether teachers or students—lay an intangible spirit peculiar to Latin School. An *esprit de corps* emerged out of the struggle and remained for life in those who had been through it. Probably the development of toughness and the consciousness of triumph over obstacles account for the pride produced in self and in the school. Whatever the reason, graduates of Latin School—either great or small in the eyes of their peers—have always remembered the school and the blind justice which it administered. It has probably been an excellent preparation for the jungle of the adult world, and the Dr. Panglosses among them discovered very early that this is not necessarily the best of all possible worlds.

The shortcomings of the curriculum I discovered almost immediately; and before my first term was even half over, I conferred with Pat Campbell. One of the most apparent weaknesses appeared early when I was preparing a tenth-grade class for the reading of Dickens's *A Tale of Two Cities.* I soon discovered that few if any boys knew even the most elementary facts about the French Revolution. Limited to very little time for outside reading by the liberal assignments of regular homework, most of them could not have picked up the information essential to an understanding of the background for this piece of historical fiction. After I had supplied what I considered the bare minimum, I hopefully approached the headmaster; for he had been for many years an enthusiastic teacher of history and therefore should be sympathetic to a plea for more courses in his field. Admitting that a great gap did exist in the course of study in the history of Western civilization between 1483 and 1914, he nevertheless regretfully refused to do anything about reducing the foreign language overload and substituting a year's study in medieval and in modern European history. As a result of this failure to introduce even so moderate a reform, I quickly dispelled from my mind a second suggestion that was germinating—for more science, particularly biology and chemistry. This idea had probably been stimulated by my recent reading of H. G. Wells's biography of the great scientific schoolmaster, Sanderson of Oundle, and his Jobian novel based on the same man, *The Undying Fire.*

Making a dent in the ancient armor of Latin School traditionalism was, I found, just as difficult in areas other than curriculum. Despite occasional hints at faculty meetings that each subject master limit nightly home assignments to one hour, many men with an inordinate zeal for their special field piled the work so high for students that those of us showing a reasonable respect for the office ruling found boys hurrying and skimming through our subjects. To assign outside reading under such conditions thus became increasingly a problem, even though I made the due dates for reports fall after weekends on Mondays to take the place of the usual weekly theme. As an added concession to slow readers and playboys, when dictating lists of books for suggested reading, I always stated the number of pages in each volume. To take care of the habitual reader or the overambitious lad, I advised that such giants as *Jean Christophe, Kristin Lavransdatter,* or *War and*

Peace be reserved for reviews due after the Christmas, February, and Easter vacations. This arrangement was killed by the politicians at School Committee Headquarters, 15 Beacon Street, when they ruled that no assignments were to be given over long holidays, later extended this dictum to short celebrations like Thanksgiving and Good Friday week-ends, and finally included even single days off. Thus, in straining to please their constituents, they reduced considerably the amount of homework.

A good workman, however, cannot be completely stymied by administrative tactics and blindness. My way of assuring a sufficient amount of reading by my students, especially in the years when success in the Board examinations depended on the number and quality of books read and understood, was to schedule the submission of reports on Tuesdays following such vacations instead of Mondays. Such subterfuge should not, of course, have been necessary if administrators had refused to submit to vote-hungry School Committeemen. Probably they would only have had to point out that at least boys and girls in college preparatory classes should be excused from such rulings; but the headmasters in all the Boston high schools, many of them hesitant because they were looking for promotion, would not tangle with their superiors, even on matters of principle.

Boston Latin School, largely because of the weight of its history and the pressure of its influential alumni, did not succumb completely to these outside influences and held on, for better or for worse, to long-established practices. One of these was the systematic control over the grading of the boys. This was exercised by a series of checks and balances to assure accuracy and justice on the part of all members of the faculty: (1) monthly reports, submitted to parents for signature, with grades for each subject figured on the basis of absolute percentages arrived at from marks on recitations, tests, and other papers; (2) weekly tests or their equivalents to be returned to boys, so that masters' grades could be checked; (3) conduct reports, based on a system of misdemeanor marks and censures somewhat similar to that in use at the Service academies.

A schematic arrangement of this character insures effective uniformity and excellent results; but whatever the underlying philosophy or principles of application, in the final analysis the ability and temperament of the individual master will determine what happens in specific situations. Examples by the score could be cited, but a few will illustrate why at class reunions or in chance conversations alumni disagree on general deductions about the school as well as on the influence of particular men.

In the first of his autobiographical accounts, *Persons and Places,* George Santayana describes his general unhappiness at the school, but selects as the only man who made life bearable a master known to many generations of schoolboys as "Stuffy" Groce. After merciless impressions of Headmaster Gardner, "Cudjo" Capen, and his Greek master Arthur Fiske, Santayana pays tribute to Groce in this paragraph:

> Very different was dapper Mr. Groce, our teacher of English composition and literature, a little plump man, with a keen, dry, cheerful yet irritable disposition, a sparkling bird-like eye, and a little black mustache and diminutive chin-beard. I suspect that he was too intelligent to put up patiently with all the conventions. Had he not been a public-school teacher, dependent on the democratic hypocrisies of a government committee, he might have said unconventional things. This inner rebellion kept him from being sentimental, moralistic, or religious in respect to poetry; yet he *understood* perfectly the penumbra of emotion that good and bad poetry alike might drag after them in an untrained mind. He knew how to rescue the structural and rational beauties of a poem from that bog of private feeling. To me this was a timely lesson, for it was precisely sadness and religiosity and grandiloquence that first attracted me to poetry; and perhaps I owe to Mr. Groce the beginnings of a capacity to distinguish the musical and expressive charm of poetry from its moral appeal. . . .

At seventy Mr. Byron Groce had retired, long before my advent, but his reputation was still green for only one discoverable reason. With the exception of the great philosopher, graduates were unanimous in denouncing him as a man who invariably made certain that every boy received a low monthly grade by a singularly diabolical device. By finding a question in the assigned lesson which nobody could answer and going around the class twice with it, he managed to award each member two zeroes. Thus handicapped, the unfortunate victims found gaining a high grade almost impossible.

Such cruelty or lack of judgment was almost matched by several of my colleagues. When asked why they did not pass a boy who fell one percentage point short of the required grade, they replied that the lad had failed by just that much to master the subject matter. Later, when official edict forbade the recording of grades between 55 and 60 (the minimum passing mark), such men always dropped the boys to the lower point, even if they had earned enough to put them beyond the halfway mark. When accused of being unsympathetic, these "killers," as they were dubbed by their victims, defended themselves by claiming that their treatment would stimulate the student to greater effort and was therefore better than giving him a false sense of security.

Not only in grading did the personality of each man reveal itself. To me, coming from the informal atmosphere of small private school classes, discipline at Boston Latin School seemed to present no problem at all. Like every newcomer or visitor, I was amazed to walk into a study hall seating seventy-eight boys and observe perfect decorum. During my first few months I could not quite get used to taking a set of themes with me and finding that I could give them the close reading they required; for I scarcely had to look up from my work. I assumed, from this experience, that the disciplinary system—based as it was, on the dreaded misdemeanor marks and censures—would rarely be invoked.

I was, however, mistaken. Many men had serious difficulties in maintaining order. A few of the most successful teachers rarely used the handy and effective instrument of punishment, the mark; and they went about their work with businesslike but friendly composure. They assumed that nothing untoward would happen, and it rarely did. At the other extreme were the few who were always in trouble, expecting the worst and getting it. If they imposed dozens of marks, the boys—by that time thoroughly antagonistic—still continued their wild and sometimes ingenious antics. The Headmaster, naturally enough, compounded the man's problems by concluding, when pupil after pupil was sent to the office, that this unfortunate master was thereby confessing his inability to control his classes.

How such men lived through day after day of miserable humiliation, escaped nervous breakdowns, and retained enough self-respect to continue teaching has always puzzled me. One teacher of French, who irritated boys to such a degree that they constantly invented new ways to make him miserable, came to me in sincere humility for advice as to what techniques I used to maintain a pleasant relationship with my classes. All that I could convey to him was a vague suggestion that I treated all boys as I should like to be treated myself—hardly profound or even helpful advice. I was not being evasive; but from observation and experience, I have concluded that the ability to get along with others cannot be learned from another person, a textbook, or a course in educational psychology. It depends on an almost intuitive gift which enables the happy possessor of it to determine in the split second permitted him when to speak and when to remain silent, what to say and what to leave unsaid, when to act and when to be passive, what to do and what to avoid doing.

Another man, obsessed with ideas undoubtedly culled from gadgets used to promote business efficiency, attempted to create infinite order in his classroom. He gave each of his students a number corresponding to that of his seat and his aisle, thereafter always calling him by that designation rather than by name. From home he brought old orange crates and grocery cartons which he transformed into filing cabinets; but when a master came to him for information about one of his boys, he became hopelessly lost in a wilderness of cross references, to the boundless delight of the class. His masterpiece was the invention of a labor-saving device to be used for the recording of misdemeanor marks. It consisted of a long mimeographed list of all misdeeds likely to be committed by boys, ranging from such comparatively innocent pranks as "attracting attention unnecessarily by clownish antics" and "making unseemly noises" to such major crimes as "cheating" and "exploding fire crackers or stink bombs." After he had placed his check mark in the appropriate space and affixed his symbol, he sent it by special courier to the offender's homeroom master, from whom a receipt was requested. One sardonic colleague, in an effort to slow down the steady intrusion of such messengers, put a stop to this particular sample of scientific management by insisting on a "receipt for the receipt."

The man least suited to deal with "tweenagers" was a near-sighted and scholarly master in the German department. How he retained his sanity or even survived each day's trials mystified most of us, for his classes were complete bedlam. During one year when he was a peripatetic, he held one of his recitations each day in my homeroom while I was having a free period. One thing I could be certain of on my return: the room which I had left moderately clean would be a shambles—with paper and other litter all over the floor, a broken desk lid or two, remains of a chalk fight. Once a juicy tomato had evidently missed its target and had flattened itself on the back wall with such momentum that its mark remained as a permanent memorial of that battle. In the beginning he came to us as a college instructor of philology and a scholar who had earned his Ph.D. with a thesis entitled "The Influence of the West Baltic Dialects on the Languages of East Poland." During his three-year trial period he had managed to meet whatever criteria were employed to test his effectiveness in his German classes. Not until a new and unsympathetic headmaster was appointed did he meet disaster. Soon after, he was set adrift as a tutor for disabled or permanently ill Boston high school children.

Before this sad fate overtook him, he showed clearly why he should have remained in college teaching rather than attempt to deal with the problems that confront the teacher of adolescents. One technique he had learned for purposes of self-preservation: he became deaf to the sounds around him and insensible to the unpleasant aspects of his environment. An incident occurred during a noon recess that illustrated how completely he had insulated himself against interruptions that might disturb the serenity of his private world. My next-door neighbor and good friend, Roland Godfrey, had been talking with me in the corridor outside my classroom on the second floor. He faced me as I stood with my back to a window which opened on a large areaway reaching from the roof to the basement. Suddenly, in the middle of a sentence, he dashed without warning down the corridor to his left. To discover what had caused his speedy departure, I turned around to look out of the window behind me. I discovered at once that he needed my help, and I ran after him. A boy was hanging by his fingertips from the window ledge while another lad was whacking his hands with a blackboard eraser in an attempt to make him let go and thus force him to drop to the roof 15 feet below.

It was just a foolish prank, but we got there in time to pull the suspended youngster into the room before anything disastrous might take place. After restoring order and dressing down the guilty with threats of dire punishment, we were about to depart when, to our astonishment and mild embarrassment, we discovered the homeroom master sitting serenely at his desk engrossed in a German text held within an inch of his thick-lensed spectacles. We asked his pardon for barging in and interfering in the affairs of his private domain. He granted it.

This member of the faculty was unique, but Boston Latin School had more than its proportionate share of odd individuals. Just below me on the first floor presided one of the best-loved but still harassed masters, "Uncle Billy" Norton, who retired at seventy in 1935 and at ninety-three is still alert enough to write me a detailed note each Christmas from Florida. I have a clear memory of his stentorian voice as it reverberated up the stairwell from Room 102 when things got a bit too turbulent. A resonant shout of "Quiet!" would shatter the air and arouse to amused attention all pupils and teachers bordering that flight of stairs. More mirth-provoking and disrupting was an equally loud but rather startling query which interrupted many a class, "Who fouls the air?"

Eccentrics distinguished themselves in many ways. One man with a ravenous appetite tried to appease it by storing plentiful supplies of cookies, chocolate bars, and bits of cheese in the upper left-hand drawer of his desk. Much to the amusement of his pupils, he attempted to extract tidbits surreptitiously, but invariably he was caught by his own clumsiness as he dropped them in his self-conscious haste. Another individualist, who left his classroom whenever he felt the need of a break, always retorted when asked how he happened to be in the Faculty Room during a scheduled recitation, "It's much quieter in here." A third, loaded down with enough papers and notes to settle the affairs between two nations, made the school and its affairs his complete world. But, despite idiosyncrasies on the part of almost every master in the school, a spirit of unity and purposeful activity prevailed.

The success of a school program depends ultimately on the strength of its faculty. Despite the eccentricities and foibles of ten or a dozen masters (and even they were partially and occasionally effective), the strong men who constituted 90 per cent of the Latin School staff assured the advancement of learning. Regardless of courses, standards, or prevailing philosophy (progressive, conservative, or reactionary), what a boy learns must depend upon who his teachers are. Teaching is an art, dependent on the emotional depth, intellectual quality, and technical skill of the artists for the excellence of its output. Thus, the development of craftsmanship will determine the degree of success the individual attains.

A good teacher is a composite of entertainer, psychologist, and public relations expert. To hold his classes and gain his ends, he must understand each member of the group before him, gain attention through interest, and make everybody feel comfortable and secure. But this process is only the beginning. Like the Ancient Mariner after stopping the wedding guest with his "glittering eye," he must tell his story. To plan the narration, to construct the exposition, and to assure an effective conclusion must become his chief concern.

The general pattern of my own classes was designed to serve these ends. First I had to determine the course the new subject matter was to take. It might be concerned with almost any aspect of language or literature. It could be a consideration of fresh material, a recapitulation or crystallization of already implanted ideas, a drill exercise on some technical point in grammar or rhetoric, the discussion of a book, or prepared talks by members of the class followed by a question period. Whatever form it took, it had to be pertinent to our objectives.

With such program planning, each meeting of a class took on

meaning, offered a challenge, and assured interest—and sometimes provided amusing entertainment. I recall an incident in early 1926 which made me certain that life among the Latin School natives would furnish a fullness and stimulus for even the most restless and eager pedagogical adventurer. In a Class V (Grade VIII) division, the writing of an anecdote was our aim. After considerable discussion of various ways to tell a story (illustrated by examples ranging from the rambling leisure of *Robinson Crusoe* to the planned precision of "The Cask of Amontillado"), we plunged into the technique of telling a "quickie" like a fable, a joke, or an anecdote. At this point I risked recounting the story of Sir Walter Scott and the button. As a schoolboy, the great writer had been frustrated in his attempts to surpass a bright classmate. Observing closely the mannerisms of his rival for the Number One position in the class, he noticed that the boy—as he arose to give his invariably correct answers—always fingered the lowest button of his waistcoat. In an inspired moment at recess one day, Sir Walter surreptitiously snipped it off. The experiment was successful; for immediately upon resumption of the recitation, the lad was called upon, but when he vainly fumbled about for the comforting button, he became confused and failed. Sir Walter, of course, came up with the correct answer and headed the class thereafter. Assuming that the point had been made, I was about to assign the writing of an anecdote for that night's homework when I saw Wasserman in a rear seat frantically waving his hand.

When I acknowledged him, he asked if I saw the point of the story. Naturally I asserted that it was simple enough for even a feeble mind like mine to grasp the implications, but perhaps he had a special slant which had escaped the rest of us. To the delight of both boys and master, he replied, "Well, that kid would never have missed the button if he weren't a Scotchman."

Such incidents occurred with sufficient frequency to keep all teachers on their toes and, as far as I was concerned, added gaiety and suspense to almost every day of my life. At times things might get out of hand, but usually laughter simply added zest to the class. Before I leave this particular aspect of a schoolmaster's existence, I must cite one of my prize classroom stories. The most talented linguist on the faculty was Ed O'Callaghan, whose knowledge of Latin and Greek was exceeded only by a natural gift for absorbing accent and inflection, even gesture and mannerism, of such disparate tongues as Russian and Italian. He was also the most excitable and dramatic. According to former students (not always the most reliable witnesses), he used every histrionic device known to actors from the days of the ancient Greeks to burlesque comedians of our times. Unfortunately his own inimitable oral report of a prime flop cannot be accurately reproduced on paper, but this account may serve to show partially how difficult it sometimes is to reach one's audience.

One day, to drive home a particularly difficult point in Latin grammatical construction—something about the periphrastic or indirect discourse—the redoubtable O'Callaghan said that he had been all over the classroom, had told jokes with accompanying diagrams, and had used acrobatic gesticulations, legerdemain, and ventriloquism. When he was finished, he strutted before the dazzled boys and inwardly took great pride in the superb job he had done. Although he felt that the customary curtain line "Any questions?" was superfluous, he asked it anyway. At once a hand shot up from one of the less promising lads, and O'Callaghan was prouder than ever at having aroused even this fellow to attentive response. Imagine, if you can, the swift and deadly deflation of the master when the question floated through the charged air: "May I leave the room?"

Teaching may look to the outsider like a humdrum, tedious task, but surprises and satisfactions constantly lighten the burden and brighten the classroom. Most practitioners have decided preferences as to subject and even as to highly specialized aspects of it. Among teachers of English most prefer discussion of books to the teaching of composition, rhetoric, or grammar; and 90 per cent at least, while admitting the necessity for correcting themes, thoroughly abhor this inescapable and time-consuming labor. Incredible though it may seem, I not only recognized as indispensable all aspects of my job, but actually enjoyed each one. To doubters I can only say that I have always preferred work to idleness and have found recreation a poor substitute. In addition,

I profoundly believe that to teach the arts of communication to the young presents the opportunity to take part in the greatest single civilizing force known to man.

This basic faith makes details of grammar, punctuation, capitalization, pronunciation, spelling, and even syllabication take on significance. At Newton, after the Supervisor of English—that old war-horse, Sam Thurber—had seen me enthusiastically put a class through the paces of a lesson on the grammatical structure of complex sentences, he admitted that he himself had never been able to work up a head of steam in himself or his classes over such matters. Many factors had contributed to my interest in grammar. I was sure that it had great value in the learning of all European languages, but particularly of Latin. Without a knowledge of the functions and relationship of words in sentences, the student is handicapped not only in the study of foreign tongues, but in the precise use of his own. Besides this utilitarian advantage, I found instruction in grammar most rewarding because the effects of my teaching were measurable and evident, much more apparent than the intangible and obscure development of taste and judgment in such areas as reading and rhetoric. If a boy entered a class without knowing the difference between a verb and an aspidistra and left it with a basic knowledge of syntax, I felt like a conqueror or at the very least like a master of my craft.

This accomplishment may seem simple, almost trivial, in the world of action, and even the pedagogy may appear to be hardly provocative. If, however, the student can be taught the structural beauty of the sentence and its relationship to similar creations of man, the importance of composition takes on color and form and perspective. The words cease to be mere parts of speech and become ideas. Taken together and in relationship with one another, the words become a harmonious unit that form a thought, the symbol of civilized communication. Lately, the study of formal grammar has been abandoned in most of our elementary schools as superfluous and scoffed at as the whim of scholars; but my long experience has taught me that not only is it valuable for precision of thought and hence a priceless instrument for speech and writing, but it serves to make more effective the teaching of the more subtle and complicated elements in language study—reading and writing.

Anybody who has ever attempted to teach youngsters to express themselves in English or in any other language will see at once the advantages of fundamental information in grammar. Even if a lad is trying to learn such a simple process as punctuating a sentence, his instructor should feel free to use terms like compound sentence, dependent clause, or participial phrase and expect to be understood. When the much more complicated lessons of rhetoric are being taught on such matters as variety in sentence structure and other elements in individual style, the teacher finds a student's knowledge of grammar a great help. He may then use with impunity the technical terms of his trade—whether they concern simple data like tense, mood, and number or finer points such as nominative absolutes, split infinitives, and periodicity of sentences. Surely it must be obvious that a teacher of English composition in the upper classes of the secondary school is badly handicapped if he is hobbled with the grammatical ignorance of the present day.

When the colleges surrendered to the progressives in allowing theory to give way to practice, and formal grammer in entrance examinations was abolished, we who were in the classrooms felt the impact. Until about 1935, in every so-called "restricted" examination paper (i.e., "restricted" to questions on prescribed books), the candidate had to give evidence of a thorough knowlledge of the grammatical construction of at least one reasonably complicated sentence. The question usually assumed a knowledge of parts of speech, complements, phrases, clauses, and types of sentences. The following examples, selected at random, will indicate the extent of the information required:

1. He was *so* absorbed in his devotion to the public business that he took *on* a quite different, a more serious, less courtly air *as* time went on. *So* it may be that the grace and gallantry *attributed* to him by those who met him socially were as *truly* his as the stocky, stuffy, ungainly *figure* ascribed to him by others.
   a. There are five subordinate clauses in the two sentences above. Tell what kind of clause each is and what its relation is to the rest of the sentence.

b. Why is there no comma after *those?*
c. Give the part of speech and construction of each of the seven italicized words.

2. The world and the customs of the world never cease *to levy* taxes upon our time, but the particular degree in *which* we suffer by this robbery depends *much* upon the weakness with which we ourselves become *parties* to the wrong, or the *energy* with which we resist it.
   a. Is this sentence complex or compound? Why?
   b. Indicate the clauses and give the relation of each to the rest of the sentence.
   c. Give the construction of the italicized words.

3. It is verily this degradation of the worker *into a machine,* which, more than any other evil of the times, is leading the mass of the nations *everywhere* into vain, incoherent, destructive struggling for a freedom *of which* they cannot explain the nature to themselves.
   a. Point out the clauses and classify them (1) as principal or subordinate and (2) as substantive, adjective, or adverbial.
   b. Give the construction of the italicized expressions.

As the answer to each question was ordinarily worth 15 percentage points, the teacher and his students recognized at once that a good start toward the essential 60 per cent could be made by mastering such concrete and easily learned subject matter. Thus, not only did this grammatical information help in class discussion of writing skills, but appealed as a simple and practical way to begin to open the college gates. It also indicated that university authorities placed some value on a knowledge of grammar.

The extent to which the abandonment of this study has destroyed all semblance of order in our speech can be heard on radio and television seven days per week. This chaos is brought about not only by the Madison Avenue hucksters who write grammatical abominations such as "Winstons taste good like a cigarette should," and by "ad-libbers" who are never quite sure whether to use "who" or "whom." It is also brought about by people who should know better and should try to restore form and good usage to a badly battered tongue. I am thinking particularly of a program called "The Last Word," which has a professor of English literature, Bergen Evans, as master of ceremonies. His only criterion for correct speech seems to be the number of people, regardless of background, who use the word or expression under discussion. With such forces at work day and night to destroy whatever regulations have been established from the early days of our language—beginning with Chaucer and continuing until recently—the conscientious teacher is helpless. Insistence on grammatical niceties becomes almost impossible.

While the structure of the sentence offers unique opportunities of a sort well known to teachers of Latin and other highly inflected languages, it represents only a tiny fragment of the task confronting a teacher of English. His major concern must be effective expression. Stimulation of interest on the part of his pupils to convey to others what they think and feel is basic. Most of my efforts were directed toward this end.

The first step was, logically enough, to make certain that every member of the class had an ample supply of ideas. Whatever the source—experience, observation, or reading—this reservoir always had to be full enough to provide the necessary flow. Thus, I had to be certain that early in the year my boys were encouraged to draw upon their personal lives (autobiographical data, family matters, neighborhood affairs, vocational or avocational interests, etc.), public affairs, mechanics, sports, music, theatre, books—anything in which they had a real interest. Usually I had difficulty with them when I tried to induce them to avoid exotic backgrounds which they had never seen (Sumatra, India, or Skid Row), plots borrowed from horror comics or movies, and odd characters whom they invented out of whole cloth. After a time, however, they discovered that the more successful writers and speakers among them used familiar material that was often commonplace, but always clear and substantial.

As soon as I convinced a boy that he was different from every other person in the room because his home, his street, his family, his community, his friends, his experiences—in fact, all aspects of him—were unique, we were on the road to successful expression. The most obvious examples might be drawn from sports-mad statisticians in my classes who had accumulated enough historical information, facts, and figures relating to standings of teams and individual players, and technical minutiae worthy of professional coaches to make them sound like vocal encyclopedias. This category often included large numbers of frequently bespectacled, round-shouldered, chubby bookworms who compensated for their lack of athletic prowess by their vast knowledge of one sport or another. They gained standing or acceptance by their classmates when in talks or themes they displayed their wares in analyses of Red Sox weaknesses; discussions of controversial figures like Ted Williams; explanations (with diagrams) of plays in basketball or football; anecdotes of past greats; or humorous incidents connected with gridiron, diamond, or court. Clearly this type of boy had inexhaustible subject matter that would serve him continuously and would be fascinating to the majority of his audience or readers. This source material supplied his needs permanently in both oral and written composition.

The sports-minded group invariably constitutes a large proportion of any American student body, and experts on athletics are legion among male teen-agers. As a result, to achieve distinction in this specialized field was difficult. A few other areas were somewhat overcrowded, too, such as jazz, auto mechanics, fishing, and photography. In discussing less popular activities, an expert gained immediate attention and prominence in the class if he had unique knowledge. Zisk, for instance, commanded respect when on numerous occasions he described his electrical experimentation and, for purposes of demonstration, brought to class a home-made motor or a radio set which he himself had constructed. Toomey, who worked after school in the research laboratories of the Harvard Medical School, introduced a pungent stench into our workshop which remained for days after he had lugged in cages of experimental rats to show us what was being done only a few steps away at the head of Avenue Louis Pasteur. Robinson, with ambitions to become a professional photographer, regaled us with a series of highly technical talks on the construction of cameras, production of pictures, artistic composition, costs, and other relevant topics. Christian, a shy lad who rarely was vocal otherwise, became eloquent when given the chance to discuss his chief interest—the breeding of carrier and racing pigeons. On one memorable day he brought into my classroom a number of his prize birds to explain their anatomical characteristics and to give us an exhibition of his ability to train the pigeons for particular tasks. He climaxed his talk, which continued far beyond the time limit of three minutes, when, to our amazement, he went over to the window, opened it, released all five birds, and announced that they would fly directly home to their nests on his rooftop in Allston, some four miles away.

The most striking instance of how ordinarily taciturn adolescents will talk freely about their real interests was furnished by Bill Callaghan when he blazed forth brilliantly as a freshman. The son of a ship's captain, he knew as much about ships at thirteen—at least in theory—as did Joseph Conrad or Eugene O'Neill. With a staggering vocabulary, an astounding knowledge, and scale models which he had built to illustrate the history of shipping, he fascinated us. I postponed all other work and let him go on for three recitations in his exposition of every type of vessel from quinquireme to dreadnought.

Once I had discovered interests as deep as these, I made certain that such specialists used their vast knowledge. My own ignorance of many technical fields steered my teaching of these boys into an important facet of writing and speaking—namely, constant consideration of one's readers and listeners.

Professional recognition came with success in the classroom. In 1937, when a new course of study in English was to be developed in the Boston schools, I was asked by Superintendent Campbell to serve as chairman of the committee for composition in Grades VII through XII. To plan how Boston children in all classes of the junior and senior high schools were to be taught one of the basic intellectual skills seemed important to me at that time, and still does. As chairman, I not only presided at all meetings to plan our several projects; but I soon found out that, in common with committee chairmen everywhere, I should have to co-ordinate the many facets of our subject matter and write the final draft of our findings. Although it proved to be a painstaking and time-consuming job, I felt that it was a contribution that a teacher who had faith in his methods should make. When the results of our collaboration were printed, I was satisfied that they represented good doctrine; but I was sure that application of the underlying principles or implementation of the suggestions would, as always, depend on the will and the skill of the craftsman in the classroom. They were scarcely revolutionary; in fact, I am sure that teachers of rhetoric used them in ancient Greece. However unoriginal, a statement of first principles can never harm the learner.

4. CONTACT

IN MY TWENTIES I ADDED AN UNFORGETTABLE PUN TO MY WELL-stocked inventory. To the question "Is life worth living?" an anonymous quipster replied, "It all depends on the liver." Aside from the physiological implications, this Delphic response contains invaluable advice for the impoverished schoolmaster. I have taken it; for I believe that although a teacher may not, as W. E. Henley avows, be "master of his fate," he must do more about it than remain in his ivory classroom.

Extracurricular activities, whether at home or at school, provide balance and prevent academic isolation. Sports are undoubtedly the most effective of them. Not only are tensions eased, but even personal behavior in such matters as tact in victory and graciousness in defeat may be shaped by the mores of the group. The British emphasis on games was justified by my experiences as a coach; and I believe that if our public schools were able to institute an athletics-for-all program, many of our juvenile problems would disappear.

Under present conditions, however, sports cannot reach a sufficient number of boys and girls. Even in the independent schools, where an inclusive program theoretically provides for every pupil, I found youngsters physically or temperamentally unfit for the rough-tough contact sports like football and hockey, for the team games requiring skillful ball-handling like baseball and basketball, or for the individualistic contests like tennis and golf. From this group, unless members of it were completely incapacitated, hiking groups or managerial staffs were formed. Although meeting the immediate need, this procedure did not satisfy these boys, who, like every one else, craved distinction and recognition.

Sometimes such craving acted in reverse. An athlete might like to shine in some other area. One such boy comes immediately to mind. An all-around star in sports, he was particularly eager to take part, despite a badly neglected cleft palate, in activities which would call into play his deep baritone voice. I had satisfied him partially by giving him a suitable assignment as third-base coach, and he had responded with more than adequate effectiveness. When the Dramatic Club approved my suggestion to put on as their big annual production Shaw's *Androcles and the Lion,* I leaped at the chance to choose Cy for the second of the title roles. He roared with a vehemence, volume, and joy that were unmatched, I am sure, by any other performance of the play, amateur or professional. Such ten-strikes come only rarely, but extracurricular activities offer a wide variety of ways in which the urges, talents, and energies of adolescents can be intensively and effectually engaged. If they cannot fit into one pattern, they can usually find another. It is important that the school discover a suitable spot for each boy and girl, so that satisfactions may be realized, talents brought to light, and identification with and recognition by the group achieved.

In the course of the years, I have had innumerable experiences to illustrate how a comprehensive program of activities works. Before my arrival at Boston Latin School, I had devoted almost every afternoon and many evenings to such projects as a purely social club (one of the two which any boy at the academy might be invited to join), interscholastic debates, a short story club, school forums, contests in the presentation of one-act plays, several full-length plays, and a literary magazine. I was convinced, by virtue of these rewarding ventures, that I should have to become part of the after-hours life at the ancient school. I could rule out at once participation in athletics, first, because by that time I had determined to be more teacher and less coach; secondly, because conducting five classes of from thirty to thirty-five pupils at the fast-paced Latin School was enough to engage even my abundant energies; and, thirdly, because Charlie FitzGerald was already well launched on his long and successful career, which still continues. Musical organizations, among the largest and most effective I had ever seen, I was not qualified to direct. Other activities, like dramatics and magazine, which I felt able to manage, were already in the capable hands of Mark Russo and "Gunner" Dole. Therefore, I decided to form a new club, modeled on one at Newton which had been founded by my old mentor at Harvard Graduate School, Charles Swain Thomas.

The Literary Club was launched during my first year in the school (1926-27) with a large membership—over sixty enthusiastic juniors and seniors, to whom it was limited. Among the most active participants were lads who have made their presence felt in the worlds they later have entered: Archbishop John J. Wright, now one of the most eloquent intellectuals in the hierarchy; Bill Harrison, editor of a Negro newspaper and an alleged Communist so militant that he has been named by every witch-hunting committee of the Massachusetts General Court; a long line of college professors, including Arnold Isenberg (philosophy at Leland Stanford), Carroll Quigley (history and government at Georgetown), the Halpern brothers (one in foreign affairs at Harvard, the other in anthropology at California), Bill Callaghan (philosophy at Michigan State), Wilfred Kaplan (mathematics at Wisconsin), and Sydney Freedberg (fine arts at Harvard); Donal Mark Sullivan, a reporter who succeeded Heywood Broun as president of the Newspapermen's Guild; Grover Cronin, leading merchant of Waltham; and many others who have made their imprint on our times. Their interest and participation were stimulated by a sure-fire program of speakers and controversial topics.

In that first year alone we heard Joseph B. Connolly, famous author of sea stories about fishermen out of neighboring Gloucester; Henry Thomas Schnittkind, well-known anthologist of college verse and editor of the *Stratford Journal;* "Doc" Stanger, a

Tufts classmate and production manager of the *Christian Science Monitor;* Leighton Rollins, a poet and at the time literary adviser to the Henry Jewett Repertory Company, a powerful force in the theatrical life of the city. After the club had become well established, it depended less and less on drawing cards from the outside and more and more on its own membership and the faculty for lively discussions of debatable topics in literature, traditional and contemporary. With this development came consideration of such questions as a modern psychological approach (Freudian, perhaps) to the personal problems of Hamlet, or the objective *vs.* the subjective theories on the subject of his tragic dilemma; obscurity as exemplified in such experimentalists as T. S. Eliot, Ezra Pound, and James Joyce; or the problems of an author in the writing of historical fiction. With the club well organized after four years, I felt free to take on a much more complex assignment as adviser to the two school publications—the magazine, the *Latin School Register* (oldest literary journal among secondary schools) and the annual, the *Liber Actorum.*

When I was drafted for this duty in 1931, I had little idea that it would continue for more than twenty-five years and that it would prove to be a fruitful and fascinating association with a long line of extraordinary lads. In the course of that quarter-century (constituting, as it did, one-third of the entire life of the *Register*), the editorial board and the business staff became a closely knit, loyal, and unique outfit. From Wilfred Kaplan, now a mathematics professor, to my last editors in 1957—Herbie Ginsberg and Henry Romberg, at present Harvard undergraduates—my staffers could provide enough material for another book.

The labor pains connected with the birth of each issue will be understood by all publishers. Particular sympathy will be felt by those unfortunates who have attempted to meet deadlines of a monthly in a school such as ours, where homework was piled mountain-high each day and able boys were usually unwilling to add to their prescribed burdens. When I attempted, in the face of this situation, to institute writing for the magazine as a regular assignment in the course in English composition and thus to make publication of the best themes a motivating force and practical goal in routine class work, the authorities immediately informed me that the *Register* would have to remain strictly extra-curricular and could not become in any way part of the English course of study. As a result, so long as the magazine continued to be a monthly, we had to resort from time to time to such subterfuges as printing long essays submitted in annual prize competitions, letters from prominent alumni, or themes selected from my own collection of weekly papers. In desperation, occasionally I ignored the official dictum by offering to my four sections special credit for any acceptable material substituted for the regular exercise in composition. My boys always came through with a sufficient number of stories, articles, humorous sketches, poems (of a sort), and other printable stuff to enable us to fill creditably the minimal 24-page issue.

When I recall some of the students who made publication possible, I realize why we won national acclaim in competitions. Just before I took over the direction of policies, a student in one of my classes, Arnold Isenberg (whom I have mentioned previously several times) received country-wide publicity by winning some five first prizes in contests conducted by "Quill and Scroll" for the best fiction, editorials, verse, essays, and special articles published during 1927-28. When interviewed at his home by Boston newsmen, this brilliant but ingenuous fifteen-year-older greeted them with "Whatever you guys do in this write-up, don't call me, in all other respects, a normal boy." This initial remark was perfect copy for the reporters and, of course, made front-page headlines; and he learned to regret his impetuous comment for at least the rest of that year. Snide remarks from envious classmates and even members of the faculty continued to plague him, but he proved equal to his trial and persisted in the production of his amazingly mature stuff.

Fully as interesting youngsters kept coming along to make life gay, lively, and challenging. The *Register* sanctum soon became, with my active encouragement, a haven for most of the off-beat originals, eccentrics, and outsiders in a school scarcely sympathetic to their breed. The procession was continuous. Withdrawn introverts, blatant exhibitionists, unpopular intellectuals, athletes ambitious to be writers or sportscasters, musical long-hairs or swing fans all made their way to my door. Daily contact with these unpredictables assured surprises and prevented dullness. On one typical morning a mild shock was provided shortly after I had entered my classroom at the usual time—precisely eight o'clock—and crossed the floor to hang hat and coat in my locker. As soon as I had opened the metal door, a rigid body fell out. It was my editor-in-chief, Hays, all six-foot-six of him, who had observed each day my opening routines. Before he had time to open his eyes, I had recovered composure enough to say, "You really flubbed that one; you should have been naked." This same jokester later achieved national distinction while a freshman at M.I.T. by breaking all records of that mad era when he swallowed thirty-six raw goldfish.

Not all members of my magazine staff were addicted to bizarre habits or practical jokes. Fortunately, most were reasonably stable citizens upon whom I could depend for the solid work that had, willy-nilly, to be done. Among the more persistently industrious of them during one memorable year was a youngster, Freddy Richmond by name, whose unbridled brazenness enabled him to get interviews with any celebrity who might enter the city. He scaled any wall, impregnable and insurmountable though it might previously have seemed. His greatest exploit is unforgettable to anybody who was connected with the *Register* of 1936-37. During a regular school day in March I was busily engaged in a routine recitation when the "intercom" buzzer interrupted the even flow of the period. It was the headmaster, Joe Powers. His words, despite my readiness for almost anything, startled me: "Phil, do you know of any one on your staff who is calling the White House? The main office chief operator of the telephone company is on the wire. She informs me that somebody from our school has tied up all the trunk lines to Washington." When I had recovered sufficiently to get the soles of my feet back on the floor, I stammered, "The only one I can think of who might have that much moxie is Freddy Richmond. He has insisted—despite my attempts to dissuade him—that he is going to get an interview with F.D.R. during the coming April vacation." Yes, my guess was correct; and, what is even more amazing, in spite of the refusal of the White House secretaries to grant this thirteen-year-older permission and despite the vigilance of secret service men, Freddy overcame all obstacles, eluded guards, sneaked into the President's office, and produced an exclusive interview. Although the rigors of Latin School forced him to leave our halls the next term for the less restrictive climate of Roxbury Memorial High School, this exemplar of American aggressiveness has since become one of the younger financial wizards to whom *Time* and *Fortune* have given international publicity.

As the final arbiter of what should be included in each issue, I was held responsible for everything; but only a few unpleasant moments in the course of my long tenure do I remember. One unpleasantness occurred when a respected and ordinarily placid Latin master, Leon Glover, came to me in a livid rage. Trembling, he confronted me and with shaking voice informed me that he had been mortally insulted by the "Register's Raving Reporter." The Latin aphorism, placed on his blackboard each day, had evidently appealed to our staff man; but, in copying it, the student made an error and used the dative instead of the accusative case. Thus, Mr. Glover had been shamed and humiliated.

Another tense moment came when John Cray, a member of the same department and admittedly one of the faculty "killers" who terrorized boys in their classes, insisted to the Headmaster that I be reported to the Superintendent and be forced to make a public apology for printing in the Alumni column a highly creditable poem which he had written for his college magazine, the Boston College *Stylus*. When I was called to the office, he claimed I had held him up to ridicule before the student body. Presumably he wished to create among his pupils an image of adamant ruthlessness and forbidding rigidity; and by reprinting, at the suggestion of his classmate, Dr. John Collins, now dean at Teachers College, a poem that expressed a sentimental love of flowers, I was destroying that image and interfering with his discipline. After assuring him that I had no such intent and considered it a harmless prank, I apologized for any discomfiture I might have caused him; and for many years thereafter we continued to be good friends.

By far the most significant unpleasantness in selecting "all the news that's fit to print" for the *Register* was one that illustrated the political and social tensions of the period. During the Spanish Civil War, one of our boys, Walba '34, was killed in battle while serving with the Abraham Lincoln International Brigade. When a classmate of his wrote from Paris to inform me of what had happened to this boy, who only a short time before had been turning every assigned theme, regardless of subject, into a piece of Communist pleading, I turned over this newsworthy item to the alumni editor. After the appearance of the next issue of the *Register,* in which this was printed, I met the Headmaster in the lower corridor near his office and entered into a casual chat. The small talk over, Mr. Powers introduced his real reason for engaging me in conversation: "By the way, Phil, I didn't like the last number of the *Register.*"

"I didn't either," I quickly countered. "Of course, I never do; for I always feel, with the boys we have here, that we should be able to do better."

"No, no; I don't mean that at all. It was excellent generally, but one item spoiled it entirely." Knowing that Joe Powers, a devout Catholic, was in complete agreement with the vast majority of his coreligionists on the issue of the Spanish Civil War, I was by that time fully aware of what he was driving at, but not quite prepared for what was coming.

"That bit about Walba should never have been permitted to appear in a Latin School publication," he said. "I consider that fellow as having written himself out of the alumni, and his name should be stricken from our records for good. I trust you will not allow anything like that to appear again."

While he was delivering himself of this incredible statement, my sense of fair play reasserted itself and I managed to reply, "I'm afraid we've reached the point of no return on that one, Mr. Powers. I can't disagree with you more completely. Walba may be right or wrong; but in any case he died for his convictions. As long as I am in charge of the magazine, I shall have to O.K. any item concerning any graduate, whatever his politics or religion. If you cannot see your way clear to accept this on principle, you'll have to pick another man as adviser to the *Register*." The conversation ended, I was still seething as I continued on my way to the Faculty Room.

When I repeated this startling colloquy to my colleagues, I got an immediate outraged response from a good friend, Bob Drummey. Also a Roman Catholic, Drummey was an outspoken liberal, long a subscriber to the *New Republic,* and explosive in temperament. I had difficulty in preventing his storming out of the room and continuing his profane denunciation of the Headmaster all the way to the office. He finally subsided, and I heard no more about the incident.

Although the *Register* harbored probably the most highly individualistic nonconformists in the school, they gradually became the closest-knit unit of all. This enthusiastic loyalty stemmed from an idiosyncrasy of my own—a tendency to associate people's facial characteristics with those of other members of the animal kingdom. Many times boys in my classes seemed to take on canine, feline, bovine, and porcine features. In a happy moment I hit upon naming the most active clown in each section the class "aardvark." As several of my writers had earned this distinction, we decided that we should form an exclusive society to be known as "The Amalgamated Order of Aardvarks." One of the charter members, Lerner (now a high school teacher), gave impetus and character to the movement while in my homeroom. Occupying the last seat in the last row for purposes of isolation, he quietly developed on the blackboard panel directly behind him a daily newspaper, called simply "The Aardvarkian." When it proved to be clever, witty, and pertinent, I rode with the punch and enjoyed watching classes enter at the beginning of each period, turn at once to the southwest corner, and read avidly Lerner's merry script.

With the passage of time and the cumulative effect of refinements and new ideas, the order took shape with constitution, bylaws, coat-of-arms, Latin motto, and other appurtenances. To become a member, the applicant had to possess unusual characteristics—physical, intellectual, or personal. Unlike other organizations, everybody joining had to prove that he was different from all others. Above all, he had to have these minimum requirements: an ugly face, a long and/or irregular nose, poor or indifferent school grades—in short, any characteristic that might disqualify him as a faculty favorite or as a candidate for the Honor Society. I served as faculty adviser from the beginning. To be elected to office, a member felt called upon to prove worthy by virtue of offbeat behavior or personal eccentricities. Many likely candidates were always available for the offices specified in the by-laws: Prominent Proboscis, Master Clockstopper, Imperial Flybait, Chief Beak, Master Ant Brain, and Chief Sniffer. When annual choices were made, the new incumbents were elated and promised original action. Membership was coveted, as was evident when many boys stopped me in the corridors to ask what qualifications one must have to become an Aardvark. Always I had a stock reply: "I am sorry that I cannot reveal the methods used in selecting candidates; but, as you probably know, it is a secret order. All that I can say is that you must have certain intangible qualities that set you off from everybody else." Some facts became well known: that our patron saint was Cyrano de Bergerac; that our annual banquet was strictly insectivorous; and that our Latin motto, always prominently displayed in color on my front board, *"Facies tantum a matre amata,"* meant, according to one master's free translation, "A face only a mother could love." The student body became aware of how important the fraternity had grown to be when in the *Liber Actorum* pictures and write-ups showed that new chapters had been formed at Girls' Latin School, Harvard, and Dartmouth. A characteristic vignette appeared in the 1951 yearbook:

THE AARDVARKS

With the pomp and dignity of a medieval coronation, a new and mystic order took its place as the school's leading inspirational force. The Amalgamated Order of Aardvarks is dedicated to the most tranquil and independent animal which God has put on earth. . . .

Induction ceremonies were held in December. Membership depends on the four qualities which best characterize the Club's symbol—dullness, laziness, ugliness, and olfactory excellence. Self-elected officers included Joseph Johnson as *Grand Snoot,* Warren Miller as *Lord High Nasal,* Thomas Doherty and Sumner J. Ferris as *Scriveners.*

A coat of arms was drawn and adopted: an aardvark rampant on a field of flies' eyes and bees' knees.

The exercises were highlighted by an address delivered by the faculty adviser, Mr. Philip Marson, the *Wise Old Aardvark,* on "The Aardvark in American Literature," which he illustrated with samples from his vast library of *aardvarkiana.* It is hoped that the society's influence for less activity and more indolence in school affairs will continue to grow.

Clearly such an activity, with its overtones of mock-heroic exclusiveness, would appeal to the type of boy who might write imaginative fiction, romantic verse, humorous and satiric sketches, or draw illustrations and cartoons. As the group met daily and by special permission ate their box luncheons in Room 235, my headquarters, a harmonious team spirit and gay tone pervaded the editorial offices and gave the boys not only comic relief but a freedom which contrasted happily with the repressive rigidity of the rest of their school day. The results of this unique arrangement were gratifying: serious efforts rewarded by public acclaim and a gay abandon that made the surrounding monastic discipline bearable.

When in 1935 Billy Norton and Bill Henderson, classmates at Latin School and at Harvard, were retired from the faculty at seventy (they are still alive and alert at ninety-three), the conduct of a traditional and well-publicized activity fell into my convenient lap. Declamation, which alumnus Charles W. Eliot had said was one of the most valuable skills acquired during his stay at the school, could hardly be classified as extracurricular. It was a hybrid study—conducted in every homeroom, graded and recorded on report cards by the presiding master, and yet not considered by faculty or student body as part of the course of study in any subject, even English. Each boy, however, was required to memorize and recite a new, approved piece for each of the first five months of the school year. Thus, by the time he was graduated, he had recited either twenty selections during the four-year course or thirty during the six-year course.

Requirements were specific: (1) the selection had to consist of twenty lines of prose or twenty-four lines of poetry as a minimum; (2) it was not to be repeated by any classmate during that round or by the boy himself during a subsequent one; and (3) it had to be approved by the master. If a lad showed unusual talent in these preliminary recitations, he was encouraged to enter the trials for public declamation held in the Assembly Hall two weeks later in the hope that he would win one of the coveted honors at the final prize competition held in April. This day was a gala event when I first came to the school; in fact, early programs were on exhibit under glass in the library with such famous oratorical names among them as Edward Everett, Ralph Waldo Emerson, and Phillips Brooks. It was considered a truly important day, and members of the twenty-five-year and fifty-year classes considered it an honor to return to the school and serve as judges of the Prize Declamation.

To co-ordinate the various phases of this school-wide program, one man was needed; and when Billy Norton, who had handled details connected with it, left us, I was asked to take over. Out of this duty came many illuminating incidents. In my own classroom I soon learned that boys spent more time searching through anthologies for pieces (usually poems with refrains) containing exactly the minimum twenty-four lines, preferably in trimeter or at most tetrameter, than it would take to learn a passage of moderate length selected at random. Naturally enough, boys resorted to innumerable dodges to escape the rigors of this superfluous abomination. When the late Fred O'Brien, a former coach and English master, learned that I had been placed in charge of declamation, he hastened to give me an account of how he had managed this particular source of irritation while a student. Instead of memorizing the thirty required pieces, he restricted his efforts to one and only one obscure twenty-four-line poem by a little-known American versifier with whom no master would be likely to be acquainted. The piece was so undistinguished in both matter and manner that no one in the room, including the master, would pay any attention to its recital. To perpetrate his hoax, he invented a new title for the selection each time it was due. For six years he used this one piece and was never discovered. Surely he could claim indisputably to have been the most artful of dodgers.

Many lads, especially those who were gifted or looked forward to becoming preachers, politicians, or other practitioners of oratory, took declamation seriously. At one period the declaimers, presumably having exhausted what they considered the best possibilities in our own language, turned to foreign languages for selections. Some took the Philippics of Demosthenes in the original Greek and the diatribes of Cicero against Catiline in Latin; but, finally, when Lee Harris (later an economic adviser to the state of Israel), after performing these two feats, climaxed his declamatory career by reciting the *Song of Songs* in Hebrew, I decided to call a halt to these foreign flights. I was certain that, despite the clarity and eloquence of the speakers, none of the judges understood more than a word or two of what was being said and were, of course, entirely incapable of evaluating the skill with which these great passages were being interpreted. Overawed by this dramatic display of assumed erudition, they were likely to believe that these competitors were far superior to those who confined themselves to the plain English of "Spartacus to the Gladiators" or Darrow's defense of "Big Bill" Heywood.

The seriousness of such occasions could in all instances be matched by the comedy. Once a lad giving Kipling's "Recessional" reached the refrain "Lord God of Hosts, be with us yet,/Lest we forget; lest we forget." At that inauspicious point, unfortunately, he forgot; and I could not withhold the conclusion that the Lord God of Hosts had obviously forgotten him. The most hilarious of all such incidents occurred at a public declamation when Howard Abramson, a brazen youth, outdid himself histrionically in a rendition of Gilbert's "Yarn of the Nancy Bell." Having worked out a "jolly tar" routine, during which he combined a miniature hornpipe with well-timed hitches of his middle, he had lost himself completely in his colorful interpretation of the speech and antics of the sole cannibalistic survivor. In so doing, he forgot a package of cigarettes in the small-change pocket of his trousers; and during a particularly vigorous hitch shot the pack in a perfect parabola through the air and onto the floor near the feet of the presiding headmaster. Fortunately for the declaimer, that dignitary was sitting with his glass eye toward him. Abramson, with rare presence of mind and rarer aplomb, took advantage of this circumstance by making a wide sweep of his arm and, without loss of effect, picking up the package to return it to his pocket. The audience, composed largely of boys, mystified the headmaster by a sudden explosion of laughter and wild applause.

Bit by bit declamation has lost its place as a major contribution to making Latin School a unique institution. With the increased use of original oral compositions in all English classes, the value of the memorized pieces has gradually diminished and the need for such exercises has all but disappeared. Now only those boys who volunteer engage in this time-honored but diluted and inferior exercise, and compulsory homeroom declamations no longer exist. A trick drill team, a noisy but effective band, and two crack regiments now regularly win prizes in the annual schoolboy parade through Boston streets and more nearly symbolize the tone of the school today.

Full as my life at school had proved to be within and without the classroom, it could not satisfy material, social, or recreational needs and desires. Personal, family, and communal responsibilities had to be met. A teacher's salary may provide a couple with the bare necessities of food, clothing, and shelter. Two people may be willing to exist on a subsistence level; but with the arrival of children, other considerations are forced upon them. Questions of neighborhood influences and proper schooling must be answered. And when personal tastes and cravings for theater, books, music, and social life demand satisfaction as well, the idealist must turn pragmatist.

Our expenses for such luxuries were kept at what is probably an all-time low until many years later (in 1937, to be exact) when an odd turn of events substantially raised my income. Up to the time of this twist, we had no car, using our legs and the trolleys whenever necessity demanded. This method of locomotion served me well each Saturday on excursions to bookshop bargain counters. The invariable weekly route began with remainder sales in department stores; followed a trail of long-established shops on Beacon Hill and Cornhill; and ended on Franklin Street with Lauriat's neat displays or on Milk Street with Goodspeed's dog-eared volumes on the sidewalk open shelves. Religious adherence to a top price limit of fifty cents prevented runaway extravagance, but on one occasion I was good-naturedly threatened with divorce by my long-suffering wife when I arrived home on a particularly fruitful day with ten or a dozen volumes. Over a period of years the accumulated treasures made bookshelves our most conspicuous furniture and wall-space a crying need. When the change in our fortunes permitted us to build a house, we began shaping our architectural dreams around a living room with floor-to-ceiling shelves. To this day the vice which has led me closest to penury has been a monomania—to surround my family with books in every room of the house, including, of course, the bathroom.

Although my wife matched my obsession with two of her own—an unquenchable desire to shower people with gifts and an overpowering urge to collect remnants of beautiful materials for future use as clothing or as décor—we shared equally one costly taste, the theater. Luckily, during our salad days Boston provided its residents with many playhouses, which served excellent repertory, stock, and Broadway companies. At prices which today seem incredibly low, we were able to satisfy our ravenous appetite for dramatic entertainment. For fifteen to twenty-five cents we enjoyed Shakespeare, O'Neill, Ibsen, Barrie, Shaw, and Galsworthy. Among others, they were acted to the hilt at the Castle Square by John Craig, Mary Young, Alfred Lunt, and Donald Meek. The Copley had the Henry Jewett and E. E. Clive companies of British actors, including such present-day celebrities as Alan Mowbray, Philip Tonge, Viola Roache, and the Americans who were then beginners, Richard Whorf and Rosalind Russell. We also had the ill-fated Repertory Theatre, built by public subscription but ruined by internal bickering and strife between management and players. By going wild and spending fifty-five cents, we became acquainted with the structure of every second balcony in the city—from the dizzy heights of the Colonial, Hollis, and Shubert to the peculiar curvature of the Plymouth—but we managed by our lofty climbing to see and hear, with admitted straining, unforgettable performances by the greatest of companies and the most illustrious of stars. As they crowd my memory, I jot them down as fast as my pen can write: the Moscow Art Theatre in *The Lower Depths* and *Boris Godunov;* the Abbey Theatre Players in the dramas of Synge, Lady Gregory, Lennox Robinson, and Sean O'Casey; the Yiddish Art Theatre, with Maurice Schwartz in *The Dybbuk* and *Yoshe Kalb;* and a parade of superb actors including Minnie Maddern Fiske, John Drew, the Barrymores—Ethel and John, Jane Cowl, Blanche Yurka, Sarah Bernhardt, Charlie Chaplin (in a British Music hall sketch, "A Night at the Opera"), and on and on.

Despite debts and worries, we always managed to find the few pennies needed for these irretrievable matinees and evenings in the theater. Climb we certainly did; in fact, we scaled the highest peak in theatrical architecture at the huge but recently demolished Boston Opera House. To hear either the local company or the Metropolitan for fifty cents, we lay flat on our bellies in the low concrete arches located well above the third tier of galleries. Although only one-half of the stage could be seen from this vantage point, the bird's-eye view seemed to give the corpulent forms of the singers more youthful shapes and compensated somewhat for other disadvantages of hearing opera from the brink of a precipitous ledge. Our visual and auditory reception of *Otello* or *La Bohême* might have been distorted, but these inexpensive adventures gave us great joy and permitted us to share in some measure our wealthier friends' experiences.

Another source of pleasure, even less costly than these, was available to Bostonians. Lectures and forums were free or almost so; and they were so popular that the halls were filled to standing room only when controversial subjects were discussed by well-known speakers. During a period of some fifteen years (*circa* 1925–1940) we haunted auditoriums, particularly on Sundays. At times unusually provocative programs lured us into all-day binges. The morning was spent at Community Church; the afternoon, at the Old South Meeting House; and the evening, at Ford Hall.

A history of the times is suggested in a partial listing of speakers and their topics during a five-year span at the Ford Hall, a hotbed of debate:

Father Corrigan—"The Menace of Divorce"

Oswald Garrison Villard—"Europe Collapsing"

Scott Nearing—"Is Life Worth Living?"

Norman Thomas—"Why the Workers of the World Do Not Unite"

Rabbi Stephen Wise—"How Shall America Deal with the Ku Klux Klan"

Edward A. Ross—"The Social Revolution in India"

Clarence Darrow—"Crime and Its Treatment"

Dhan Gopal Mukerji—"The Asiatic Menace"

John Haynes Holmes—"A Pacifist Looks at the World"

Anna Louise Strong—"Russia's New Life"

Arthur E. Morgan—"What Is Civilization?"

Roscoe Pound—"The Task of the Law"

W. E. B. DuBois—"The Hypocrisy of White Folk"

Harry F. Ward—"China and the Orient"

Maurice Samuel—"Palestine's New Message"

Roger Baldwin—"Is Democracy Failing in America?"

Arthur Schlesinger—"Conservatism and Radicalism in America"

Zechariah Chaffee—"Free Speech versus Violence"

Lincoln Steffens—"Armistice and No Peace"

Horace Kallen—"Men Who Have Seen God"

Carl Sandburg—A Lecture-Recital

Joseph Wood Krutch—"The Drama of the Modern World—Ibsen to O'Neill"

Count Michael Karolyi—"Fascismo—Menace to World Peace"

Harry Overstreet—"What Shall We Do with Our Old People?"

Kenneth MacGowan—"The Theatre of Today and Tomorrow"

Countee Cullen—"Color"

Norman Hapgood—"Professional Patriots—Seeing Red"

Morris Hillquit—"Socialism and Soviet Russia"

Rev. W. A. Bolger—"The Menace of Birth Control"

John Langdon-Davies—"Communism and Fascism—Policies of Despair"

Bertrand Russell—"Are Parents Good for Children?"

Dr. Fritz Wittels—"How the Psychoanalyst Cures His Patients"

Stuart Chase—"Men and Machines"

Not only did such programs serve as an inexpensive form of recreation and an endless source of pleasurable discussion; they proved to be a stimulus to weekly meetings with friends. For years we had Sunday night suppers in a nearby restaurant before heading for Ford Hall. Sometimes it was an over-hasty meal; for we had to enter the building before 7:30 to take advantage of our special privilege as members—that is, before the general public was admitted. By the time the doors were flung open to the hordes who wished to get in, the double-line stretched from the entrance on Ashburton Place for blocks almost to Cambridge Street at the bottom of Beacon Hill. When Chairman Charles W. Coleman rose to open the meeting, the atmosphere was charged with an electrical excitement generated by the tense crowd, which not only filled every seat, but sat on steps, stood four-deep at the rear, and overflowed into every available aisle and nook.

During the throbbing thirties, unforeseen thrills often punctuated the sessions. Our lives were at the time dominated by mighty men: F.D.R. was in the White House, and Adolf Hitler had fired the Reichstag. On one memorable evening a spokesman for the Unspeakable One—in fact, a member of the German Government who had left his professorial chair to help his Führer—had been engaged to present the Nazi case at the Forum. At a dinner party given the week before at the home of the present moderator, Judge Reuben Lurie, I had argued vigorously that a bad error was being committed. I voiced the fear that violence was almost certain with an outspoken protagonist of the indefensible authoritarian monster before an audience consisting at least 90 per cent of New Deal Democrats, militant liberals, long-standing but emotionally aroused Fabian Socialists, horrified middle-of-the-roaders from neighboring school and college faculties and student bodies, and—worst of all—large numbers of Jews who were daily receiving anguished pleas for help from persecuted relatives. Nothing I said could swerve Rube a fractional degree in his stand that this meeting sustained a Ford Hall principle—the most important one of all—that every point of view, no matter how distasteful or even destructive of civil liberties, must be given a hearing. While agreeing with him in theory and practice, I continued to insist that this particular demonstration of liberalism was ill-timed and ill-advised. I predicted serious trouble.

My prophecy was fulfilled. A full-scale riot occurred outside the hall when hundreds of citizens—not predominantly fellow-travelers, although undoubtedly the mob was egged on by well-placed Communist agitators—first shouted their disapproval, then began milling about, later threw punches and rocks, and finally brought on the mounties of the Boston police force with their high-stepping steeds and swinging clubs. Among the dozens arrested, some guilty, many innocent, was a boy in one of my classes, David Walba, who as a member of Pioneer Youth had been drafted by his elders to take part in this wild demonstration. Inside the hall, there were no fisticuffs, but verbal brickbats flew fast and furiously. Throughout the evening there were shouted interruptions during the main speech, angry murmurs of disapproval audible enough to make the speaker's words unintelligible in the far corners, and vitriolic comments which expanded into diatribes during what was inexactly called the question period. Anybody who was in the audience will never forget that night of nights.

Ford Hall Forum was the best of its kind, but it was characteristic of the turbulent times that discussion groups were meeting all over the country. Throughout that decade and the next, commentators and debaters in open forums, on radio programs, and in print were heard and read by millions. All controversial subjects were freely explored in a manner and in a volume we have sorely lacked since. Certainly the availability of such food at so low a cost and of so high a quality was an invaluable boon to us and others like us.

This side of our lives was satisfied, as I have intimated, with no unbearable strain on the family exchequer. As bills for other necessaries mounted, however, I felt greater and greater need for supplementary income. Concern for our daughter's education became more specific and insistent. Boy-girl relationships in the coeducational atmosphere of Brookline High School, we were sure, became in many cases a major interference with serious study. As Betty had an inordinately high I.Q. and was headed for Radcliffe, we determined to enroll her at the rigidly classical Girls'

Latin School in Boston. Although it is, like its masculine counterpart, a public school, we as nonresidents would have to pay tuition fees. The eight-year stretch of continuous term bills at school and college made additional funds mandatory.

A teacher should, of course, receive a salary sufficiently high to be able to devote himself exclusively—like men in other learned professions—to his work. Also he should have time for rest, recreation, and travel; but school budgets do not provide funds adequate to supply these needs. Therefore, whatever his personal desires or the general welfare may call for, the taxpayers will not supply adequate funds and the teacher must take on additional chores, however unsuitable or exhausting they may prove to be. Many of my colleagues have had to resort to part-time occupations at best embarrassing and in some instances degrading—to wit, gas station attendant, hotel doorman or bellboy, cashier at race tracks, usher at ball parks, barber, bartender, drummer in a dance band. These men were all driven to such extremes because taxpayers refuse to pay the price for their children's proper education and thus, in effect, permit teachers to subsidize the schools.

I had come to the point that these men had reached and had worked in successive summers as a bookkeeper in a factory, contract clerk in a shipyard, and correspondent in a jobber's office before I began my apprenticeship as a camp administrator. This experience, gained at a tutoring camp on Squam Lake, was valuable but harrowing and costly. It was so disastrous financially that it nearly discouraged further ventures in this field; for I received no salary and lost half of my investment. To add to my woes, it was at this time—just prior to my beginning my tenure at Latin School—that my wife gave birth prematurely to twins, who died almost immediately. All in all, the summer of 1926 was unprofitable, unhappy, and discouraging to a man who wanted desperately to continue to teach.

5. FREEDOM

EXTRACURRICULAR ACTIVITIES WERE UNDOUBTEDLY SAFETY valves and balance wheels in the lives of Latin School boys and served as happy, important supplemental factors in their development. Nevertheless, studies and personalities created the dominant and pervasive atmosphere. In the early years of my tenure, the long-standing influence of rigid Puritanical attitudes toward work and duty—as inculcated by crusty, hard-bitten Yankee schoolmasters—permeated the building. Inflexibility, born of tradition, ruled policy and shaped spirit; but with it came also the rewards of unremitting toil, respect for authority, and a feeling that the work of the school was important, uncomplicated, and effective.

No matter how peculiar or tyrannical the individual master might have been, he knew—and his charges knew—that he represented unwritten laws and traditional procedures bigger than both of them. Fear and resentment they surely evoked, but the relationship between boy and man became highly personal. A measure of its nature may be deduced from the nicknames earned, achieved, or foisted upon some of the more colorful members of the faculty: Stuffy, Bingo, Cudjo, Doggie, Itchy, Bunk, and Skunko.

Intolerant and unfair they often were; but no boy ever doubted their seriousness, integrity, or sense of duty.

What the boys were not aware of, however, was that these men took for granted and with a good grace their miserably low pay. Before 1935 I heard no complaints. Inherent dignity and respect for their profession prevented the formation of any organization that might be militant enough to take on the coloration of a trade union. Undoubtedly these attitudes accounted for low salaries and some political exploitation, but they also set the tone of the school and reflected the gentility and academic interest of its faculty. Our headmaster, Pat Campbell, was characteristic of his generation. He had simple tastes and frugal habits and was satisfied with his lot. Throughout his life, even after he had been elevated to the superintendency, he continued to reside in a modest two-family home nearby. On numerous occasions, such as faculty dinners or class reunions, he had solemnly declared that "there was no promotion from the Latin School." At the time he probably believed it. I certainly did.

The statement mirrored the pride felt by masters, student body, and alumni in the history and persistent reputation of the school. Prestige and acclaim made up in part for lack of monetary recognition; but good men were often lured into leaving the school when promotions provided bigger salaries. Pat Campbell's own story illustrates, at least in one case, why great teachers—most of whom are born, not trained—are too often tempted to leave a school of which they have become truly an organic part and to give up their profession to become administrators. Pat loved people, particularly boys, and he reflected this love in his dealings with individuals and with groups.

At the annual pre-Thanskgiving dinner of 1957, I heard former Ambassador Joseph Kennedy as a member of the fifty-year class cite Pat Campbell as the man solely responsible for keeping him at the school and thus making it possible for him to become a Harvard man. The details are worth recalling. Joe Kennedy, crack first baseman of the school team which Pat was directing, was flunking badly in Latin and slipping in other subjects sufficiently to endanger his eligibility. When the report cards were issued, the worst had happened. Joe, sensing fully the probabilities, had been in touch with the English High School coach, who had gladly promised to provide for his transfer to the rival institution. Not a word had been spoken at home to inform his parents of the planned move, and Joe had decided to surprise them with the *fait accompli* on the day the report cards would have to be signed and returned. The ever-alert Pat Campbell, however, had learned of his player's scholastic problems and his plans for escape. Jumping the gun, he took streetcar and ferry to his native East Boston, where the Kennedys had always lived, to talk with them of Joe's intentions. When the unsuspecting miscreant arrived, he was confronted by Pat and a thoroughly aroused mother. The sequel is well known to Bostonians: Joe played first-base at Harvard, remained undistinguished as a scholar, but went on to become an internationally known alumnus. This incident was only one of hundreds in which Pat Campbell took a personal interest in his boys.

His concern did not diminish with the years. A quarter-century later I was a partner to one of his good deeds. We were both interested in a boy we had watched grow up from the time he entered the school in 1926. The boy was a typical youngster of that era when he enrolled in Ralph Taylor's class, which occupied half of the study hall in Room 206. My own class met in the other half, but I could not help noticing this oversized, beautifully built Jewish lad. He soon made his way in the school; and by the time he became a senior, his athletic prowess had earned him a place as tackle on the all-scholastic team, and his outgoing personality had won him the football captaincy as well as the class presidency. As he did well in his studies, we were confident that with a reasonable showing in the all-important entrance examinations, his admission to Harvard was assured. Unfortunately, however, his grades were just a fraction of a point below the inflexible 75 required by Harvard for Jewish candidates; and in mid-July the glorified clerks in the admissions office automatically sent him the politely phrased stock note stating, in effect, that "we regret to inform you that your grades are not sufficiently high for matriculation in our freshman class."

As he was a counselor at camp with me when he received this crushing news, he rushed immediately from his post at the waterfront to my office to express his dismay and confusion. Infuriated by such obvious injustice, I sent an angry but factual letter to the Chairman of the Harvard board of admissions, Mr. Henry Pennypacker, predecessor to Pat Campbell as Latin School headmaster. The only other action I could think of was to call the redoubtable Pat (by that time Assistant Superintendent of the Boston public schools) for advice. His immediate response was, "They can't do that to our Dave; I'm heading for Cambridge as soon as I hang up and give Henry a going-over he won't forget." My letter and Pat arrived at almost the same moment. The happy result was that Dave got his bachelor's degree from Harvard, was an outstanding tackle on Barry Wood's 1932 eleven, and like his captain went on to the Medical School to prepare for a successful career. The directness, the intimate knowledge, and the personal interest needed for such action can come only to those in daily contact with boys and girls. When schools, because of lack of money, must permit born teachers to forsake their calling and enter the political lists for promotion, they have lost their most essential property.

At the time that Pat Campbell succumbed to the temptations of high office, the Boston Latin School faculty still consisted predominantly of unselfish men. They considered teaching a worthy and respectable calling, accepted a modest income as an inherent attribute of their profession, just as preachers did of theirs, and gladly dedicated themselves to helping boys grow up—at the very least, intellectually. Like monks, they paid little attention to the world outside and devoted themselves strictly to the advancement of learning. As I used to suggest to my classes, "You and I are here for only one purpose—*your* education."

Unfortunately, however, almost all schoolmasters in this country find it necessary, especially if they are married and have children, to supplement their incomes. I have been no exception. To maintain a not unreasonable standard of living, I have had to work in whatever spare time I could find during the academic year and to spend every summer pursuing elusive dollars. In an earlier chapter I have recounted my attempts to find satisfactory means of removing a great source of worry and discontent. It was not until I discovered camping as a suitable part-time occupation that I had any hope of freeing myself from the constant pressure of financial shackles that bound me.

My ill-fated summer investment of 1926 did not, I am glad to say, destroy my faith in camping. I would return to it; but my first year at Boston Latin School was to begin with gargantuan handicaps, traceable in part to this speculative disaster. In part, I say, for, despite a rugged physique, I was flattened by an acute inflammation of the throat called *quinsy*. It was probably brought on by worry about mounting medical expenses, about my wife's condition, and about my new job. During the first two weeks of the term I had to appear at the doctor's office to have my tonsils painted with iodine—an irritating nuisance, but a trifle in the maelstrom of surrounding difficulties. Above everything else, I had to earn extra money.

The gods, I quickly discovered, had not entirely forsaken me. Bill Pierce, head of the history department, as considerate and capable a man as I have ever met, offered me an appointment in English and American literature at Central Evening High School, of which he was principal. Not only would the work provide fifteen dollars each week, but it would keep me on my toes. The classes of adults were tired after a day's work and had to be kept alert or at least awake. The three courses—English literature, American literature, and types of literature—necessitated the delivery of a lecture at each session; but the subject matter had become so completely part of me that the chore was not impossible. For five years I continued, without skipping one night, to rush through dinner, which had to be served not later than six to enable me to meet my first group at seven-thirty; catch the trolley to Copley Station in the subway; walk along Dartmouth Street for better than a half-mile to the building which housed English High School during the day; perform my duties; and then drive home with my boss, who dropped me about ten o'clock before continuing his route to Needham.

The program sounds grimly forbidding as I record it; but the eagerness of the men and women in my classes and the satisfactions that come from working with appreciative adults repaid me for energy consumed and time expended. Most of these people I have forgotten, the memory of some of them is dim and blurred, but a few remain distinctly and sharply etched in my mind. Among them were housewives, nurses, secretaries, salesmen, truckdrivers, waitresses—in fact, every segment of the population, including a sizable group who had nowhere else to go and enjoyed the warm, comfortable, congenial surroundings. One such gentleman was a perennial who had attended classes for many years before I came and who continued after I had left.

During my five-year stay, he never failed to register at the first session and seemed to enjoy himself throughout the course. Occupying the same rear seat with unfailing regularity, he asked at least one big question at each session. His supply of problems never ran out, for his vocational pursuits and his avocational interests were many and varied. An imposing and massive figure as he slowly rose from his squat chair to his full six-feet-four, he always gave me a start when he addressed me as "Perfessor." Usually, in framing his query, he drew upon his rich experience in three major occupations: as an itinerant preacher, a part-time lawyer, and an exterminator of bedbugs and roaches. He might, for instance, ask me if I could furnish him with a list of novels which "stressed the brotherhood of man and the fatherhood of God" or what I thought of the disgraceful condition of the Boston streets. Whatever it was, he never disappointed me by omitting to pose at least one problem per session.

In attempts to stimulate collateral reading, I often suggested current books or classics which my students were not likely to have read before. On one such occasion I assigned for a scheduled report the study of a Shakespearean play ordinarily not studied in high school, naming as possibilities such dramas as *Lear, Othello, Cymbeline,* or *A Winter's Tale.* After considerable explanation of the purpose of the assignment and its preparation, I assumed that everybody understood; but I had forgotten one listener. My friend, with perfect understanding of the problem, began in characteristic fashion: "Perfessor, would you object if

I reported on *The Merchant of Venice?* I have just been reading it, and I find it mighty interesting. How about it, sir?"

I had long before learned to go along with whatever he suggested, and I readily consented. Little did I know, even on the basis of long experience, that he was about to create a unique masterpiece of misinformation and confusion. It would serve me well as an example of what a teacher of English is up against. I grant that fortunately we do not meet many of his peers, but now and then insoluble mysteries of pedagogy do appear. Many times I have used his critique to enliven a class dinner, and I submit it here for "posterity."

THE MERCHANT OF VENICE

A Report

Subject: The Action of a Skilful Woman Causes Her Lover to be Discharged in Court.

A man will forget the language you use but he will not forget the pictur you make. Our pictures we make are like love which exist between man and woman. It forever stands.

The word dollar means more to the average man than money, fleish more than a dollar. Cornflakes more than breakfast food.

Shakespeare vary beautifully and vary apprately said that Hiawatha's canoe would float upon the river like a yellow water lily, like a yellow leaf in autumn, but if you were offering a canoe for sale you would emphasize its utility as well as its beauty in no less expression but slightly different comparison.

I do not criticise the work of Mr. Shakespeare's promoter. But I take much plesure in abstricking from Mr. Hudson's abstract.

A on his voyage to B City, having in mind to call on X while in B City, meets C, who were vary wealth and beautiful. He falls deeply in love with C and returns to V in City to get a loan of 10,000 dollars from M, giving M a note dated a certain date, promising to pay on date stated or he would give one pound of his fleish from his body. Should he default in his payment. A gains the love of C and marrages. He fogets the promes he made and hasten to the loaner. When reaching him he finds him rigiving and requested the one pound of fleish. Hereupon A, who were Giannetto the barran and the one who marraged the wealth beautiful lady on his voyage to Belmont.

Now he is much overjoyed at the happy issue, yields up to the Judge in token of his gratitude a ring which his wife had give him on their marriage day, and the Judge, on returning home and putting off the disguise rails at her husband in fine terms about his parting with the ring, which she says she is sure he must have give to some woman.

This goes to show what a skilful woman can do. Because of she having meet Giannetto while on his voyage to Belmont and by becoming deeply in love with him she marriage him and through her actions and polished language she disguist herself and played the part of judge to save her husband and cause him to be discharge in Court. She disguises herself as a doctor of laws and gets herself introduced as a judge into the Court where the case were on trial in Italy, at which time nice and difficult points of law were determined, not by ordinary Judges but by doctors of law from Padua, Bologna, and other Roman law schools.

The lady C, unrecognized by her husband, learns of the nature of the case, and, after reading the bond, calls on the Jew to take the pound of fleish, but tells him he must take neither more nor less than exactly a pound and that he must shed no blood. A executioner is at hand to behead him in case any blood be drawn. The Jew then says he will except the 10,000 offered. But he had declared up and down that he would have nothing but the one pound of fleish. The woman Judge refuses to allow any repayment of money whatsoever. And the Jew in a rage tears up the bond and quits the Court.

Therefor I will say that a man who is bone of a woman, as all men are, they are compell to love them. Because a woman is more than wealth or beauty, a man will forget his language and statements he makes to a woman, but he will not forget his love to her.

After five years I had taken leave of the classes, but one additional tie with them was established by my successor, the late Paul Thayer. After he had accepted the post, Bill Pierce had implanted in him a kernel of insecurity by lauding my methods. He had attributed to my approach and procedure the large enrollment and maintenance of membership throughout the year. As a teacher of evening courses is rated on the number of students who continue to attend his classes, Paul was naturally eager to duplicate my success; and so that he might be briefed on my procedure, we arranged an afternoon coffee date. After our conference he had settled on an opening talk about Shakespeare and the Elizabethan theater.

Two weeks later Paul reported the outcome of his well-planned first-night performance. After pulling all the stops and utilizing fully the humor and "schmaltz" on a subject with infinite possibilities, he proudly concluded with the efficient teacher's finale, "Are there any questions?" With his usual aplomb, our friend rose majestically and astounded his instructor by asking in resonant tones, "Perfessor, when's we gonna have spellin'?" The teacher of such classes needs both an acute sense of the ridiculous and a sympathetic understanding.

After a prolonged tour of duty in adult education, a man looks for an escape hatch. Not only does he find the work a burden and an invasion of the peace that should be his after a strenuous day, but the remuneration does not solve his financial problems. Thus, when in the spring of 1928 I was asked to become director of the first camp organized by the Associated Y.M.H.A.'s at Middleboro (Massachusetts), I gladly consented. Not until I was actually on the job as a full-fledged director, did I begin to understand why my boss at Squam Lake (Ed Ogden) had never smiled, had spoken only when forced to, and had looked as if he were carrying the burdens of a god on his back. Now that I have completed my thirty-third year as a camp director, I assert that no man should be asked to assume the responsibilities inherent in the position. Regardless of rewards—material and intangible—I would advise no one to take on its duties and obligations; they are too great, too many, and too unpredictable.

As I begin to write this detailed account of my life at camp, I am aware that the purpose of my book may seem to have been side-tracked. To justify what may appear to some an irrelevancy, I offer two considerations: first, I wish to show how one teacher solved the problem of insufficient income; and second, although it should not have been necessary and took too much of his time and energy, I wish to indicate how he avoided engaging in unrelated occupations and how, on the contrary, he found in camping a means of making himself a more effective teacher. I could learn much more about human behavior in camp than in the classroom.

That first season at Camp Avoda should have supplied me with sufficient warning signals. If I was not dissuaded and discouraged then, I probably could never be. The board which had selected the site on the shores of Lake Tispaquin should have been presented with some appropriate prize, to symbolize ability to ignore every requirement essential to effective camping. The small area was flatter than a prairie. Naturally, then, we could anticipate drainage troubles, and we were not wrong. Any rains reduced the athletic field to a bog of ankle-deep mud. On the other hand, during a prolonged dry spell it became a choking dust bowl in which the parched athletes often were lost to view. The utter flatness of the terrain prevented normal sewage disposal, and Mr. Mahoney arrived from Brockton with his "honey cart" to dig out at too frequent intervals the cesspool connected with the eight-holer that served sixty-four campers and fifteen adults. To add to our problems, Lake Tispaquin, like many Cape Cod ponds, was cursed with a muddy bottom. As a result, bloodsuckers and huge water snakes were abundant; and boys and counselors often emerged from the water with one type of pest clinging tenaciously and bloodily to their backs and the other wrapped lovingly around their legs. To complete what should have been a refreshing bath, an oily film covered them and necessitated their heading for the home-made barrel shower which we had been forced to improvise almost at once.

With such deterrents to even reasonable comfort, the possibility of a happy summer would seem remote, if not unattainable. Natural handicaps were not the only ones. Man-made obstacles, like hard, unbending, mattress-free bunks in screenless shelters, added problems. In spite of everything so far mentioned and other abominations, the nine-week season was unanimously adjudged a success.

It is hard to explain why camp produces so much enthusiasm. Whether it is the freedom, the release from the complexities of civilized life, the independence of action away from family and community prohibitions, the easy camaraderie, the manifold opportunities for socializing and engaging in sports, or any combination of these—I do not even now profess to know. But if we could make a go of it for some eighty people with the handicaps under which we conducted our program, there must be something in the institution itself that accounts for its wide acceptance as a valuable supplementary agent in the maturation of youngsters.

Before concluding these brief notes concerning my first directorship (for which service, incidentally, I was paid five hundred dollars), I must add a few significant memoranda. One concerns a physical inconvenience as viewed by a resourceful camper. "Kesty," an interesting and curious lad, was my most frequent visitor. I could rely on seeing him several times each day, his intermittent appearances usually heralded in identical fashion. His head would be stuck through the partially opened screen door of my office, and his opening gambit was always the same. A stammerer, he invariably began, "M-m-mr. M-m-m-marson, I've g-g-got an id-d-dea!" Although I had learned early in our association that his suggestions were rarely workable, I always managed to restrain the impulse to send him on his way by merely pointing to the mountainous pile of paper-work that was a permanent adjunct of my job; and I asked with feigned interest, "What have you got to offer today, Kesty?"

The prize colloquy of the season opened in standard fashion, but this time his inventive mind had come up with an unorthodox curio which would be a credit to Rube Goldberg: "W-w-well, Ch-ch-chief, y'know th-those m-m-m-mosquit-to nets th-th-that c-c-c-cover us. Th-they're j-j-just ab-b-bout d-drivin' me n-n-nuts! Th-th-the darn p-p-pests k-keep b-b-buzzin' around on the outside s-s-so I c-c-can't s-sleep. L-l-last n-n-night I g-got a f-f-flash through m-my b-b-brain. I c-cut a h-h-hole in the n-n-net, and wh-when the stinker c-comes th-through—wham! I g-g-give it a c-clout and k-k-kill it!"

No season since has produced another Kesty. We have had our full share of individualists; and I am glad that we have, for to retain our perspective, we need people with oddities and quiddities. They help supply the relief one needs when too many wrenches are thrown by perverse monkeys in the forest. I had a particularly persistent thrower that summer who taught me an invaluable lesson. As the most active busybody on the board, he visited camp every few days from his convenient home in neighboring Brockton; cross-examined counselors as to what was going on; made innumerable suggestions of an unworkable nature; and interfered generally. After several minor explosions on my part and his, I hinted to an equally influential trustee that if his confrère did not stay away from me—in fact, away from camp—I should regrettably depart and give him free rein. I was not troubled again; but when I was asked to return for a second round the following year, I consented to consider it only after the board had met my stipulation that the gadfly be kept from buzzing too loudly or at too close range. When, however, a committee from a Boston orphanage waited on me before I had made my decision and offered me the opportunity to direct their new camp at Alfred, Maine, I was happy to accept.

Not only was I to receive twice as much salary, but a cottage was to be available for my family. During the previous summer at Avoda, I caught only occasional glimpses of my wife and my daughter by making flying visits to Onset, where they stayed at rates that were reasonable but still too high for us. Therefore, an offer which would make possible our being together, would relieve us of costs for food and utilities, and would net us a thousand dollars in cash seemed like a climactic turn in our fortunes. It was undeniably a windfall, but, as we were to discover, not enough to provide what we considered essentials to the good life.

Camp Emoh (appropriately enough, its name spelled H-O-M-E backwards) occupied a good site. Located in the woods on the shores of Lake Bunganut in Maine, it was three miles by dirt road from the highway—whether approached from the county-seat Alfred, from Waterboro, or from the Sanford-Biddeford road. The hilly terrain permitted good drainage, so that sewage disposal was possible by gravity flow. Our water supply was pumped from the lake to a large concrete tank and chlorinated before being piped to the cabins, which contained the fabulous luxury of flush toilets and wash basins with running water. Such accommodations, I earnestly believed after my previous camp ventures, were as good as a director in Utopia had any right to hope for. With essential buildings, ample playing fields, and adequate swimming and boating facilities, we had a highly satisfactory plant.

When I considered my campers and my personnel, I felt that life at camp could become interesting and complete. This outfit had characteristics all its own. Most unusual of them was that we were really operating two separate camps: one in July, made up of 150 boys and a male staff of some thirty-five; and a strikingly different one in August, when the same number of girls and female counselors changed the appearance, the tone, and the tempo. All-summer residents included the director, his wife, his daughter, his dog, the physician, the nurse, the bookkeeper, the waterfront director, and the commisariat. The roster of campers in both months had a common factor: one-third of them came from the orphanage, while the rest were youngsters of moderate means whose parents paid fees sufficient to cover costs of operation. Actually, at the end of each year the audit showed several thousands of dollars in surplus, which was used for improvements or as a contribution to the maintenance of the orphanage. This noteworthy result was accomplished from 1929 to 1936 by means of seasonal fees for each paying camper of not more than 150 dollars. With a total income, therefore, of about 10 thousand dollars, we managed beautifully, and without sacrificing quality or quantity of food, personnel, or activity. For the benefit of business managers of similar projects, I hasten to add that Camp Emoh, being classified as a charitable institution, was not subject to local, state, or federal taxes. Furthermore, one does not have to be an accountant to be aware of the fact that, during the period under consideration, prices were at an all-time low. Otherwise, these results might look like an unbelievable miracle. Finally, as efficient as my wife might have been as dietitian and buyer and as careful as I might have been in spending other people's money, we could not have run camp without the generous spirit and substantial co-operation of our staff. Partly because they could afford the luxury of spending the summer at camp and partly because they wished to contribute a social service, they worked for almost nothing.

After five summers of operation, Camp Emoh became a full-season all-boys' camp. The decision was based not on any smaller degree of success with the girls, but on two major factors: fewer and fewer counselors were interested in the short one-month term of employment and, as the depression deepened, parents cut expenses by keeping their daughters at home rather than their sons.

So happy was our life at camp, that I came to accept this part-time occupation as a permanent arrangement. A series of events, however, combined to bring about a change. First, the removal of the girls forced us to find a suitable camp for our daughter Betty, then twelve years old. Secondly, we felt the need of enrolling her at Girls' Latin School, where serious preparation for college was possible. As the cost of school and camp would thus be increased by almost five hundred dollars, the need for more income was apparent.

Up to that point I had refused all offers that might tempt me into the commercial side of camping. Some people attributed my obstinacy to lack of ambition; I myself suspected that my earlier financial flop at Aloha might have had subconscious effects. As I think about these matters now, I explain my stubbornness in neither way; I believe that inertia, caused by the contentment with my life at Emoh, accounts for it. The satisfactions were many, deep, and invisible. I was vaguely conscious of them, but even now am hard put to name or describe them specifically. Perhaps they may be accounted for by the successful blending of gratifying work, joyous play, and rare people. Never have I felt, for instance, like one young man—an accomplished pianist and at the time a candidate for a doctor's degree in philosophy—when he made an unforgettable remark, "Chief, do you realize what a wonderful camp this would be if the kids weren't here?" This revelation indicated, of course, his own weakness as a counselor. He should not have attempted to work with children, for he obviously disliked them. In fact, he avoided them at all costs, even going so far as to do heavy manual labor like digging a well or, when possible, escaping into the deep woods with a comforting book.

A counselor or a teacher must find all youngsters, however odd or maladjusted, at least interesting and usually likable. Unless one feels that way about the growing child, he should avoid life at camp as he would a school of man-eating sharks. Without this sympathy and friendliness for children, the anguish connected with my job as director would long ago have driven me out. A recent correspondent described it by means of a mathematical formula:

$$\underset{\text{(Seasonal Anxiety)}}{A} = \underset{\text{(Seconds)}}{60S} \times \underset{\text{(Minutes)}}{60M} \times \underset{\text{(Hours)}}{24H} \times \underset{\text{(Weeks)}}{8W}$$

The satisfactions of the work compensate for the toll it takes, but I still found myself in a financial quagmire. If we were to maintain a reasonable standard of living and send our daughter to Radcliffe, I should have to find a source of much greater income. My chance came in the spring. While my wife was shopping one Saturday night, I remained outside in the car and, absorbed in a book, did not notice the man parked next to me until he shouted a greeting. It was Eli Yoffe, a neighbor. After some small talk, he surprised me with a sudden question, "Phil, would you be interested in running a camp of your own?"

The question might be academic, pleasantly conversational, or seriously pointed. Whatever it would turn out to be, I answered it as evasively as I had on other occasions, "Well, I might if I weren't a schoolmaster. I haven't that kind of money; and even if I had, I have no stomach for business."

"Anyway, think it over. I might be able to supply the capital. Look around during the summer for a possible camp site. Maybe you'll find something really good."

With that, our wives returned and I dismissed the subject from my mind. After all, we were scarcely more than casual acquaintances. They had just moved into their home a few doors up the street. Two years before, we had built the first house on Wallis Road in the newly developed district of South Brookline. The story of our home, which I had named "The House that Hitler Built," is worth telling.

One great advantage of teaching in a big city is the sabbatical leave of absence granted after each seven-year period of service. I had vowed that I would never fail to take advantage of this privilege whenever it came due. The only fly in the ointment was that one had to get along on about three-fifths of his salary that year while devoting himself to study at an approved university; but by 1933, when my first one was impending, we had managed—by forced savings in a co-operative bank—to accumulate some twenty-five hundred dollars for the anticipated decrease in income and the increase in outgo. *Outgo* it was, for the plans called for my family's residing in Berlin while I studied comparative literature at its great university. But these best-laid plans went sadly awry.

That particular year the Nazi madman cut loose, and Germany became a country to be avoided. When in December my mother, who was to accompany us and visit with family and friends in her native land, was fatally struck down by an automobile, we decided to forego the sabbatical entirely. Instead, we used our hard-earned savings to build a house. Collaborating with a rising young architect, Sam Glaser, we determined to construct a huge fireplace, around which a pine-panelled living room, bookshelves, and other necessary appurtenances would grow. The result was so beautiful that both exterior and interior of what finally turned out to be a modified Costwold cottage were pictured in the Boston *Transcript* (an honor which even a *Proper* Bostonian would covet) and later in the *Architectural Forum.* In January of 1934 we moved in and lived happily in it until we transferred title and mortgage to our daughter and son-in-law sixteen years later. Thus, I am able to record one good deed for which the unspeakable Hitler was unconsciously responsible.

Not only the house itself, but the friendships it brought were unforeseeable blessings. Permanent ties were cemented with people who are now among those closest to us; and, as stated previously, paved the way for a venture which is still a major part of my life, Camp Alton.

A Welsh prescription for personal success itemizes three ingredients—"the gift of the gods, man's energy, and events to suit." None may be omitted. According to the formula, then, a teacher may have the natural endowment and may be a human dynamo; but without what the sporting world calls "the breaks," he cannot reach his goal. One element must certainly be sufficient income to enable him to devote himself exclusively to his profession. It follows that to escape financial worries of crushing force, he must be lucky enough to have been born wealthy, to have married an heiress, to have remained a bachelor, or . . . to have become a camp owner. This last stroke of fortune, in my case, made possible—beyond the removal of debts—independence of spirit and freedom of action.

The gods had decreed, for reasons known only to themselves, that I was to become a camp tycoon, or more accurately, one-third of one. The advent of Hitler, the cancellation of my sabbatical, and the building of our house on Wallis Road had paved the way for a triple alliance of good neighbors—the Yoffes, the Riesmans, and the Marsons. The first two were wealthy; the last-named was impoverished and in 1936 was struggling to meet mortgage payments as well as remain afloat in a steady flood of bills. When Eli Yoffe had suggested in his quiet, offhand way that I look for a suitable camp site, I dismissed his offer as polite conversation and did nothing about it. In mid-July, however, when I received a letter from him asking if I had seen any likely plants, I realized that he was not fooling. After many fruitless expeditions through northern New England with agents, whom I had driven almost mad, I finally saw what I did not expect to find—the ideal site. Oliver Baxter, who looked like, talked like, and acted like the all-time Yankee horse-trader David Harum, drove me from his Farmington office to a millionaire's showplace off Route 28, seven miles beyond Alton Bay towards Wolfeboro, "the oldest summer resort in America." The estate was at the time a white elephant owned by Helen Hopewell, widow of Frank, who had been president and treasurer of the Goodall Worsted Mills (manufacturers of Palm Beach cloth) and whose chief interests had been boats and horses. It had, *mirabile dictu,* everything I was looking for. As a result, no other place, however suitable, pleased me thereafter. It was beyond my most Utopian dreams, but it had a price tag that we could not afford. The lady was asking seventy-five thousand dollars—not too much for the 65-acre peninsula (called Clay Point) which jutted out into Lake Winnipesaukee. Located in indescribably beautiful country among the foothills of the White Mountains, it had almost perfect terrain. Continuous pine groves bordered a mile of shore front, a sizable portion of which was a sandy beach with a hard bottom, a gradual slope, and no rocks or holes. Deep-water docks for yachts permitted the U. S. mailboat to stop daily on its rounds and provided an 18-foot depth for diving. A 3-foot rock breakwater bordered a filled-in stretch of land on which stood a pavilion, and immediately I envisioned an outdoor stage facing the natural amphitheater which sloped toward it from the main building.

The open fields which we had seen as we entered had served the late Mr. Hopewell as a polo field and a level spot for training his jumpers. The fields would, of course, be perfect playing areas for our boys, with enough acreage to provide baseball and softball diamonds; a soccer or football gridiron; a quarter-mile track; tennis, basketball, and volleyball courts. The sturdy gray-and-white buildings, all of which could be easily adapted to our purposes, had been perfectly maintained and were in excellent condition. The biggest of them contained the lodge, dining room, kitchen, and sleeping quarters for the family. Two small adjoining cabins housed guests. Separate structures were provided for male and female help. Other buildings included a four-car garage (a possible craftshop?), stables, sheds, bathhouses, and sundry storerooms. These basic facilities, as well as electrification and good roads, were great assets; but they could be only a beginning for a camp of 150 boys and 50 adults. To do the necessary rebuilding of what was already there and to build new cabins and a large recreation hall would involve a greater capital outlay than my associates might be willing to provide. When, however, they went over the property and saw its possibilities, they could not resist making an offer.

This offer, far below the asking price, was accepted; papers were passed before the end of the year; and I was faced with a huge project. Construction should have been started at once, but could not be begun before April after what natives call "mud time"; for dirt roads are impassable for passenger cars, let alone trucks. Thus, all building would have to be done between mid-April and the first of July. When I found that the caretaker, Charley Roberts, was a contractor willing to tackle anything—carpentry, roofing, roadwork, forest-clearance, masonry, plumbing, construction of tanks and filter-beds, boat repairs, electrical work, and grading—I had no hesitation in turning the project over to him. The basic work included the erection of fourteen cabins; a large hall, which would serve a dual purpose as an auditorium and gymnasium; a remodeled dining room and kitchen to provide meals for 200 people. A big undertaking it certainly was; but Mr. Roberts, a strong and vigorous man, tackled it with the confidence born of experience.

Unfortunately, this rugged and heretofore healthy man fell ill just as the work began, so ill that physicians doubted his ability to survive. My compassion for his plight (with a family of six) led me into a major error when I permitted his wife to attempt to carry on. On May 30, the sum total of new construction consisted of the framework for two cabins. When I visualized the realities of the situation I should have to face one short month later, I quailed. Contrary to my own doubts and to anybody else's extravagant estimates, I had enrolled more than 125 campers. After explaining to Mr. and Mrs. Roberts the implications of this registration, I had to act with dispatch and without sentiment. I engaged Charles Palmer of Farmington to finish the job. This man proved to be fast, efficient, thorough, and honest; but he could not accomplish the impossible or perform miracles. With fifty men constantly at work and closely supervised, he managed by the end of June to have finished sufficiently the dining hall and the cabins to permit us to move in. But that was all.

When I arrived with a half-dozen stalwarts on the twenty-fourth of June (the day school closed), I was faced with difficulties which appeared to be insurmountable. No pipes had been laid, ditches were only partly dug, new metal septic tanks were lying on their sides above ground, and no plumbing had been installed. To add to the pervading gloom, the heavens opened and rain poured down on us without cessation for six days and nights. Digging trenches was slowed, if not stopped. Charlie Palmer kept punching, though, with his clothes drenched and his vision dimmed by continuous streams. To hire extra laborers, pipefitters, and plumbers, he traveled as far as Nashua and Lowell and worked them around the clock.

When "D-Day" arrived, we were almost ready for the invading hordes. While we were on the way to the railroad station at Wolfeboro to pick up with buses and beachwagons the 157 campers and 35 counselors to make up our initial roster, the sun came out for the first time that week. Even if our matter-of-fact minds could not accept its appearance as a good omen, it helped to cheer us and make the hurly-burly of those first days a little less trying.

Buildings were certainly not ship-shape (although with the amount of water they had absorbed, they should have been), but they were habitable. For six weeks thereafter boys and counselors might be awakened before reveille by the banging of hammers instead of the blowing of bugles; and then might discover—as they rubbed their eyes incredulously—the head of a workman jutting out of an opening in the floor. A total of fifty plumbers, carpenters, and laborers continued to be under foot for three-quarters of the season before they put the finishing touches on the last of their works, the recreational hall.

How I managed to survive that summer and remain upright I still do not understand. As a matter of fact, until the Christmas holidays, I was numb—going as mechanically as a robot through the motions of living. I had little interest in work or family; it was evident that the strain had taken its toll. That I bent under it should have occasioned no wonder; for I had opened a new camp and had attended single-handed to all preliminary details (selecting a site, planning and supervising construction, buying equipment and supplies, enrolling a capacity membership, engaging a staff), and then had directed its operation under indescribable handicaps. Its direction involved a many-sided set of tasks: orientation to our new surroundings; establishment of congenial relationships with neighbors, shopkeepers, express and freight agents, physicians and hospital officials, and others; building a spirit of co-operation and happy camaraderie among counselors and campers; organization and administration of a comprehensive recreational and educational program; and the successful performance of all these functions while Charlie Palmer and his men continued their operations.

The success of Alton, despite the difficulties of that first season, became apparent from the beginning. Financially, it is solidly established; in fact, its annual audit has led one of my associates (who have been the most silent of silent partners) to repeat on several occasions that the federal authorities ought to consult the director of Camp Alton on budgetary matters. Only a few facts concerning this aspect of camping will be mentioned here, for I thoroughly dislike it, and if the educational phases of the project were not so gratifying, I should have given it up long ago. We have realized a sizable profit every year—substantial enough *in toto* to have permitted the repayment of all indebtedness to my partners within five years and the elimination of the mortgage two years later. The figures are of little consequence to anybody else; but the reasons for them are important to the head of every school or camp, public or private.

Many times I have been asked to account for this uninterrupted success, and I have usually given evasive or incomplete replies. Analysis of so complex a project must, in any case, be partly subjective; for I must view it personally and necessarily from inside its very core. As I am convinced, however, that generalizations growing out of the experience have valuable implications for all engaged in the educative process, I am now succumbing to the temptation of acting like an expert.

After a camp director or a school principal has been provided with adequate facilities and has been supplied with sufficient working capital, he faces his greatest problem—human beings. Let us assume that he is not afflicted with interfering busybodies on the board and he does not have to cope with fond (in its original sense of "foolish") and overprotective parents. This is probably too big an assumption for any administrator to accept; but whether he does or not, he still has to deal with his immediate and chief concern—the children. When fathers and mothers express their complete confidence in me by entrusting their priceless possession to my care, I take on a frightening responsibility. In addition to providing for their safety and physical well-being, I am contracting to create an atmosphere conducive to their growth in all ways—social, ethical, aesthetic, and intellectual. What they are to learn, by whom that learning is to be imparted, and what means and methods are to be used become urgent considerations. Therefore, I must exercise great care in selecting a staff and devising a program.

A camp, like a school, is as strong as its personnel. Fortunately, through my academic connections, I have always been able to find men and women to put into practice principles born of experience. The qualities of leaders have to be inherent, but the necessity of gaining their confidence and of assuring co-operation is crucial. From the beginning, I have had people on whom I could depend for adherence to principle and for conscientious performance. To name them all (their number must total at least three hundred) is not feasible, and to select a favored few is unfair to the rest. They have fully justified my judgment of them as men and my confidence in their ability to lead others. They may be found in the front ranks in a wide variety of occupations: among professors, research scientists, internists, obstetricians, anthropologists, attorneys, philosophers, oral and orthopedic surgeons, philosophers, clergymen, writers, engineers, mineralogists, businessmen, and artists—and I have not begun to exhaust the categories. Interestingly enough, they have continued their belief in the values of our camp; and in the summer just ended they have expressed it positively by sending their sons to us. A more gratifying compliment cannot be paid than the confidence of people who know every aspect of Operation Camp. Further proof of the binding relationship has been demonstrated by the formation of an alumni body of more than a hundred former counselors who meet regularly to continue their friendship and their ties with Camp Alton.

The proper selection of a competent staff is fundamental, but indoctrination of every newcomer is also essential. In camp, as well as school, basic ideas and practices have determined the direction my teaching must take. Three principles are always in evidence: respect for individual differences, encouragement of personal achievement, and insistence upon social responsibilty through co-operative effort. To imbue each member of the staff with enthusiasm for these articles of my educational creed, I must act myself toward them as I would have them act toward the children. Before engaging a counselor, I must believe that he is intelligent, sympathetic, and likable; but after his arrival at camp, I must make sure that he is conscientious and contented in the application of our basic objectives. These concepts mean that I must accept him as he is and avoid trying to make him over into what I might like him to be; and that I must treat him with understanding, sympathy, and tolerance before I can expect co-operative effort and constructive action.

The results of putting these policies into practice have been as gratifying as they have been effectual. In the long run they are undoubtedly good doctrine in the classroom as they are at camp; but in their day-to-day application, compared with authoritarian absolutism, they are more difficult, more wearing, and often exasperating. To overlook or pretend not to see errors and faulty techniques, to correct serious but forgivable errors, and to wait for the less precocious youth among them to grow up takes patience as great as Job's and hope that one's luck will not run out. These generalizations grow out of the knowledge that I am at the mercy of my counselors and out of specific memories of the more colorful eccentrics and the more dismal failures.

One oversized Boy Scout from M.I.T., in applying for the job of counselor-in-charge-of-campcraft-and-trips, brought with him a volume as thick as the Boston Directory of Residents as a documentary display of his plans for a complete Indian-lore program. He impressed me as an earnest and personable fellow; and as his outlined project promised to supply a long-felt lack at camp, I hired him with enthusiasm and forward-looking thoughts. When the season was under way only a short time, I began to recognize an error in judgment; for he had turned out to be the camp goat. His *chef-d'oeuvre* was an elaborately prepared Indian campfire. He had daubed half the camp population with warpaint, equipped everybody with feathers and blankets to impersonate tribal braves, and issued detailed mimeographed directions. On the great night he appeared as the Great Chief on the highest step of the recreation hall at the top of the hill. With appropriate sound effects, he led a long line of carefully chosen braves in an authentic ceremonial dance toward the rest of us who waited eagerly in a circle on the plateau where the sacred fire-making rites were to take place. We could not anticipate the climax. As the long procession approached, the suspense mounted. After the proper incantations had been intoned and The Great Spirit invoked, the Chief prayed to the fire gods for favor. Presumably the Chief was not in their good graces, for he continued to rub sticks and tinder for endless minutes without results. Finally, a helpful ten-year-old brave came to his rescue by producing a sorely needed match. The hysterical laughter which followed signalled the final discrediting of the Great Chief. Needless to add, he could not regain the respect that a counselor must have.

We have had a steady procession of colorful people who have made life much happier and more interesting than it could have been without them. Despite the trials they have sometimes proved to be and the trouble they have caused, I still believe that we need a few of their species to disturb the deadly calm that would prevail if everybody were as quiet, as dependable, and as balanced as are those priceless individuals who have to predominate—the well-qualified but colorless workers in the hive. The big trick that the director must perfect is, of course, to make every one feel that he is appreciated and approved. To bring it off, he will have to employ every psychological device that he knows; and, above all, he must have a program.

Facilities may be perfect, surroundings may be beautiful, children may be normal, and staff, excellent. But without a well-conceived, accurately aimed, and workable program, the director would be lost and the camp a failure. From my first year, I have continued to use, with very little change, the same general plan. Theorists have disapproved, parents have sometimes questioned, and new counselors have occasionally doubted; but I have not swerved from the plotted course. It works. Children and adults who live by it are happy, and it is consonant with my own philosophy and what I believe to be in the best interests of the individual child.

Comprehensive in scope, it includes activities valuable to all children; but unfortunately what may be good for them *en masse* may not be what each and every one of them can readily do or what may at times seem attractive or desirable. If I were a believer in good "progressive" doctrine that only what interests each child at the moment should be taught or in the "permissive" axiom that he should do only what comes naturally, I should ignore what I consider essential to his welfare and be guided solely by his desires. Many present-day directors have been fatally afflicted with both viruses and determine each day's events by consulting with each individual child to decide what is to be done. In some cases, his preference might be to do nothing but remain in his cabin and read, perhaps comic books. With old-fashioned perverseness, I do not approve of a growing boy's imitating a vegetable or worse. I reason from completely different premises: an experiencd adult who has made a life study of educational practice and theory is a more competent judge as to what should be done, and children—especially those who have not yet reached adolescence, and even most of those who have—are confused by being forced into making constant choices and actually prefer guidance, direction, and at times compulsion. As a result, I have built a framework which is largely prearranged, permanent, and unchangeable.

Some critics have voiced objection to the basic framework as being too exciting, as emphasizing rivalry instead of co-operation, and as overstressing athletics. In the course of thirty-three years, I have given this phase of our program serious thought and have observed it closely and analytically. My conclusions are not merely defensive replies, but are as objectively honest as I can make them. I admit, of course, that the object of competition is to make games purposeful and interesting. By daily repetition and consequent conditioning of youngsters to this sort of play, the objective is attained without undue stimulation. Excitement there certainly must be; for playing tennis, baseball, or any other form of sport (even indoor varieties like chess or bridge) involves the desire and will to win. An important by-product will perforce be to learn how to accept graciously either victory or defeat. As for selfish aims as opposed to co-operative effort, I am sure that the mixture of both (present in almost all human endeavor involving two or more people) can be brewed successfully on playing fields. It seems highly desirable to provide youngsters with the chance to acquire individual skills at the same time they are teaming up with others to produce a favorable result. Overemphasis on sports is undoubtedly an evil of the present American way of life—particularly among boys and among adolescents of both sexes at all ages. Among teenagers the standing of any male is measured by his athletic skill, interest, and knowledge. Much as we may decry this overemphasis, we cannot deny the importance of sports to the growing boy; nor can we do anything effective to make a fact disappear. Therefore, anything we can do to help boys feel at home in this area is a contribution to their adjustment.

Regardless of convictions or theories, however, the proof of the workability of the program is clear and unmistakable. The most important evidence is that year after year both campers and counselors return; in fact, some of them aver that they suffer through the rest of the year so that they may enjoy the following summer. Many boys have grown up at camp—beginning their life with us at six or seven; continuing until they have ceased to be campers at fifteen; and then becoming in turn counselors-in-training, junior counselors, and finally (after a year at college) full-fledged counselors, to serve until they have received their doctor's degrees from some graduate school or other. I have, as a matter of fact, suspected in a few instances that one reason they aimed at doctorates was to be able to return to camp for three or four more flings.

Unanimously they all declare that two benefits stand out above all others: (1) they became independent birds, able to fly on their own, away from the sheltering wings of the family, especially Mom; and (2) they learned to live with others peacefully, harmoniously, and happily.

6. TURNING POINT

THE FINANCIAL SECURITY DERIVED FROM CONTINUOUS SUCCESS as a camp director permitted me to devote myself exclusively to my profession, which was and always would be teaching. No longer did I have to search for after-school jobs like conducting evening courses for adults, giving private instruction to slow or negligent teenagers, or lecturing entertainingly on current books before women's clubs. I could at last look upon teaching as a true profession.

With this change in my personal life, came a feeling of independence as well as complete identification with the Boston Latin School. From the beginning of my association with it I had felt that this was where I belonged and where I wanted to spend the rest of my days as a teacher. I understood the boys, and they responded enthusiastically. The faculty was capable, congenial, and co-operative. The aims of the school were continuing to be realized, and its well-merited reputation made being part of it a privilege. I was content.

Powerful forces were at work, however, to disturb this happy state of affairs. The peace of mind which I enjoyed during these halcyon years and my complete absorption in the life of the school engendered a false sense of permanence. I assumed that the solution of my personal problems and my solid establishment as a respected member of the faculty had set the stage for a satisfying existence in the best of all possible worlds and had assured a happy life. I certainly did not foresee the turn of events which would inevitably change the plot line.

A facetious critic once defined a dramatic climax as the point in a play when "the beginning begins to end and the end begins to begin." My life as a teacher may be plotted in similar fashion. The turning point is reached at just about mid-channel. The first act—largely expository—consists of four important scenes, which take place at Needham, Saint Paul, Newton, and Brookline (Rivers). It was a period of development personally and professionally, when basic philosophy was formed, reputation established, and technique perfected. The rising action, which followed at Boston Latin School during the next ten years, took place under almost perfect conditions in a stimulating atmosphere conducive to maximum effort and excellent educational results. As a consequence, the most gratifying accomplishments of my life as a teacher were made possible. About 1935, however, corroding influences, which had spread insidiously through the rest of the American educational system, began to be felt in our academic citadel, and erosive elements rusted away the strong metal bit by bit. Climactic revolutionary changes, both within and without, finally made true teaching impossible. By 1954, when John Doyle made his entrance as Headmaster, the tragic denouement had already taken place; and even had he been a superman, he could not have prevented the final outcome. It surely must be called a tragedy, when one of the last outposts of sound education in the public schools was destroyed and the faculty defeated.

The decline and fall of a great school can be demonstrated by my own story, for I saw it in its original glory. It is impossible for a faculty by itself, however well-meaning and however conscientious, to prevent the collapse of standards and the adulteration of principles. When an institution as sturdy as the Latin School can be undermined by internal and external forces, then the whole structure of education is weakened, and our entire way of life endangered. What I am going to say deals with my own experience in the Boston school system, but the principles involved are applicable to all school systems in the United States.

In teaching *Hamlet,* I have always called attention to the two prongs of the protagonist's tragic dilemma. While discussing his insoluble problem, I have pointed out that one school of criticism insists that his fatal weakness is within himself; while the other, that external circumstances surrounding him are beyond anyone's strength to overcome, especially Hamlet's. The longer I have grappled with these conflicting theories, the more I have become convinced that here Shakespeare reveals every man's dual problem: (1) Is one's own ability sufficient to cope with his peculiar environmental difficulties? (2) Is there a point at which the most capable may not be able to surmount them? Thus Hamlet's defeat has lighted the way to an understanding of life.

I was positive, by 1935, that I had conquered the subjective obstacles to teaching success. Unlike Hamlet, who refused to return to the university at Wittenberg, I had continued my studies with greater and greater interest as time went on. Furthermore, I had not forsworn female companionship by advising my beloved to "get her to a nunnery"; nor had I driven her quite mad. On the contrary, I had married the girl, begotten a daughter, and enjoyed a normal life among family and friends. Professionally, too, I was unlike the great Dane. Depressed by grief and disgust, he had refused to work at his job. In contrast, I almost knocked myself out; but my labors were fruitful, and I prospered. In short, he was a melancholy loafer; I was a happy worker.

Hamlet's inability to adjust his life to the impenetrable gloom which surrounded him was enough to bring about his personal tragedy; but the obstacles to his adjustment were much greater than mine. As he put it, the time was "out of joint"; and he cursed the irony that demanded his setting it right. Yes, his timing was bad: he had been born in an evil hour. As a consequence, the march of events had prevented his completing his education, having the normal young man's complement of companions, becoming a varsity athlete (say, on the fencing team), living a full life as a happily married man, and functioning as a prince. On the other hand, I had timed my entrance into this world with enough foresight to escape a sufficient proportion of the "slings and arrows of outrageous fortune" to enable me to reach my goals personally and professionally. Up to this time, I had reached a point where my own drama appeared to be building up to a happy ending; but, like all men, I could not foresee or prevent the build-up of external forces.

Bit by bit, with changes in the tone and temper of the times, the character and attitude of most members of the Latin School faculty had shifted. As world events gradually produced an ever expanding and crushing economic inflation, local politics and conditions brought about a concurrent educational deflation. Our school suffered with others in Boston and the nation. Not only were individual teachers finding it more and more difficult to keep out of debt and consequently being forced into other or additional occupations, but collectively their interests shifted from worrying about the school to worrying about finances. With many men the lack of money blurred their vision, and the injustices suffered at the hands of those in control of school budgets became an overpowering obsession. They could think of little else, and discussions in faculty rooms and corridors almost invariably turned to that subject. Harassed by the necessity of providing for growing families, the men became discontented, militant, and organized.

The change in tone and temper was many-sided. The number of "cultured gentlemen" had noticeably decreased, while more and more ill-prepared temporary teachers, who looked and acted like City Hall clerks, took their places. Instead of concern for their classes or the school, they became preoccupied with the size of their salaries. Constantly they talked of what they were getting instead of what they might be giving. Unprofessional they certainly were. Any one who showed interest in his work was suspect: he must be a bit balmy; he was looking for promotion; or, worse still, he was doing so much that others might be expected to emulate him.

The reasons for the changes in tone and spirit are not easily or simply accounted for. One might assume too quickly that the weeding out of the Puritan martinets and the invasion of easy-going, affable Irishmen (who until recently had been excluded by the

Proper Bostonians) resulted in the gradual erosion of principles. Or one might conclude that the creeping inflation had made all of us aware of the financial facts of life. Either assumption would be oversimplification. Deep-rooted causes—attributable no doubt to two world wars, the 1929 crash, the great depression, and their effects on the public—are too complicated for discussion here, but they left unmistakable marks on the school and on the individuals who comprised it. Whatever a man might have thought and however intensely aware he might have been of the shifting of principles and the disappearance of ideals, he was powerless to stem the incoming waves as they began to cover him. Like every one else, I found it difficult to keep my head above water and remain afloat.

Regardless of what goals a man might have in mind or what values he might have established, the American economy forced him to consider money as one of them. Try as I would, I could not deny the importance of eating, sleeping, and playing. Neither could I avoid clothing myself and my family or paying medical bills. As a result, I was always in debt; and, subconsciously at least, I was constantly aware of my insolvency. The year I entered Latin School, I added two thousand dollars to my financial overload when doctors and hospitals demanded payment for services rendered in a vain attempt to save twin girls born to my wife. To raise cash, I had had to borrow to the limit at 6 per cent my own money accumulated on insurance policies, to teach evenings for five years, and to tutor continually. Besides these time-consuming and wearing labors during the academic year, I was forced to supplement my income of less than four thousand dollars with what I could earn during the summer. Personal experience thus strengthened and intensified convictions that teachers—particularly men with families—were victims of indifference and selfishness on the part of the public.

Theoretically I had always been with the underdog in other occupations, and politically I had invariably voted for candidates who favored labor. Therefore, when the men organized to fight for salary increases, I entered the lists with enthusiasm and vigor. Much as I deprecated the need for such action, I saw no other way to gain even minimum justice.

Unfortunately the ends of education or of professional standards were not served in these mass efforts. They called attention to the plight of the male teacher; but they reduced him at the same time to the status of a worker who measures his labor in terms of dollars and hours instead of service, and they removed him from the ranks of professional men. I learned much, however, from my associations with agitators, company men, political connivers, educational bosses, and civic leaders.

My first big lesson came from a group in the Boston school system known as the Junior Masters Association, consisting of all high school men below the rank of head of department. Despite the fact that we were well aware of the disadvantages of the existence of ten or more such splinter groups in the city, our problems, we felt, were peculiar and required a separate organization. It was headed by a brilliant but frenetic fellow-alumnus of Tufts, appropriately known as "Wild Bill" Roche, who, about every five minutes, had a new idea and usually acted upon it. At one of our frequent meetings we hit upon a plan which made our efforts unique and effective—the publication of a sheet in which our targets were displayed and the accuracy of our marksmanship recorded for the reading pleasure of our members. But, more important, the publication specifically noted the votes cast by legislators, city councillors, and school committeemen on all educational measures. This periodical proved to be much more powerful than we had dreamed it could be.

The first issue of *The Junior Master,* published in 1933, had an impact and an independence unusual for teachers' utterances. A sample or two of my own contributions as associate editor show why. The lead article on Page 1, captioned "Junior Masters Organize for Action," fired the opening shot:

> The schoolmen of Boston must either act or submit to conditions imposed by vested interests. We are at present the victims of a steady, organized, vicious propaganda imposed on the unsuspecting public by a strong group of influential bankers and real estate operators who control the local press. The *Herald* and its evening sheet, the *Traveler,*

are controlled by banks which refused loans to the city administration in anticipation of taxes. As a result, these two papers have persistently given their readers a one-sided picture, resorting to distortion of news, ridicule of any person daring to raise his voice in protest (for example, P. T. Campbell, our superintendent, or Payson Smith, state commissioner of education), suppression of our contributions to their Mailbag, and constant repetition of abusive references to our attempts to prevent violation of our rights. Other journals, depending on these same banks for financing, have simply fallen in line—not militantly, but obviously helping by silent consent to poison the minds of the public against us. The only paper in the city favoring us at all has been a Hearst publication, not subject to local dictatorship. In the face of these tremendous odds, it is small wonder that we are losing ground rapidly, ground won by long, bitter struggles and hard to regain. . . .

On the editorial page was printed in bold type the *Credo* which I had composed shortly before the deadline:

CREDO

1. WE BELIEVE that the greatest single contribution America has made to civilized life is the establishment of public education as the keystone to democratic government.
2. WE BELIEVE that it is our privilege and duty as teachers to provide the most effective schooling possible for the children of Boston.
3. WE BELIEVE that to be effective teachers we must maintain standards of scholarship, of workmanship, and of living commensurate with our high calling.
4. WE BELIEVE that we must fight every subversive influence aiming to undermine our standards.
5. WE BELIEVE that we must unite with a dignity, an energy, and a will consistent with our purposes and promoting our ends.

These pronunciamentos were followed by pertinent news items and by legislative roll calls on bills affecting teachers, coupled with advice and warning to our members on rewarding our friends and punishing our enemies.

It was at this time that a highly significant incident in the history of Boston teachers' salary fights took place. The Schoolmen's Economic Association, which represented all male teachers, elementary as well as high school, determined to fight the antagonistic Boston *Herald* with the only weapon that they had—mass action. The Executive Committee, of which I was a member, advised all men and women in the School Department to cancel subscriptions or to write to the newspaper to state that they were discontinuing to buy it. Much more important, charge accounts and purchases in all stores advertising in the *Herald* were to be stopped. Whether this action constituted an illegal boycott was never determined, for the situation came to a head in dramatic and revealing fashion.

After the owners of the paper had appealed to Mr. Campbell to call off the dogs of war, those most active in the fight by virtue of printed and vocal opinions were requested to appear in the Superintendent's office for a meeting with a representative of the *Herald*. Three of us were called in—Bill Roche; Tom Winston, who up to that time had always been a loud and eloquent champion of the men but unfortunately was trying for promotion; and I. Pat Campbell, who had long before given up his independence and peace of mind when he became superintendent, introduced the subject by an explanation that the fight was already lost and that, in view of the fact that we needed all the friends we could gather for the future, we should do well to accept what he considered a magnanimous offer by the *Herald*. If we agreed to call off what was evidently proving to be an effective campaign, the paper would give us an entire page in the following Sunday issue to present our views.

Pat turned to me first: "Phil, I'd be happy to have you take on this job. What do you say?"

"Count me out, Pat. Unequivocally, no. After the plastering

they've given us, I want no part of this acknowledgment of the beating we've suffered."

"How about you, Bill? I'm sure you can put your case well."

"It's too late, Pat. I'm sorry, but I'm one hundred per cent with Phil."

Before Pat had a chance to put the question, Tom had consented to the deal. Shortly thereafter, Tom became Head of the History Department at Hyde Park High School. Perhaps, though, the turn of events was sheer coincidence. Perhaps, too, my recalcitrance in this situation might account in part for my remaining a classroom teacher throughout my tenure. Other factors—like not being of the right persuasion, not playing the political game, not being obsequious to superiors, and not surrendering principles—were undoubtedly taken into account when rated lists were formed; but I am sure that being in the forefront in these brawls did little to ingratiate me with the top brass.

Actually it was a matter of small moment to me, for I had no ambitions to be an administrator and wanted to continue to be a teacher of English. If administration meant leaving the classroom and consequently losing direct contact with students, I wanted none of it. If advancing one step as head of department involved my leaving Latin School, I was not interested. My experiences with rated lists, however, are worth recording; for they point up why most teachers throughout the land are opposed to so-called merit systems and why those in the Boston system in particular have become discouraged, debased, and demoralized by theirs.

The competitive examinations conducted by the Boston Board of Examiners for candidates wishing to be placed on lists for appointment to teaching positions have always been sufficiently searching and fairly administered. They have been graded objectively, and the lists of eligible teachers have been impartially formed according to the grades earned. From these lists principals of elementary schools and headmasters of high schools are required by the School Committee to appoint teachers in the order of their places. Unlike civil service regulations, which permit the employer to select one of the first three candidates, the Boston rules have always provided that Number One must be chosen before any one below him on the list can be appointed to a teaching post. Presumably no subterfuges could be worked or injustices take place.

Strangely enough, my initial encounter with this usually fair mechanism was exceptional. By means of memorizing a minutely detailed outline of English and American literature, which I had recited over and over again on long walks through Franklin Park with my fiancée, I managed to stand at the head of the English list. When I was assigned to East Boston High School in the fall of 1916, I was content. For more than a month I taught with serene disregard of anything but preparing lesson plans and correcting papers. When, however, I was informed that pupils had not enrolled in sufficient numbers to warrant my permanent appointment, I woke up to what had happened. While I had been temporarily placed on a *per diem* basis in a school where registrations were uncertain, two men below me on the list had already been ensconced in safe spots. When I protested my dismissal and relegation to the substitutes' daily bench at headquarters, Miss Mary Mellyn, Director of Practice and Training and then in charge of appointments, expressed her sympathy but informed me that nothing could be done.

The following two months I spent as a substitute in any spot where I was needed—whether it was to teach my own subject or such exotic electives as Spanish (of which language I knew no more than ten words) or typewriting (for the students of which I distributed paper for insertion into their machines with aplomb and precision). For these and similar exertions I was paid five dollars for each day employed. Disappointment and disgust soon took their toll; and when in December I was offered a steady position at Needham to teach five regular classes in English at eight hundred dollars per annum (180 days in the academic year), I jumped eagerly at the great opportunity. That decision took me out of the Boston schools for ten years.

In fairness to Miss Mellyn, whom I have always considered one of the most intelligent and kind administrators I have ever met, I believe abuses of the merit system were accidental and unavoidable at the time. When I again took the examinations and landed over one hundred points ahead of my nearest competitor, no hitch in the proceedings developed as I took my place at the Latin School, which I was not to leave for thirty-one years. With the administration of the examinations, the forming of the lists on the basis of them, and the resulting appointments, I have no quarrel. But the provisions for recognition and promotion later are an insufferable abomination and should be abolished completely. They have destroyed individuals and undermined morale.

Despite my own interesting encounters with the system in some of its worst manifestations, I am not making these observations with the bitterness of a disappointed office-seeker. I had no ambitions to become an administrator or to leave the school. The sole reason for my being rated for head of department was to be prepared to take over in the event of the retirement or death of Ed Benson, who occupied the post when I came to Latin School. The position itself, as it has developed in Boston, held no particular attractiveness. It consists of conducting perfunctory meetings each month, distributing textbooks, and visiting new teachers. Although nominal prestige, a lighter teaching load, and a higher salary are its rewards, the position meant little to me.

A description of the promotional system is necessary to an understanding of its operation. A teacher, if he wants to become a head of department or superintendent of schools, must study its workings and must devote himself assiduously to building a great structure of credits. Usually a board of examiners consists of three well-picked conformists and has jurisdiction of an intricate compilation of papers, recommendations, and ratings. Theoretically, it is possible for a candidate to make a perfect score of 1,000 points, 600 of which he can accumulate by his own doing and the other 400 of which are in the hands, minds, and hearts of others.

To accumulate the maximum 600 points within his control, he must submit to the board evidence of his right to be credited with them. In my case, I was able to assemble all the necessary data. These included a wide variety of important and unimportant items, arranged in five categories, as follows:

1. Educational preparation.
2. Teaching and executive experience.
   (A strange paradox developed in this category when I was given credit points for my one year at Needham as head of a department consisting of one other teacher besides me and refused credit for the infinitely more complex and valuable duties as a camp director for many seasons. This anomaly led me to write the following letter.)

Brookline, Massachusetts
January 1, 1943

Board of Examiners
15 Beacon Street, Boston

Dear Sirs:

I am submitting as executive experience not only three years as Head of the English Department at Rivers School, but also a number of other items: (a) Supervisor of Activities and Associate Director, Camp Aloha Summer School, Holderness, N. H.; (b) Director of Athletics, St. Paul Academy; (c) Director of Student Activities, Rivers School; (d) Director, Camp Avoda, Middleboro, Mass.; (e) Director, Camp Emoh, Alfred, Maine; (f) Director, Camp Alton, Wolfeboro, N. H.

Believing that this experience has been extremely valuable from the standpoint of administrative and executive responsibility, I am offering it as evidence of ability pertinent to the position of head of department. That these positions involve every sort of educational problem may be clear from the following descriptive notes:

(a) Camp Aloha Summer School . . . is a tutoring camp, preparing boys for College Board examinations and helping them to make up deficient school work . . . I had charge of studies in English and history and supervised the recreational program.

(b) At St. Paul Academy, as at all country day schools, athletics is compulsory for all pupils . . . The director has to supervise a corps of coaches and administer a department more complex than that of a curricular study.

(c) At Rivers School, a department of extracurricular activities was organized to include student government, publications, dramatics, musical organizations, a forum, and an athletic association. I was appointed director of this department.

(d) More important than any of the positions mentioned above, I consider my present summer work as camp director. Besides

> selecting and supervising 50-60 employes, I plan and administer a program of physical, recreational, and educational activities for 175 campers . . . This program includes such subjects as nature study, . . . arts and crafts, music—vocal and instrumental, and tutoring. To organize and administer the affairs of a community of 225-235 people must require more executive ability than does any position for which I might apply in the Boston school system.

I respectfully suggest that experience such as I have outlined should be considered as significant and pertinent, even though the rating schedule does not state specifically what credit should be given. It would seem that such experience is more valuable to a candidate for an administrative position than the taking or the giving of courses, belonging to organizations, traveling, and a number of other items for which I am automatically given a number of credits.

Yours respectfully,

(As indicated, this letter availed me nothing except the satisfaction of writing it.)

3. Professional interest and growth.
   Included under this topic were a mixed bag of contributions, such as directing the formation of a new course of study in composition for Grades VII-XII, inclusive; and inconsequential memberships in the National Education Association and other professional groups (in evidence of which I had to include cancelled checks in payment of current dues).
4. Outside activities.
   Under this topic were included letters and programs which indicated an interest in communal affairs, amateur theatricals, philanthropic and political organizations; lectures delivered before women's clubs and other organizations; service as judge in public-speaking contests or in dramatics competitions; and attendance at class dinners and other school functions.
5. Travel.
   As evidence that I had made a trip to Germany and had traveled in this country, I presented affidavits signed by members of my family.
6. Academic leadership or scholarly achievement.
   Papers written, reading lists compiled, addresses given to professional groups, and other such contributions were included.

With the submission of this mass of documents, I encountered no difficulty in gaining full credit for this section of the rating. My difficulties soon became obvious: they were based on the personal opinions, prejudices, or politico-religious affiliations of those who sat in judgment on the candidates and manipulated the remaining forty per cent of the 1000-point total.

Not only were the victims of this "merit" system subjected to innumerable indignities; but they had no appeal from the verdict after the rating lists were published. The figures were rigged so cleverly that exposure of their falsity and the chicanery underlying them became impossible. A visiting supervisor might spend only ten minutes in a classroom before passing judgment. He might, as in the case of one of the greatest teachers we ever had in the school, grade him so low for a piece of scrap paper dropped on the floor by a careless boy that the poor man was put out of the running. (Incidentally, this outraged scholar and gentleman refused ever to be rated again.) Or the visitor might have had an unpleasant incident just before his visitation and is in a venomous mood as he enters the classroom of the ill-fated victim. But even if these possibilities are ignored, the candidate is still faced with the final reckoning at the judgment seat.

As it works out, no dirty work can be proved and no outcry is therefore in order. If one finds, as I did in each of the four times I was rated, that he has been accredited with well over nine hundred points of a possible thousand, he has apparently no cause for complaint. After all, no human being should believe that he can attain perfection; and if, as in 1940, I was awarded fourth place among thirty-five candidates with 917 points—just one point below the man ahead of me, I should surely be happy about or at least resigned to the outcome. Normally only one or two positions were available during the three-year period during which the list was in effect; and invariably, when the new one appeared, for some strange but not incomprehensible reason, three or four names—up to that time unknown or unimpressive—suddenly appeared at the summit. The only rational explanation of such magic was that these nonpareils had certain intangible qualities which became visible during the intervening three-year period and which deserved recognition by the Board of Superintendents and the School Committee. What they were we rarely discovered; and when we did, it was obvious that they varied with the candidates. He might, as in one case, belong in the same parish as the assistant superintendent who visited him. This man was given poor marks until one Sunday when the omniscient official discovered that his assumption that the candidate was a Protestant was wrong. The next rating enabled him to go ahead. Doubts as to the validity of this implication may be dispelled by noting the roster of high-ranking administrators: the conclusion is inevitable that to be promoted, a man might not have to be a graduate of either Boston College or Holy Cross, but it would certainly help. By 1954, the superintendent, his five assistants, all supervisors, and all high school headmasters except one (Kelley of Tufts) possessed this helpful qualification. No Protestant or Jewish candidate during the preceding twenty-five years seems to have been able to overcome the handicap of being an alumnus of Harvard, M.I.T., Tufts, or other "inferior" institutions. Objective evaluation had little to do with where one landed on the list.

This perversion of what had begun as a merit system had devastating effects on the morale of the men, who depended upon promotion for increases in salary. Disillusionment, despair, and bitterness appeared and affected their attitudes and, finally, their work. Until the pinch of poverty or the itch for power disturbed a good teacher, he was happy in his work and contented to remain at his post. Many men who had observed the workings of the system refused to be browbeaten into taking courses, to be subservient or acquiescent, or to be subjected to unpleasant extra duties. They either did not present themselves for rating or ran the gauntlet only once and ignored it thereafter. Usually these insurgents had outside sources of income or fewer obligations and hence refused to submit to the rigmarole of accumulated credits, meaningless visitations, or incidental indignities.

The effects on the school system were many when objectivity gave way to political maneuvering. We had witnessed a striking change while the free-wheeling James Michael Curley was mayor. Not only had City Hall become a bargaining center for hundreds of plums distributed to the faithful, but even School Headquarters —until about 1920 a sacrosanct and inviolable sanctuary of incorruptible men—had become a replica of the noisome political swamp down the hill on School Street. The climax came when widespread scandals connected with job-selling and favoritism were publicized. Later the rated lists came under scrutiny when a disappointed but capable candidate for headmaster exposed the workings of the system. Among other things, he pointed out that a comparatively unknown newcomer had jumped in one rating from the bottom of the list to the top, leaping over some twenty-eight candidates who were ahead of him. With such goings-on, the schools were sure to feel the effects.

At Latin School we felt the impact almost immediately. Heads of department appeared who were unschooled and ineffective. In only a few accidental instances were they qualified; and in several cases, large staffs were headed by mediocrities who were outclassed in scholarship, pedagogical skill, and executive ability by four or more men under them. In the early years of my tenure, the momentum furnished by the traditional standards of the school sustained us; but when one headmaster, during the last five years of his term, refused to fight, the end of qualitative work was assured.

7. DECLINE

THE FACTS JUST RECORDED, REPREHENSIBLE AND REGRETTABLE as they were, could not of themselves have destroyed the spirit or affected the quality of the Boston Latin School before 1940. Despite many factors beyond their control, the veteran members of the faculty continued—long after most schools had given up the ghost—partly from habit and partly from pride, to insist on substantial study and high standards of achievement on the part of their students. Retirement, promotion, and death had removed from the illustrious roster of great teachers many well-remembered names. But a sufficient number of excellent men had remained to carry on the traditions and values of the past. Other stalwarts who joined them were in complete agreement with the long-established objectives of the school. Compromisers had no place among them.

Their best efforts, however, proved to be unequal to the combat. The anarchy of our times—already reflected in our painting, sculpture, music, and literature (both prose and verse)—finally invaded and replaced the orderly life that we had enjoyed for three centuries at Boston Latin School. The progressive revolution reached its last victim, and the strong conservatism we had come to take for granted began to disappear. Many of us had understood the weaknesses, the cruelties, and the indifference of ancient reactionary practices, and we were happy to see them go. We were not prepared, however, to have the whole system destroyed and replaced by something worse. Specifically, the following table lists five of the more striking substitutions:

Replacement

of

Bad Elements of the Past	*by*	*Worse Elements of the Present*
1. Lockstep regimentation.		1. The license of permissiveness.
2. Repression of the individual.		2. Uncontrolled abandon.
3. Rigidity of the classical curriculum.		3. Lawless choice of electives.
4. Inflexibility of standards of promotion, even to the point of placing in the same class a 16-year-old giant and a 10-year-old Lilliputian.		4. Social promotion, as a result of which everybody—from dullard to genius—moves from grade to grade at the same pace, regardless of academic achievement.
5. Absolutism of precise grading, by virtue of which schoolmasters made the fine distinction between success at 60 per cent and failure at 59.		5. Abolition of all systematic and honest grading and adoption of the "Numbers Racket" of relative scores, curve pitching, and percentile palaver, so that nobody knows where anybody stands.

The radical changes led not only to adulteration of subject matter and destruction of standards, but reduced the teacher to a state of utter helplessness. He was caught in a powerful trap from which escape was impossible. It was set by theorists, statisticians, administrators, and indoctrinated fellow teachers who were inexperienced, believing, or ambitious. The trap was complicated, destructive, and complete. It proved to have several moving parts; but no matter how clearly the teacher understood its operation, it did its work so well that there was no escape. No matter how strong or capable the individual teacher might be, he could find no way out and could discover no effective means to relay his anguish to the world outside.

In the particular trap at the Boston Latin School, one of the last to be sprung, the old-timers continued to go through automatic motions of workmanship which resembled those of the past. They attempted to teach as much and as well as when favorable circumstances had stimulated the interest and energies of their students. The practices of the past, they soon found, could not be applied to classrooms of the present.

A fundamental assumption of a master at Latin School had always been that he must impart a definite and substantial body of knowledge to his class—whether seventh-grade Latin or senior English. In either case, he would depend on efforts in previous years of both teachers and boys to supply the reservoir of information essential to educational continuity and growth. By the time the changeover had been completed in 1940, the youngsters who came to us from the elementary grades knew so little of the subject matter that we had to begin the learning process at incredibly low levels and lay foundations that should have been set and completed several grades below. Teachers of first-year English or Latin were forced to start from scratch, whether in grammar or other fundamentals of language.

Before 1935, it could be taken for granted that boys, admitted from the sixth grade, would be able to arrange a list of authors in alphabetical order with reasonable accuracy; for there were still in the primary grades a sufficient number of old-fashioned teachers who had taught them their A-B-C's. Also, when reading, they could be depended upon to pronounce new words because of their knowledge of sounds and syllables. As a result of valuable training in phonetic principles, pupils could be expected to tackle with confidence the spelling of unfamiliar words and come at least close to accuracy. They could even be relied upon to recognize the eight parts of speech and identify subject and verb; and some of the group had acquired still more advanced grammatical information. But, above all, they had fundamental knowledge of sentence structure, so that papers in all subjects were written at least in complete sentences, fully supplied with capitals, periods, and sometimes even commas. In short, the mechanics of writing had been mastered sufficiently to enable us to teach some of the finer points of composition and rhetoric.

It was comforting to know that when I told a lad that he was suffering from a bad case of "adjectivitis," he could understand the implication because he was familiar with the word and what it meant. Or if I were teaching the elements of punctuation—say, some principle involving dependent clauses—I could feel certain that everybody in the class had already learned the necessary distinctions between *phrase* and *clause* as well as *dependent* and *independent*. In discussing, for instance, variety of sentence structure, I did not hesitate to turn from such simple terminology as "long" and "short" to the more abstract "simple, complex, and compound." Such assumptions were safe, and they were sound; for boys and girls in elementary schools had been taught a well-defined body of knowledge according to a graded course of study, the minimum essentials of which had to be covered before they were permitted to go on. Thus, when they came to Latin School with honest grades of A or B earned from teachers who had completed the prescribed year's work, we were able to proceed with confidence that our boys possessed the basic information.

Although we began to sense that changes had been taking place, it was not until the revolutionary ideas of the progressives had gained control of our elementary schools that we saw concrete evidence in our students of a devastating reduction in essential knowledge. By 1940, the boys who came to us could rarely spell, punctuate, write, or read with reasonable facility or accuracy. Grammatical information was either nonexistent or so limited that we were compelled to start all classes at the very beginnings of the subject. In fact, their knowledge was so hazy at one point that I asked the master in charge of program assignments to give me a seventh-grade division in place of a tenth. I wanted to help the poor lads who were miserably handicapped in beginning a curriculum so heavily loaded with languages. That year they would begin Latin, followed later by French, German or Greek, and that other foreign tongue—proper English. Almost totally innocent of the facts of grammar, they were also poor readers. They had, for the most part, been taught with "flash" cards and could recognize only those words which they had memorized. Very few could read rapidly enough to cope with the sizable assignments of collateral reading they would be getting for proper college preparation; nor could they read accurately or comprehendingly the prose and verse given for intensive study. To descend many notches lower in the scale of minimums, spelling—actually a minor accomplishment, though handy—had become sketchy, as may be deduced from an entertaining but revealing little experiment I tried with the upper classes during my last five years in service. I merely had them answer a question originally given as part of a final examination for the seventh grade many years before; but when I tried it on each of my graduating sections from 1953 to 1957, not one of those seventeen-year-olders was able to achieve a perfect score—in fact, not fewer than three errors were made in any single paper. The question follows:

Some of the words below are spelled correctly; some, incorrectly. Correct the misspellings as you copy ALL the words in the list:

SPELLING

yeild	supercede	reccommend	indispensible
receive	changeable	goverment	superintendant
weird	athelete	counterfiet	regretable
disatisfy	independence	diphtheria	concensus
disappearance	grammer	exciteable	accomodate

The evidence of the constantly deteriorating standards of achievement and grading in the elementary schools had become so overwhelming that successive headmasters of our school had protested. Their just claims, however, brought no change in the admission requirements; for neither the school committee nor the board of superintendents would consent to the recommendations proposed. In the past the restrictions consisted of the simple device of demanding that the candidate have marks of A or B in four major subjects during his sixth-grade or eighth-grade year—that is, in English, geography, history, and mathematics; and it had served fairly well to weed out the wholly unqualified. (It was possible for a boy who had grades below this level to gain admittance by passing examinations.) When, however, it became apparent to the faculty that (a) little had been taught or learned before arrival at our doors and (b) dependence on the marks donated by kind teachers had become worse than useless, our head was prevailed upon to petition that students thereafter be admitted by examination only. But we got nowhere, partly because some people presented specious arguments that such a method would be undemocratic, some feared political consequences inflicted by voters whose sons might fail, but most of those in control were either indifferent to our plight or incapable of seeing the problem. We were not surprised at the refusal to give serious consideration to our request; for few, if any, of those who would decide the matter were qualified, either by education or interests, to pass fair judgment, even if they had wished to. They consisted largely of political hacks ambitious for greater power or privilege. But for a long period of years we had at least one member who tried to perform his civic duty creditably. Unfortunately, despite his good intentions, he was regularly outvoted four-to-one.

With a school committee made up, for the most part, of well-meaning fools or scheming politicians, the teachers of the city could scarcely be expected to be bubbling over with confidence and hope that help for the ailing schools would come from that source. Neither could they count on appointments that were within the committee's jurisdiction or subject to its sanction to reflect sound judgment. The result was inevitable. With rare exceptions, the administrators and the headmasters were conformists, unoriginal mediocrities, congenial joiners who belonged to the right organizations or who managed to be seen at every important wake, and invariably compromisers trying to perpetuate and protect the escalator system. The system was, as a matter of fact, self-perpetuating; for no man who hoped for promotion dared to cross his immediate superior or indicate disapproval of any aspect of the way the schools were operated. It was a rare man, indeed, who could afford the luxury of originality, intellectual vigor, political independence, religious deviation, or educational nonconformity.

As a result of such circumstances, faculties in any school knew that the promotional sweepstakes were more likely to produce a winner who was closer to a nag than to a thoroughbred. When the headmaster's chair was vacated through death, retirement, or advancement, the staff could only hope the new man would prove to be better than they had any right to expect—in a word, adequate. At Latin School, he should have been much more than that; at the very least, he should have the highest academic standards, unfailing integrity in educational theory and practice, and unqualified independence. Particularly during the stormy years I am now considering, we needed such a man if we were to maintain our historic eminence. Through the administration of Pat Campbell and for a few years thereafter, the momentum of the past and the still formidable scholastic demands of the present supported and strengthened our position at the top of the public schools preparing for college. An editorial which appeared in the *Boston Globe* of January 28, 1933, contained these paragraphs expressing what was the generally accepted opinion:

> Out of the 25,000 candidates taking College Board entrance examinations in English, in Latin, in Greek, and in Mathematics the top mark each time went to a Latin School boy.
>
> How is this done? These lads are not housed in cloistered dormitories, with proctored study hours, and rural seclusion. Their masters have them only five and one-half hours a day. They walk, or ride on rattledy-bang streetcars, and study at home in chamber, dining-room, or kitchen, with persons talking in the same room. They have to concentrate! In a large proportion of these households the language spoken is not English. Thirty years ago the majority of the boys were Yankees. Today it is hard to find a Yankee in the school. The names now begin with *O'* and end in *-ski*. But the Latin School goes straight on doing as it did in the days when Ezekiel Cheever was Master.
>
> Yes, but how? Very strangely! Faith, e'en with teaching them to use their heads. Its instructors do not call themselves "educators"; they are just plain schoolmasters. . . . It is notorious that these masters work like a blend of drayhorse and Pegasus; for if a teacher expects a boy to work, he must work himself . . . And they get results. . . .
>
> To get into B.L.S. is fairly easy; it is very hard to stay there. This is true democracy in education, a public school which offers to any boy such instruction as he would receive in an expensive private school

and offers it to him free—provided he can take it. But it does not tell him he is a shining star if he is a burnt-out planet. The mark he gets is the mark he earns: no more, no less. This gives him intellectual standards. It also stiffens the teachers in their exactions.

In the 1920's, when the school more than doubled its enrollment and had to increase its faculty, there was anxiety as to whether it could make Latin School teachers of these new masters. The difficulty proved to be the other way round. It was necessary to put on the brakes a little to keep them from out-Latin-Schooling the Latin School.

Here in our midst is this topmost school of America, so much a part of the city's cultural routine as to be taken for granted, like the moon and the tides. Not for its sake but for our own we shall do well to pause and take account of it. Praise can mean little to the men engaged in such an enterprise. Their minds are too occupied with matters more important. What they do value is being allowed to go on doing a great work in a great way.

To fortify this estimate of the school in those still fruitful years, an item which appeared in the alumni column of *Latin School Register* concerning boys in the Class of 1935 is pertinent:

Harvard

Our reputation in our "mother school" has not been let down by our recent graduates, as is evidenced by the staggering list of honors obtained by our sons last year (1939).

(3) *Summa Cum Laude*

Albert H. Cohen (Sociology)
Lawrence F. Ebb (Government and Philosophy)
Harry Pollard (Mathematics)

(12) *Magna Cum Laude*

Norman H. Brisson (Economics)
Harold Brown (Biochemical Sciences)
Bernard Fisher (Geological Sciences)
Stanley G. Geist (English)
Robert Kaplan (Government)
Julian J. Leavitt (Chemistry)
Leon Levinson (Biology)
Irving J. Lewis (Government)

Robert M. Ravven (Philosophy and Psychology)
Elliott L. Seegall (Biochemical Sciences)
William B. Saunders (Economics)
David C. Sullivan (Germanic Languages and Literature)

(19) *Cum Laude*

Leonard Bernstein (Music)
Seymour Bunshaft (History)
Jacob B. Dana (Economics)
Leonidas H. Demeter (Classics and Government)
Sherwood D. Fox (Sociology)
Sylvan E. Golden (Sociology)
Benjamin S. Golub (Sociology)
Edward A. Goodwin (Government)
Bernard D. Grossman (Government)
James J. Horowitz (Government)
Melvin L. Levin (Economics)
Joseph Levine (Astronomy)
Robert L. Lubell (Economics)
Eugene F. Murphy (Romance Languages and Literature)
David J. Oppenheim (Biology and Literature)
Fred Rogosin (Music)
Bernard S. Resser (Economics)
Sidney Sullivan (Philosophy)

To continue the quality of work implicit in such performance called for a favorable climate and able leadership. Unfortunately, the men who followed Pat Campbell were not strong enough to combat the two-headed hydra of interference from headquarters and of the fast-moving forces that were to overcome secondary and college education as they had elementary. The beloved and capable Pat, after having administered the affairs of the school for nine years with firm adherence to the traditional standards of the past, left us in 1929 to become Assistant Superintendent and later Superintendent of Schools.

Shortly after Mr. Joseph L. Powers had succeeded him, one of my student editors received a most gracious letter from an illustrious member of the Class of 1882, the great philosopher George Santayana. Its contents have made me hesitate to record the details of what ensued the following two decades, and I am consequently withholding the most unpleasant ones and including only those which I must to explain the erosive strength of the outside influences on the life of the school. The letter to Gaynor O'Gorman, the lad who had requested the contribution from the famed scholar, follows:

Hotel Bristol, Rome
Feb. 1, 1932

Dear Mr. O'Gorman,

Here is the promised article, which I trust will reach you safely. I think it is well under 2000 words: in fact I cut out a paragraph at the last moment, and a great deal else earlier, because I felt that I was getting too far away from the Register and the School, and becoming too personal. I remember a lot of things about my teachers and friends, which are set down in my autobiography, but it would be indiscreet to publish them when any one is still alive who might be wounded by little details—and all the salt is in the details—about his dear departed relations.

I shall be interested in seeing the anniversary number, and rely on you and your proof-reader to correct my proof for me. Don't hesitate to correct any obvious slip, I mean in my manuscript as well as in the proof; and of course you may change the spelling to conform to your usage, if there are any divergencies.

Yours sincerely,
G. Santayana

Although Joe Powers was dignified, gentlemanly, and just, he either did not see the gathering storm clouds as they formed; or he did not acknowledge that he had the influence or the strength to prevent the deluge which they visibly and audibly proclaimed. I am sure that if during the closing years of his rule he had had the vision and the energy and the will, he might have marshalled the thousands of influential alumni and the strong members of his faculty to fight a final battle for the school and all that it stood for. At one crucial point, when he was president of the New England Association of Colleges and Secondary Schools, I pleaded with him to propose to that influential body that they combat the abolition of the essay examinations; but, in spite of the fact that he showed me a letter from Williams of Exeter making the same plea, he refused to attempt to reverse what he claimed was already a *fait accompli.* That he represented a school which carried weight he undoubtedly knew, but at that stage of his life he had expressed on more than one occasion that he wished to avoid controversy and strife. It would have been better for all concerned if he had pursued another tack, such as suggested by the late Elmer Davis in his essay *On Having Arrived at Sixty.* His idea is, I believe, much more sound: that our elder citizens, having arrived at the stage of their lives when they can be both independent in thought and indifferent to criticism, should be in the forefront of every battle for justice and freedom.

It had become increasingly clear to the Old Guard that we were caught in a crossfire between the poor preparation of our students by the elementary schools and the abandonment of responsibility for secondary education by the colleges. We should, therefore, be fatally injured or completely destroyed if those in executive power failed to act. With the headmaster's refusal to bring the necessary pressure on the colleges, our only hope lay in the determination, the ability, and the energy of the faculty to insist on the continuance of the traditional principles and practices within the school itself. To this objective, Joe Powers—for twenty-three years an uncompromising martinet as a teacher of mathematics before he became headmaster—was entirely agreeable and did what he could to sustain the academic strength gathered by three hundred years of steady achievement.

When his successor, George McKim, took office, the end of an era was in sight and within a short time was assured. Although a successful teacher of history in two comprehensive high schools, he soon indicated to those of us who had taught in the school when it was at its peak of performance that changes were inevitable. Coming at the critical moment of retreat by the colleges—particularly Harvard, towards which we had always looked for guidance and support—his policies helped the debilitating processes that were at work.

During his six years in office, the final effects of the educational revolution made teaching, in the true sense, almost impossible. I am not, of course, holding the headmaster of the Latin School responsible for events beyond his control. But in his unique position as head of the oldest school in the nation with a well-earned reputation for scholarship and integrity, a man of understanding and courage—with the help of a remarkably influential alumni—could have defended the school and its faculty against the forces of destruction. For whatever reasons, he felt obliged to submit to pressures from his superiors at headquarters.

It was not long before we felt the impact of his policies by specific items in his practices. One of the first directives demanded that each master submit monthly reports on specially printed cards, issued by the Board of Superintendents, indicating how many A's, B's, C's, etc. were distributed in each class. If a master's percentage of the marks did not conform to the predetermined curve of probability, he could be called to account. Whether it was a class consisting of unusually bright students or unusually slow students, the same proportionate figure must prevail. This procedure is not only arrant nonsense. It also destroys absolute standards of scholarship and the master's control of the tempo and progress of his classes. With these and other radical changes that we feared might affect both the quantity and quality of the work in the school, the faculty elected a committee of seven to wait upon the headmaster and offer our co-operation in fighting all attempts, from within or without, to adulterate our instruction. As chairman, I experienced at first-hand the difficulties that confronted George McKim. He was always forced to bow to the demands of the Assistant Superintendent assigned to Latin School. As his aim was to make the procedures on such matters as promotion, grading, etc. uniform throughout the school system, the unique institution known as the Latin School would eventually disappear. When we voiced our fears of the future, the headmaster—recognizing that the committee consisted of men highly respected by colleagues, student body, and alumni—listened respectfully to everything we had to say; but when we had concluded, he declined our help and asserted that he would have to comply with whatever orders he received from his immediate superior, regardless of what we might believe their effect on the school might be. With that ultimatum, we departed, later decided to disband permanently, and individually withdrew into our own classrooms to fight lone rear-guard actions.

This was our last attempt collectively to fortify the administration, but we hoped to be able to teach our subjects effectively for those boys whom we faced each day. Within narrow limits, our hopes were realized, but the results were necessarily a far cry from what we were able to accomplish in the now dim past. The final blow to effectiveness was dealt when the colleges defaulted. That story deserves special treatment; for no matter how able, conscientious, or efficient the faculties of our secondary schools may be, the dilution of the admission requirements for the colleges has delivered a lethal blow to education.

Unseen influences, however, far beyond the control of individual teachers, had been at work since the turn of the century to destroy educational foundations laid when the Latin School was young. These rocks of our structure had been imported from Europe and were still the materials basic to our strength. Our school and all others had used the *gymnasia* of Germany, the *lycées* of France, and the grammar schools of Great Britain as academic models. We turned to them when curricula were determined, courses of study arranged, and standards established. Not only were elementary and secondary schools patterned in accordance with long-established European precedents, but our best universities adopted the strict scholastic requirements of Heidelberg, Paris, and London when they considered the merits of candidates for admission. As a result of these age-old practices and procedures, we teachers continued to believe until it was too late that permanent principles had been established and that nothing radical would disturb or could change our academic stability. Like the nobility during the years preceding the French Revolution, we were complacently inactive. This complacency was born of assumptions that the dogmas of the Columbia "encyclopedists"—the torch bearers of progressive education and their followers—were theoretically unsound, practically unworkable, and only temporarily fashionable. Therefore, their theories would die an early death. The experimentation might continue indefinitely, but their wild recommendations would certainly not be widely adopted and could not possibly injure badly or destroy the solid educational structure which had been so painstakingly and conscientiously erected over the years.

Many of us were aware of the revolutionary effects the teachings of Freud and Dewey had had on all of our thinking, especially in pedagogy. We recognized that changes were long overdue and welcomed them. To eliminate the lockstep regimentation, to pay more attention to the individual child, to make the rigidly classical curriculum more flexible, and to reduce the absolutism of fixed standards of measurement were all ideas with which we could agree. My own early reactions to the establishment of experimental schools (i.e., Chicago's Parker, Baltimore's Park, Boston's Beaver, and New York's Lincoln and Little Red Schoolhouse) were enthusiastically receptive, for I believed we needed academic laboratories to test each new idea before adopting it.

Not only was I a sympathetic listener at meetings where the new religion was being spread by avid missionaries, but I became so convinced of the truth in some of its tenets that I became actively involved. While at Saint Paul Academy, I had limited my zeal to arguing with John Briggs about the rigidity of his curriculum as applied to boys who were creative in either the fine arts or in technology. Later, however, I had an opportunity to apply a pet theory when I had become influential enough at Rivers to be consulted on matters of policy. I induced the headmaster to accompany a selected group of the faculty to the Dalton School in New York, where we studied the system originated by its founder in a small town in Massachusetts and then given full scope in her own private venture. Convinced that the plan solved one of the great problems of pedagogy—namely, the educational advancement of each child at his own pace—we adopted it hook, line, and sinker. I cite this exploratory trip into the land of experimentation for two reasons: first, to show how attractive the new faith was to those of us grappling with old questions which continued to puzzle and thwart us; and, secondly, to indicate that although we had been brought up according to orthodox dogmas, we were willing to examine and to test the more rational proposals in the New Jerusalem and accept those that had value.

Little did we anticipate that, by 1935, the theorists and statisticians would overrun all of our schools (public and private) and our universities to such an extent that the *ancien régime* would crumble and the revolution would be effected. When we Americans adopt a new fad, we act like adolescents. Characteristically, in this case we went wild—throwing into the discard everything we had previously established as valid and grabbing at everything that was glitteringly new—sometimes simply because it was new. Monotonous drills must be abolished, for children should be happy at all times. Drudgery must disappear; for studies should be pleasant, uninterruptedly happy, and always easy. Discipline must be sparingly administered as permissive attitudes are adopted towards unruly children or unwilling students. If a youngster says he does not like Latin, let him elect Spanish or Yiddish—whatever is spoken at home; if he cannot or will not study languages, let him try woodworking or cooking. If he dislikes manual arts or domestic science, find something—perhaps baton-twirling or social conversation—in short, anything he might enjoy. Whatever it is, he must be happy. So long as these practices were confined to experimental schools or classes, voluntarily approved and adopted by parents for their children, no one had cause to complain. If school authorities could afford them and could find a sufficient number of fathers and mothers willing to have their boys and girls used as guinea pigs, why should any one object—least of all, teachers?

It was not long, however, before whole school systems were invaded. Graduates of teachers' colleges, thoroughly indoctrinated with the new ideology, entered the elementary schools by the hundreds. New principals and superintendents poured out of the schools of education (especially those from influential ones like Columbia, Chicago, and Harvard) to propagate the faith and convert the heathen in every urban community, suburban town, and country village. By 1940, Dewey-eyed zealots had swayed large numbers of docile oldsters who feared for their jobs or were on the make for better ones and all the innocent neophytes who had no convictions to disturb them. Thus, over the years, majorities were created in faculties, and final victory came when all departments of the all-powerful National Education Association were captured.

The revolution accomplished on the elementary level, the vanquishing of the secondary schools constituted the next goal. This conquest would not have followed without help from an unexpected source. The *coup de grâce* was delivered when the universities—the best of them—went over to the revolutionaries.

8. UNITY

SCHOOLMASTERS ALL OVER THE WORLD HAVE ALWAYS BEEN FACED with the great problem of overcoming the natural resistance of the young to academic disciplines. The intellectual tone of the school and skillful teaching do much, but often they are not strong enough. During my first fifteen years at Boston Latin School (1926-1940) the faculty had a great and powerful ally—the College Entrance Examination Board. No boy wishing to enter Harvard or similar colleges could withstand the pressure of its demands. As the majority of our students had this ambition, our course was precisely mapped and followed.

Authorities in all member colleges were obviously interested in the preparation of entering freshmen, so much so that every detail was specifically outlined. A teacher, then, facing a class of thirty-five candidates, would feel a heavy responsibility. To make certain that he waived none of it, moreover, school officials and parents would insist on careful planning and effective instruction. They would also support the teacher whenever he demanded study from his pupils. The entrance requirements dictated action and defined it. With academic objectives precisely stated by the colleges, everybody concerned knew exactly what ground had to be covered, what quality of performance was expected, and how the results were to be measured.

The directives issued by the College Board established order, unity, and system. If they seem at first glance to usurp local authority or suggest tyrannical domination by colleges over secondary schools, the order created was infinitely preferable to the chaos which followed their abolition. Some idea of the way instruction was outlined and teachers guided may be gained from a typical booklet issued by the Board: *Definition of the Requirements for 1930*. The paragraphs below give a clue to the pervasive and co-ordinating effects of the Board:

> In order to facilitate the comparison of admission requirements with one another, the Board has given its approval to the following statement . . . descriptive of a unit of admission requirements:
>
> > A unit represents a year's study in any subject in a secondary school. . . . A four-year secondary school curriculum should be regarded as representing not more than sixteen units of work.
>
> This statement is designed to afford a standard of measurement for the work done in secondary schools . . . It assumes that the length of the school year is 36 to 40 weeks, that a period is from 40 to 60 minutes in length, and that the study is pursued for four or five periods a week. . . .

It is clear that the Board concerned itself with specific details to assure quantitative measurement of what the schools were teaching; but even more, it insisted on the quality of the instruction. Consequently, a section was devoted to each of the subjects in which examinations were to be offered: English; French, German, Greek, Italian, Latin, Spanish; History, Civil Government; Biology, Botany, Chemistry, Physical Geography; Mathematics; and Drawing—Freehand or Mechanical. A secondary school, therefore, had a wide variety of courses upon which it could build its curriculum for college preparation.

To indicate how closely the Board concerned itself with the supervision of each subject on the list, I cite below the requirements in my own field—English. A candidate might select, after completion of the course, either of two types of examination—the Restricted or the Comprehensive. In the booklet of 1930, the major requirements for both types were stated as follows:

(a) *Habits of correct, clear, truthful expression*
This part of the requirement calls for a graded course in . . . composition and for instruction in the practical essentials of grammar. In all written work constant attention should be paid to spelling, punctuation, and good usage.

(b) *Ability to read with intelligence and appreciation works of moderate difficulty; familiarity with a few masterpieces*
This requirement calls for a carefully graded course in literature. Two lists are provided: (1) *For Reading* in the earlier years . . . . ; (2) *For Study* for closer reading in the later years. The progressive course thus formed should be supplemented by home reading . . . It should be constantly kept in mind that the main purpose is to cultivate a fondness for good literature and to encourage the habit of reading with discrimination.

1. *Books for Reading*

Fiction: *The Last of the Mohicans, A Tale of Two Cities, The Mill on the Floss, Ivanhoe* or *Quentin Durward, Treasure Island* or *Kidnapped, The House of the Seven Gables*

Drama (Shakespeare): *The Merchant of Venice, Julius Caesar, King Henry V, As You Like It, The Tempest*

Verse: Selections from Chaucer, *Lady of the Lake, The Ancient Mariner, Sohrab and Rustum,* representative narrative and lyric verse, *Idylls of the King* (any four), *Beowulf* (translation), *Aeneid* or *Odyssey* (translation), *Tales of a Wayside Inn*

Miscellany: Old Testament narratives, *The Sketch Book* (about 175 pages), *The DeCoverley Papers,* Macaulay's *Lord Clive,* Franklin's *Autobiography,* Emerson's *Representative Men*

Modern Works: a novel; a biography; a collection of short stories; an anthology of verse; a collection of scientific works; a collection of plays

N.B. All selections from the last group should be works of recognized excellence.

2. *Books for Study*

Shakespeare: *Macbeth, Hamlet*
Milton: *L'Allegro, Il Penseroso, Comus, Lycidas*
Browning: specified selections
Burke: *Speech on Conciliation with America*
Macaulay: *Johnson*
Carlyle: *Essay on Burns,* with some of Burns's poems
Lowell: selected essays
Lincoln: selected speeches

The chief differences between the restricted and the comprehensive examinations were that in the latter no books were prescribed and the selection was left to the discretion of the English department of each school. A list of suitable books was suggested merely to indicate "the kind of literature secondary school pupils should be taught to appreciate." These works, besides well-established classics, included Hardy's *The Return of the Native* and *The Mayor of Casterbridge,* Galsworthy's *Forsyte Saga,* Conrad's *The Rescue* and *The Nigger of the Narcissus,* selections from Thomas Huxley, and Bryce's *Hindrances to Good Citizenship.*

Even superficial consideration of the above requirements demonstrates that the colleges were deeply concerned with what was taught and how well it was learned. Teachers were guided and helped by the directives. The contrast between the concern and helpfulness of the universities at that time and their indifference today is nowhere better illustrated than in a 42-page booklet published in 1922 as Document #100, entitled *Suggestions and Aids for College Candidates in English.*

In a prefatory note, H. R. Steeves (Columbia) states: "It is unnecessary to suggest a method for using this publication, for the reason that it is not intended as a basis for a course either in literature or in composition. Its aim is primarily to aid the individual candidate to recognize and remedy the flaws in his preparation. The pamphlet might, nevertheless, be used profitably in classroom discussion as a supplement to regular and methodical teaching."

In a second prefatory note, Clark S. Northrup (Columbia) contributed more light on the general point of view: ". . . in the five years since the first edition appeared—the period of the World War, with its demoralization of well nigh every organization and system of ante-bellum days—there has been no great advance in standards or in average achievement. . . . Since 1916, moreover, the Comprehensive Examinations have been instituted; and an effort has been made to furnish some suggestions helpful to teachers and candidates. . . ." This comment certainly establishes the consciousness of responsibility felt by the colleges toward the secondary faculties and their students.

The rest of the publication is devoted to specific recommendations. The opening paragraphs contain these statements:

> The division of the discussion undertaken here will fall under three heads, representing the three subjects of examination—Grammar, Composition, and Literature. It should be remembered that deficiencies in any one of these subjects may—and frequently do—cause a paper to fail, regardless of the merits of the answers to questions under the other subjects.

Any conscientious teacher of English—realizing that admission to college could not be gained without a passing grade in his field—would cover the ground and impress upon his classes the importance of all three divisions of the subject.

What about grammar, that long-neglected element in modern schools? The explicit directions leave no doubt as to what was expected by the professors of those days:

> What is required in grammar is simply a mastery of grammatical principles and terminology sufficient to enable a student to discuss intelligently the functions of words and members of sentences. It is not necessary to apologize for this requirement, although teachers have objected even to reviewing in high schools what they regard as the work of the lower schools. The justification of the requirement lies simply in the fact that an instructor in college finds it impossible to discuss questions of sentence structure and syntax with a student who is not acquainted with the names of the tools. The ability to write with fair grammatical correctness, however, is not evidence of an acquaintance with grammar sufficient for purposes of instruction in

composition; and it is a fact which reflects the direct value of the study of grammar in connection with practice in composition that the readers in English have always observed a fairly consistent correlation between competency in writing and adequate command of grammatical terminology. Insufficient preparation in grammar is extremely hazardous, for many candidates fail every year because of inability to meet this part of the requirement.

Every teacher felt obliged to heed this warning of possible disaster and provide his students with a solid foundation of grammatical information.

Part II of the pamphlet contained in complete detail a series of directions showing what was expected in matters of composition. After an introductory sentence stating that "the first requisite in composition is correctness in mechanical details," subdivisions were explicit regarding standards of perfection. The following excerpts will serve to show how precise the directions were:

SPELLING

Errors in spelling count seriously against an otherwise acceptable examination book. Ten actual misspellings are as a rule sufficient to cause a book to fail, although this rule is not followed without consideration for unusual merit or generous length. It must be understood, however, that the readers in English regard misspellings as a mark of illiteracy; and the best of books may fail or receive a low rating for this reason alone. . . .

It should be said in passing that few experienced teachers can approve the notion that any large proportion of students "cannot spell." Spelling may be difficult for many, but it practically never happens that a student fails in spelling unless his memory or observation is defective; and if he is weak in either of these respects, his fitness as a student is probably so much the lower in other subjects of study. By far the greater number of "bad spellers" will be found to be frankly untrained, inattentive, or indolent.

Although I agree in large part with the basic ideas expressed above, I question the validity of attaching so much importance to this aspect of the study of English. In at least 95 per cent of the thousands of students I have met, the ability to spell could be developed; and the injunction of the Board was followed successfully. Only one boy do I recall who could or would not be taught and did not learn to spell even reasonably well. Fortunately, he was strong enough in all other respects, so that he was admitted to Harvard, majored in Fine Arts, and is now Curator of one of our best museums. Evidently his "memory and observation" were adequate.

ABBREVIATIONS AND CONTRACTIONS

As a matter of form, sentences should always be written out in full. The "telegraphic answer," in which connectives or other important words are omitted for the purpose of brevity, is in a connected piece of writing altogether reprehensible. Words also should be written in full. Such forms as *&* for *and, writg.* for *writing, Chas. II* for *Charles the Second,* and the *U.S.* for the *United States,* are thoroughly bad; and even the fairly general *Pres.* and *Prof.* are questionable.

Surely no doubt can be left that the Board considered even such minute matters of propriety important enough to make their wishes clear to secondary school teachers.

PUNCTUATION

If it is kept in mind that punctuation serves simply to add to the clearness of composition, one will be less likely to make needless blunders than if he regards the rules of punctuation as merely a set of conventions. As a matter of fact, there is no aspect of composition that is governed more completely by common sense than is punctuation; yet there is no single matter in which candidates show more faulty practice.

Rules and examples of punctuation and mispunctuation follow.

USE OF WORDS

The candidate should use simple, every-day, but specific words. Slang and "gush" should be avoided. Pretentious words are never especially effective and are ludicrous when not correctly used.

As a result of original convictions and the added emphasis of this suggestion, I have long had the reputation of being a teacher who preferred Anglo-Saxon roots to Latin derivatives and who rigidly insisted upon sincerity, simplicity, and economy of expression. One former student, in discussing my methods with a friend recently, expressed his shock when, after having received from previous teachers the highest possible grades for pretentious verbiage and purple prose, he received his first theme of the year in my senior section with an extremely low mark and the comment, "Cut out the crap, and get down to business." I am sure that I was being misquoted, for I never used vulgarisms or profanity on duty; but I am equally sure that the sentiment was accurately recalled.

SENTENCES

The candidate must demonstrate his ability to write clear and well-constructed sentences.

I cite this statement only because at the present time, the candidate is not called upon to write a single complete sentence in any college entrance test, even in English composition.

PARAGRAPHS

A paragraph is not a formless or haphazard aggregation of sentences. A good paragraph, certainly, will deal with one idea. It will proceed straight to the point without needless words or sentences, and it will stop when it has made its point. . . .

THE WHOLE ESSAY

We have still to consider the organization of an entire theme or answer. Upon this point there is little to suggest that is in principle different from the ideas of propriety and effectiveness so far discussed. The theme as a whole must also deal with one idea—an idea of greater inclusiveness than that of the paragraph—and must deal with that idea in a logical, coherent fashion. A student who has mastered the problem of writing well-organized paragraphs should have little difficulty in expanding his principles so that they will fit the necessities which he confronts in treating a larger subject.

In the following pages are reproduced four typical themes, which will serve to give the candidate a concrete notion of how the reader is impressed by varying degress of merit.

Then follow the themes which represent both failure and success with reasons for the grades given. Briefly, the first writer failed very badly, according to the explanation, because he was careless, if not illiterate; not wholly relevant in his treatment of the subject; organized his material in generally haphazard fashion; and gave no serious thought to limiting the substance or determining the order of his treatment. In the second theme, which fell below the passing grade of 60, "there is again bad planning"; "the paragraphing is faulty, and the conclusion is quite irrelevant"; "there are also a few mistakes in punctuation, spelling, and construction"; "these deficiencies weighed . . . heavily against the candidate . . . in spite of the force and interest of the writing. . . ." The third theme, also a few points below 60, was "fairly well assembled, although there are some instances of redundancy; but the writer is more than usually careless in punctuation and spelling and has evidently neglected to revise her work." In the fourth theme, which received a 78 ("a very creditable mark") there is "thoroughly logical arrangement, with generally precise and fluent phraseology, and relative freedom from careless errors and irrelevancy."

The teacher of composition was greatly helped by the many suggestions, expressed and implied. He could rely on the specific directions for planning the year's work. Once he impressed his students with the importance and desirability of considering the writing of many papers not only an inescapable chore, but an opportunity for essential practice, the rest—the responsibility for the character of the assignments and the intelligent and constructive correction of all themes and reports—was strictly the teacher's job.

Part III of the document consisted of advice concerning preparation in literature. It began with this brief paragraph:

> It is necessary, in the first place, to emphasize a very obvious fact; that a student should not attempt the examination in literature until he has faithfully studied the books set for study and feels that he has mastered their substance. The student who depends upon eleventh-hour cramming, or still worse, upon his rhetoric, is bound to be caught, for it is one of the objects of the examiners to test the extent and exactness of a student's information.

The warning about dependence on rhetoric was particularly important; for I found the collegiate representatives among the readers savagely critical of candidates whom they dubbed "word-slingers."

Final instructions concerning the examination book as a whole were as exact as the previous ones on the specific parts: "The candidate should write plainly and neatly, for the readers are only human, and are irritated by indecipherable manuscript. They are correspondingly pleased at evident attempts at neatness. Ink should be used if possible. If a pencil must be used, it should not be so soft as to smudge the paper when the book is handled, nor so hard as to make a thin and light mark, very difficult to read."

To go to such lengths with specific instructions indicates how deeply the colleges were concerned with what was going on in the secondary schools and how seriously they took on the responsibility of directing their courses of study and judging their teaching by means of the examinations. The Board was a tremendous force for good and the only unifying agent for our thousands of sprawling, locally controlled school systems. These examinations influenced administrators when they planned curricula; guided teachers as to what aspects of their subjects they should emphasize; and helped pupils by establishing fixed goals, by enforcing adequate preparation, and by furnishing honest criteria and measurements. The proof of their effectiveness was obvious to every teacher and student who had to meet their thoughtful demands.

The cliché that experience is the best teacher may be—like most aphorisms—only a half-truth; but a lifetime in a single occupation does strengthen it as a generalization. Among many lessons learned in the field of education, some of the most pertinent were furnished while I served for nine years as a reader for the College Entrance Examination Board. This appointment proved to be a great help to me and my students, for I learned, of course, exactly what was wanted by the colleges. The examinations, which were well-conceived, were excellent teaching guides and learning goals. But beyond this advantage, I became well informed on methods employed to assure fair dealing. As the reading of the English papers has been one of the prime targets for the destroyers of the old system, I have been particularly interested in their claims. Not only did this examination give the student the opportunity to reveal his background of reading, his ability to select pertinent material, his organizing skill, and his capability as a writer; but it gave the college authorities an insight into his personality and an evaluation of his intellectual quality far beyond what they could gain in any other way.

Reading such an examination would obviously be much more expensive than running a modern multiple-choice test through a computing machine. The advantages of the one over the other, however, are immeasurable for everybody concerned: for the admissions officer, who could learn much from the paper about the candidate; for the student, both as an incentive and as a measuring rod of his accomplishment; and for the teacher, as an instrument of motivation. Educationally, there can be no argument; and to settle so important a matter on a dollars-and-cents basis is unpardonable.

The problem of objectivity the Board met consciously and vigorously. During my term of service, in the course of which 1,500 to 2,000 papers came to my attention, I saw no miscarriage of justice in the case of a single boy or girl. It is fair to say that almost all candidates received grades commensurate with their ability. The care and attention given to briefing the hundred or so readers of English examinations will serve to show how seriously the Board considered such matters as objectivity and justice.

To prepare for the reading, preliminary meetings were held by committees to discuss the problems of grading the examination of that particular year and to determine the weight to be given each question. Loopholes, possible differences in interpretation, and variations of satisfactory answers were thoroughly examined. On the following morning, when the entire body of readers was assembled, typical papers were presented as samples of each category: high honors (90-100), honors (80-89), satisfactory (60-79), unsatisfactory (40-59), and failures so complete that they required no further consideration (0-39). Every paper was graded by two readers—the first marking mechanical errors with blue pencil and the second with red—to assure accurate and meticulous correction. If, in conference after the completion of seven or eight papers, they could not agree on the grade for an individual blue book, the examination under dispute was submitted to a committee of review for final decision.

Only in two instances during my nine years as a reader did my partners for the day feel the need of assistance from re-readers. The first occasion (in 1928) was brought about by our refusal to trust our own judgment. Both Professor Manwaring (Wellesley) and I felt obliged to give the paper a perfect grade (100%), an attainment we had up to that time believed impossible and which had never been achieved in a Board examination. Later, by special dispensation, we managed to find out that it belonged to one of the Alsop brothers (I have forgotten which one). We were so bowled over by the quality of both substance and style that we could not believe the feat, accomplished under pressure, was possible. After the chairman of our table (Professor Cawley of Princeton) had read the paper, his comment was, "If we have been giving candidates 60 per cent for flat but accurate mediocrity, this book should be marked 160, 300, or infinity. There's nothing we can do but call it perfect."

I do not know whether Joseph (or Stewart) ever found out how good that paper was, but I still remember some of its unusual features. From start to finish the writing was lucid, fluent, and coherent. The discussion of books was mature in its approach and analysis, rich in content, and beautifully organized. In dealing with *Hamlet,* he began by considering opinions of great Shakespearean scholars like Schlegel, Dowden, and Kittredge on the question at hand, and concluded by giving his own reactions to the critics' comments. His handling of fiction was equally startling; for, as one of the three unusual novels he had selected, he discussed with clear insight and complete assurance James Joyce's *Ulysses.* His interpretation of sight passages in prose and verse was not only intelligent, but had the depth and scope of a sympathetic reader twice his age. For his original theme he chose as his subject "Personal Tastes and Critical Standards" and entitled it *Eclecticism.* It was a piece of writing that might have been done by a professional critic; and in it he had utilized a rich background of books, music, art, and travel. It was truly a remarkable performance for a boy not yet in college.

The only other situation which called for resolution of an impasse with my reading partner was caused by a candidate equally interesting but for different reasons. In this case a young woman, who very early in her paper revealed a desire to display her sophistication, committed a serious error in judgment and perhaps in good taste.

As I read with interest her intelligent but suggestive comments on naturalistic fiction, I began to wonder about a candidate who dared adopt her tone in so serious a situation. When I came to her analysis of verse, I was surprised again to find that she had continued with such phrasing as "The simile was as clear as a cocktail." The climax came, however, in the original theme based on the subject "Driving at Night," in which she gave a play-by-play account of a petting party she had recently enjoyed. Frankly, I was puzzled by this capable girl who lacked common sense; but I decided to convey to the college authorities what I thought of her immature exhibitionism. I would reduce her numerical grade of 85 by 10 points on the grounds of "flippancy," thus taking her out of the honors group. Although I thought that I had exceeded my authority in thus judging her manners and morals instead of her ability in composition and literature, the admissions office at Wellesley might see fit to inform her that she was penalized severely for her poor taste and judgment.

What I had assumed was severity turned out to be the acme of mildness when I met my colleague for the day, Miss Carolyn Gerrish from our sister institution, Girls' Latin School. Although up to that moment we had found our grades for other candidates almost identical, the serene atmosphere became frigid as soon as the strait-laced schoolteacher asked in clipped syllables, "What did you give this person?" After apologetically murmuring that I had reduced the grade to 75, I could scarcely believe what I heard, "I get 40; she's not the kind of girl who should be permitted to go to college." Realizing at once that argument would be futile, I replied that rather than waste time discussing the young woman's character, we should submit the book to the Committee of Review. That afternoon, one of the members (four of the five were men) came to inform me that the candidate's final grade was fixed at 80. I have since used this incident to warn students against playing with fate by assuming that judges have either a sense of humor or feelings of compassion. In this case, if the girl's paper had fallen into the hands of two unbending Puritans rather than one, her goose would have been cooked.

Some papers presented no problems at all. For instance, I once read an almost incredible hodge-podge that earned the lowest grade I have ever given in any examination—a dubious 19, which might have been just as fairly marked zero. Written by a lad from a small mining town in Pennsylvania, it was so devoid of any signs of knowledge either of reading or writing that I still wonder why he spent the time and money to take the test. His theme, one of the most original I have ever read, served a useful purpose for one of the readers, Dr. James Tupper, Professor of English Literature at Lafayette. Each year thereafter, when he began his Shakespeare course, he introduced his lecture with this masterpiece of misinformation. Not one subject on the list given by the Board even remotely suggested a biographical sketch of the dramatist; but the boy was so eager to use his material that he disregarded the omission of the topic and wrote on it anyway.

SHAKESPEARE

Shakespeare was born in a nearby town of Edinborogh, England, in the year of 1535, His father was a merchant and was the leading citizen of his district. Shakespeare as a boy loved to read novels and histories of the past. It was a great pleasure for him to go with his father on long sea voyages, for Shakespeare later it was a great advantage to his writings.

At the age of six years old his father sent him to a private school. When at the age of twelve he completed his course and entered a high school where he stayed three years. In school he wrote many novels on nature which were soon publish in the town paper. He entered college at Cambridge, but did not complete his course for a degree. He recieved a job in a newspaper office and there he wrote essays, being publish two times a week.

Shakespeare continue his work for the newspaper, which after a year of experience he quite and wrote for himself. Shakespeare's first start to progress was the writing of the English history and a few novels of Athens. This development was soon recognised by his countrymen.

In the later years to come Shakespeare wrote on Caesar in Gaul, Life of Caesar, Poems of Greece, Adventures of Ulysse, and Essays on Nature. The most important story that made him famous was the conquering of the world by Caesar.

Shakespeare describes his dramatic plots and characters so plainly that his readers may be satisfied with what takes place at different stages.

In the year of 1625 he retired and made a trip to France and Italy. Then he spent a few years in visiting the old destructions that had been done during Caesar's time. While visiting through the land he wrote many small novels about the land. He returned to England in 1628 and spent much of his time going hunting and walking through his estate. Shakespeare died in the year of 1636, leaving behind a great record that no other author has been able to equal.

No doubts disturbed the readers of English papers as to what grades candidates with such well-defined attributes should receive. Some difficulties, of course, plagued the Board; and circumstances beyond its control must certainly have resulted in some occasional errors and injustices. None ever came to my attention; and, by and large, candidates were all treated alike and were dealt with fairly. The advantages of the system far outweighed any weaknesses. Most important of all, secondary schools found it a great help in the maintenance of order, unity, and standards.

The College Board went modern in the forties. Instead of continuing to originate and compose the examinations, engage the readers, and determine the grades, it turned over the entire preparation and administration of the *tests* (as they are now called) to a statistical bureau—the Educational Testing Service. Armed with figures, charts, and graphs, the authorities decided to entrust the judging of the academic qualifications of our graduates to the impersonal pollsters with their bloodless monsters—the computing machines. The tests would now be much more efficient: mathematically checked, purified, and organized even before being printed; presented to the candidate so that he could answer each question specifically and immediately with a symbol, a letter, or a number; and graded objectively, accurately, and unalterably without the aid of erring human hands or faulty human minds. These tests, admittedly doing everything that is claimed, have nevertheless been the chief instrument of destruction in the annihilation of secondary school standards; for they ignore their effects on subject matter and instruction as well as on teachers and pupils.

The effects, both quantitatively and qualitatively, on academic standards at Boston Latin School and all other secondary schools have been evident for many years to all veteran members of the teaching profession. What was clearly apparent seemed to be of little concern to the colleges, at least to those officials who determined policies on admissions. At this point personal reactions must be introduced because no sound exposition has been offered for the disastrous about-face. The mysterious refusal to answer questions has forced a reluctant conclusion that these dignitaries wished to prevent interference with final decisions or interrogation as to who should enter their institutions.

This deduction is prompted by a number of unpleasant facts. The first is the odd refusal to submit an intelligible report to the candidate or his parents on grades earned in the tests and the equally odd insistence that schools must not convey information they receive. "The Board will not issue reports to candidates, their families, or friends. The reports are confidential and may be released only to the colleges or to the candidate's school." Why the secrecy?

The authorities must wish to avoid questioning; no other inference makes sense. A clue to explain the radical shift of emphasis from strictly academic considerations may be the shameful situation which developed at Harvard from about 1925 to 1935, at just about the time when the change was being contemplated. Up to that point almost everything except final decisions had been open and aboveboard. Each candidate was admitted to college on his scholastic merits as determined by the results of the examinations. All grades, figured on a basis of percentage regardless of his standing in relationship to other candidates, were mailed to the candidate; and, by virtue of the results, he could calculate what his chances of admission to Harvard would be. Presumably he would have to obtain, as a minimum, passing grades of 60 per cent in all subjects. At Latin School such assurance was assumed because over a number of years we had found that the examination grades formed almost the sole reason for acceptance or rejection.

In the course of our research, however, we encountered a striking discrepancy between two groups of candidates, whom we shall designate as Group A (desirable) and Group B (undesirable). We found that the first group, considered acceptable for unpublished reasons, needed to obtain a weighted average of 60 per cent (or almost that figure); but the second, evidently unacceptable because of racial or religious homogeneity, had to achieve a minimum of 75 and not a fraction of a point less. Although this refined application of the *numerus clausus* permitted the victims to beat it by extraordinary ability or effort, a few statistics from many in my possession will serve to show how the injustice worked.

From the Records of 1930

Subjects	*Eng.*	*Lat.*	*Greek*	*French*	*Ger.*	*Hist.*	*Math.*	*Phys.*	*Weighted Ave.*
Group A—Accepted by Harvard									
Candidate C. .	50	55		72	76	75	62	55	65.3
Candidate G. .	68	50	60	66	75	55	60	16	59.6
Group B—Rejected by Harvard									
Candidate B. .	67	75	79	76		71	78	35	70.0
Candidate K. .	76	78		81	82	68	73	67	73.8

From the Records of 1934

Subjects	*Eng.*	*Lat.*	*Greek*	*French*	*Ger.*	*Hist.*	*Math.*	*Phys.*	*Weighted Ave.*
Group A—Accepted									
Candidate S. .	65	58	71	82		50	72	35	65.3
Candidate V. .	50	65		78	79	60	65	60	65.2
Group B—Rejected									
Candidate A. .	70	70		75	78	80	71	55	75.3
Candidate Y. .	70	80		75	78	65	70	55	72.2

(*Note:* In this year the Harvard admissions office notified our headmaster that twenty-seven boys in Group B had qualifying records but would be rejected.)

This sad record of unfair dealing by a university which had always enjoyed the reputation of being a liberal force in this country would not now be unearthed if I could account in any other way for the current obscurity concerning grades and the emphasis placed on other criteria. Although my conclusions must necessarily be conjectural, I can see no other valid reason for abandoning the frank honesty of absolute grading or the notification of candidates and for adopting the beclouded methods of the present. My theory is simply that if the old policies had been continued, sooner or later unfavorable publicity, a nasty scandal, and deep embarrassment might have ensued. Rather than risk discovery or be subjected to hundreds of justifiable protests, the officials might well have decided to build an entirely new structure of tests, other criteria, and mysterious and unavailable measurements. The new processing of candidates would permit them to accept or reject any one on any grounds they pleased beyond the public's gaze or redress.

The reasons given school, parents, and candidates for the present system will not stand scrutiny. The fact that the new tests can be evaluated by machines and are therefore more economical to administer surely cannot be taken as a serious explanation in a country as wealthy as ours. When authorities are confronted by those who have been dismayed by their use, this specious reason is one of the first given. Is the purpose of the tests to save money? Another equally inept defense is that too many are now taking the tests in proportion to the number of readers available. Never has the supply of examiners and readers run short in other countries. Why should it in ours? Competent teachers and professors would gladly accept the opportunity to meet with their fellows and to earn much-needed extra money.

Other statements to justify the new type of tests make more sense, but do not explain why the colleges have forsaken their traditional place as advisers and guides to the secondary schools and hence to the entire educational system. To tell us that the grading is more objective when done by mechanical means than it is when teachers and professors read the papers surely begs the question as to what is best for the schools and therefore for our boys and girls. That they are as reliable on the score of predictability of success in college has been established by statistical studies, but this equal efficiency certainly cannot make up for the damage done to secondary education.

The old forms of essay examination were a tremendous force for good. They unified the efforts of the thousands of our sprawling, locally controlled school systems and thus minimized the anarchy that stems from uncontrolled independent action. They influenced administrators planning curricula; they guided teachers outlining courses of study; and they helped pupils by establishing goals, by enforcing preparation, and by furnishing honest tests and measurements. The proof of their effectiveness was obvious to every teacher who ever prepared students to meet their thoughtful demands.

9. DEFEAT

IT IS DOUBTFUL THAT ANY DIKE, HOWEVER STRONG OR INGENIOUSLY constructed, could have withstood the tidal wave which inundated the old school and drowned its faculty. Even if George McKim had emulated the little Dutch boy who put his finger in the leaky crack until help came, he could not have prevented the destructive winds that produced the final floods. The aid which he would have needed to save us did not arrive; for the colleges, which were our only hope as saviors, did not seem to know that their assistance was needed.

Within the school the stalwart men who might have been strong enough to overcome the waves of theory from without and the winds of expediency from within had either resigned themselves to the inevitable or were unable to marshal sufficient help. By the time the present headmaster, John Doyle, arrived in 1954, it was too late; and although he made life more pleasant for the men on his staff, he could not restore an atmosphere of serious study among the boys and proud accomplishment among the men. However valiant and persistent the efforts of such dedicated masters as Max Levine, Albert Van Steenbergen, Paul Pearson, and others might be, the forces surrounding them were overwhelming.

With the brightest principles, the deepest integrity, and the greatest ability, neither Jack Doyle nor his immediate predecessors—Powers and McKim—could have saved the school from the blow which the colleges had struck. Why the universities decided to remove the strongest prop we and other secondary schools had as a defensive wall against the seas of indifference, ignorance, and anti-intellectualism has never been explained or justified. That prop was the high foundation erected by the academic requirements basic to admission into the best colleges—especially, in our case, Harvard. Why a university which has always had four or five times the number of applicants that it is able to accept destroyed the old system of entrance examinations, thus removing their control of what should be taught in the secondary schools and what freshmen should know before being admitted, is still a mystery.

To forsake the practices of the best universities in the Western world, our greatest institutions should have had much better reasons than any of those which have been officially stated. If Harvard and its peers do not defend scholarly excellence by insistence on adequate preparation, then the whole educational system is lost. The only proven method of maintaining standards and unified achievement at the secondary level is to define what is wanted and then to test the results achieved. Until 1940 the College Entrance Examination Board had met both of these essential needs of the schools preparing boys and girls for the best colleges. Not only did the strictly academic requirements make the work in these institutions specific and mandatory, but they designed the pattern and set the pace for all other schools in the land. The administrative officers responsible for them have not yet divulged the causes. The only theories are that (a) they, as well as the schools of education and their disciples, succumbed to the pressures of the pedagogical revolution; and (b) they wanted to select their students on bases other than, or in addition to, scholastic excellence.

The present requirements represent an almost complete reversal of policies of the past. As Harvard is the best example of what has happened and is the chief cause of the collapse of standards at Latin School, it serves to prove this conclusion. Before 1935, the criteria were almost solely academic. Again and again, representatives of the college addressed our upper classes at special meetings in the assembly hall to assure them that if they had completed the course of study and received satisfactory grades in the Board examinations, their admission was assured. And so it was. I could say to my boys, "Study and you will be accepted. In English you must learn to write well-organized themes clearly expressed and mechanically clean. You must develop enough fluency to be able to compose at least four hundred words an hour. Furthermore, you must read a sufficient number of carefully selected novels, plays, essays, and poems to be ready for any questions that may be asked about them." These well-understood demands brought about a year's work which covered the necessary subject matter and assured the boy's readiness for the type of work he would be called upon to do at college. Besides achieving these specific ends, I was always satisfied that my boys were being introduced to the values of a true education. They were taught not only to read with understanding and to write clearly, but they were exposed to the world of thought and beauty.

This desirable state of affairs was destroyed in the years under examination. We were soon to discover that what Harvard was now looking for was quite different. As well as abandoning the old examination system as almost the sole determining factor, the authorities added several other criteria which have nothing whatever to do with academic promise. First of all, they demanded that photographs accompany the application blank, which was altered in many other respects—including increased data on the candidate's ancestry. These were trivial when compared with other considerations. Athletics could never in the past have made up for deficiencies in scholarship, but now unusual aptitude in sports weighed heavily. A few years ago, for instance, a boy ranked as the poorest student in his class happened to be a track star of the first magnitude, being at the time state 1000-yard champion. Before the close of the year, both Brown and Harvard were competing for his services. By offering the lucky runner a four-year scholarship (certainly a misnomer in this instance) of a thousand dollars per annum, the Crimson won that race. The most promising student in that same class was awarded a scholarship of three hundred dollars for just one year. This is not an isolated example; there are many similar cases. This emphasis on athletics as a criterion of quality is not confined to Harvard or other Ivy League colleges. They offend least often in this respect, as is evident from their records in sports. The importance in general of this phase of admission requirements may be gleaned from a remark made, *sotto voce,* by Latin School Coach "Pep" McCarthy at a recent alumni banquet after the headmaster had mentioned the many thousands of dollars in scholarships won by our boys the previous year: "More than half of that sum went to my football players!"

Many unprincipled institutions which stress *physical* education rather than *mental* offer inducements to outstanding athletic specialists. But why reputable colleges should stoop to such practices is unfathomable. Sports-minded alumni are undoubtedly in part responsible; and the directors of college budgets probably help them by claiming that big football crowds must subsidize those parts of the vast program of athletic activities which are not self-supporting. Nevertheless, if any self-respecting college cannot insist on the same standards of academic achievement for its athletes as for the rest of the entering freshmen, it should give up its desire for winning teams or play only those colleges which agree to similar restrictions. Otherwise, all hope for undergraduate quality comparable with that of Oxford, Cambridge, or any other European university must be abandoned. Perhaps, however, the Ivy colleges could eat their cake and have it, too; for to satisfy the victory-hungry graduates and undergraduates, they might establish a special field of concentration—physical education, with its own entrance qualifications, curriculum, and degree requirements.

Sports are not, by any means, the only additional item in the new order which has the ultimate effect of excluding many who lack one or more of the essential qualifications. A test more suitable for selecting a salesman or a public relations expert or a member of an exclusive club is now used by leading colleges eager to find ways of eliminating great numbers of candidates. This dubious method of judging the quality of a prospective student has unquestionably barred many a qualified applicant from pursuing his undergraduate studies in the college of his choice. Before Harvard had adopted this instrument of refined torture for a seventeen-year-old who knows his admission may hinge on his ability to impress his interviewer, Tufts and Dartmouth used it with decisive but some very peculiar results.

In one case, an abnormally obese lad, suffering so intensely from self-consciousness that he trembled even when he approached my desk, had decided to go to a small college. He hoped to overcome his lack of social ease in the more intimate atmosphere of campus life in such an institution. He asked me to supply a letter of recommendation to my *alma mater,* Tufts, and I was glad to do so; for in addition to standing Number 3 in a class of some 250 he was a boy of fine character and of keen sensibilities. Knowing, however, that his nervousness in the presence of his elders would in all probability cause him to make a poor showing in his interview, I suggested to him that I had rather hoped—with his intellectual ability—he would head for Harvard, where the bigness of the university was overcome by the "house" plan and where the heterogeneous nature of the student body made it possible for any boy to find congenial companions. Later, I was glad to find that he had taken the examinations which admitted him to Harvard; for, as I had feared, Tufts turned down this excellent candidate. If such a lad is refused, what a travesty the requirements become. Does it not occur to those who set them up that if he never learns to wear Brooks Brothers clothes, how to balance a teacup or a cocktail glass, or fails to make the Hasty Pudding Club, he may still conceivably become a first-class research scientist or skillful surgeon? Not all people are called upon to be good mixers.

If this boy were an isolated example of the miscarriage of justice resulting from this criterion, defenders of the new requirements might claim that, on the whole, they are fair enough. Unhappily I must record that he typifies altogether too many candidates. Representatives from Harvard spend several days conducting interviews at Latin School. Often they are ill-suited to appreciate some of our boys; for one can hardly expect an urbane young cosmopolite to understand or appreciate numbers of our students—particularly those who come from humble foreign homes and who work every afternoon as newsboys, bootblacks, or delivery clerks. I often observed the lads on my editorial staff become more and more nervous, tense, and unnatural as the time for their appointment drew near. On one such occasion a boy with an obviously Italian name returned after his ordeal clearly depressed. When I asked him why he felt discouraged, he informed me that the interviewer had set a trap for him when he asked if the lad liked operatic music. Assuming that as an Italian he was expected to, he quickly replied that he was acquainted with several operas; whereupon his interrogator fired questions at him concerning details of particular ones. To his dismay, he became confused and vague. He was sure that his goose was cooked. Regardless of the outcome, the incident points up what a many-sided weapon the meeting can become in the hands of an unskilled or unfair interviewer.

Another opportunity to observe the odd workings of this method of eliminating large groups of candidates came when two boys whom I knew very well were considered for admission to Dartmouth. One was an awkward, angular, taciturn lad who had proved himself a capable and assiduous student in class and a solid citizen —popular and adaptable—at camp. The other was a fast-talking, smooth-tongued, beautifully groomed playboy whom I had to tutor in preparation for the examinations he would take if he were turned down by Dartmouth. The second was picked over the first. I am not, of course, intimating that interviewers invariably or even frequently make such flagrant mistakes; but they err often enough to make me doubt the validity of their findings and make me certain that their judgments should have no bearing on the admission of boys to a college like Harvard.

Besides athletics and interviews, other factors have become important; for instance, extracurricular activities and personal recommendations. Neither may have any bearing on the candidate's fitness as a student. To be a member of a club which meets once a month may serve to show gregarious tendencies rather than a desire for solitude; but it scarcely should weigh much in the scale when considering a boy's academic possibilities, which should be the only important criterion for admission to a first-rate university.

This shifting of the emphasis from the intellectual to the physical, social, and recreational qualifications would alone have been a body-blow. The real crusher came when the testing apparatus to determine knowledge and intelligence became ridiculously inadequate and ceased to be important as either a measuring rod for the effectiveness of teaching or as an aid to the teacher. The mere retention of the old essay examinations might have helped to prevent complete destruction of previous standards; but Harvard, in league with the other institutions which controlled the College Entrance Examination Board, abolished them and substituted the present objective and objectionable tests of today. This blow was a final and irreparable thrust; it completed the work of the educational revolution. The successful candidate might now enter Harvard with very little scholastic substance, provided he had what the progressives believe constitutes the "whole" child, the well-adjusted conformist. If he knows how to play the game, how to get along with his fellows, how to be glib, and how to co-operate with the faculty (to get those important letters of recommendation), he is at least half-way or three-quarters in. Certainly the tests he will have to take are no challenge to a Latin School boy of the present and would have been a joke to one of the past.

To show how far-reaching and disastrous this change has been to educational aims and results in the secondary school, let us examine the specific nature of the tests and describe the effects they had on my teaching and students' learning. The multiple-choice tests (in which all answers are indicated by letters, symbols, or numbers) may serve well enough for purposes of selection or elimination of candidates for admission to college. But the fact that not one complete sentence (or paragraph) has to be composed either in the Verbal section of the Scholastic Aptitude Test or in the Achievement Test in English composition has destroyed the function of the old entrance examination that served as a national unifying force in the teaching of reading and writing. Essay examinations forced secondary school teachers in all subjects to insist on adequate ability in composition. Teachers of English were thus aided by colleagues who insisted, especially in history and foreign languages, on well-organized paragraphs, carefully constructed sentences, and accuracy in diction and the mechanics (spelling, punctuation, syntax, etc.). With no composition, even of one complete sentence, required in any subject, these teachers ceased to be concerned with connected writing *per se* and devoted themselves to having their classes memorize pertinent facts and to testing their pupils in the labor-saving way obviously approved by the college authorities and their agent, the Educational Testing Service: by means of tests consisting of questions that could be answered by one word or symbol.

The teacher of English thus found himself forsaken by his colleagues and by the colleges. He was on his own. His pupils could also thwart him by avoiding the achievement test entirely, for most colleges, including Harvard, no longer made passing the English examination a prerequisite for admission; and even if a few boys decided to present English as one of their three subjects for the tests, the elementary nature of the questions eliminated them as a stimulus to either reading or writing. It is easy to see why.

From the booklet issued by the College Entrance Examination Board in 1954 to describe the test in English composition, the following extracts show why it is of little value to either the teacher or the student as a stimulating influence or a measure of qualitative accomplishment in either reading or writing:

Each aspect [of writing] is measured partly by multiple-choice questions and partly by free-response questions. . . .

MULTIPLE-CHOICE QUESTIONS

Correctness and effectiveness of expression

Perhaps the simplest kind of question . . . presents the student with a sentence which has four parts underlined and numbered. In some questions one, and only one of the underlined parts may be wrong or undesirable. In others none . . . needs changing. The student indicates on a separate answer sheet which one, if any, of the underlined portions is incorrect or unfelicitous. . . .

1. The wind <u>would of</u> (1) blown <u>down</u> (2) the house <u>had it not been</u> (3) for the <u>special</u> (4) reinforcements.
2. He spoke <u>bluntly</u> (1) and <u>angrily</u> (2) to <u>we</u> (3) <u>spectators</u> (4).
3. There are four states with <u>populations</u> (1) <u>less</u> (2) than <u>500,000;</u> (3) Delaware, Nevada, <u>Vermont,</u> (4) and Wyoming.

A different kind of question, one that goes beyond the mere recognition of error, requires the student to choose among a number of possibilities the best correction or improvement of an indicated word or phrase. . . .

1. This apple tastes *good.*

    (1) NO CHANGE. (2) well.

2. Cod liver oil is very good for children. *It* gives them vitamins they might not otherwise get.

    (1) NO CHANGE (2) , it (3) , for it (4) ; for it

3. When I was young, I was sure that the life of a businessman was easier than a *student.*

    (1) NO CHANGE (2) of a student (3) that of a student (4) that of a student's

Organizational ability

Writing ability does not, of course, consist merely of avoiding errors of usage. It includes the arrangement of ideas in reasonable order with appropriate connectives. A kind of question that aims at this ability is the "scrambled paragraph."

> *Directions:* The sentences below are in scrambled order. . . . Decide what would be the *best order* in which to put sentences so as to form a well-organized paragraph. . . . In answering the questions, consider O to mean that nothing follows.
>
> (a) Since his day it has undergone change.
> (b) President James Monroe announced it in 1823.
> (c) Its primary purpose, security for the Republic, has, however, remained the same.
> (d) The Monroe Doctrine, one of the most famous statements of American foreign policy, has been in effect for more than a century.
>
> 1. Which sentence did you put first? a b c d o
> 2. Which sentence did you put after (a)? a b c d o
> 3. Which sentence did you put after (b)? a b c d o
> 4. Which sentence did you put after (c)? a b c d o
> 5. Which sentence did you put after (d)? a b c d o

Taste and sensitivity

The third area tested by the multiple-choice questions is that of taste and sensitivity. The questions deal with figurative language and with appropriateness of meaning, tone, and rhythm.

> *Directions:* In each of the groups of sentences . . . there is a blank space indicating that a phrase has been omitted. Select the best phrase and blacken the space beneath its number on the answer sheet.
> With a dull roar, the vessel reached the water; and, half submerged by the plunge, the stern buried itself and a white wave curled up around it. Like a ______, she reared up again, and again plunged with a pitching motion.
>
> (1) swimmer breasting the surf
> (2) stag leaping through the brush
> (3) flat stone skipping across the flat surface of a lake
> (4) diver leaping from a springboard
> (5) small child learning how to swim

FREE-RESPONSE QUESTIONS

The free-response question most frequently used is known as the interlinear exercise. It is a piece of prose from 300 to 500 words in length which has been altered to include a number of errors in grammar, clarity, and emphasis. . . . The student is to locate anything he thinks is poor and correct it. . . . He should not rewrite the entire passage, and he is specifically warned not to do so. . . .

That this completely ineffective and ridiculous test is unsatisfactory to the teacher of senior English in the secondary school can readily be understood. The confession in the pamphlet that the members of the College Board committee are "not satisfied with the test as it appears; nor are they satisfied with any English composition test they know of" is far from reassuring. Nor does it help to know that they are aware of its obvious weaknesses when they say, "As is evident from what has gone before, there is no special subject matter for the English Composition Test." These statements mean that no one on the college level is at present guiding or directing, as was the case when the old type of examinations were in force, the course of study in all subjects taught in the preparatory schools. What havoc this change has wrought in the teaching of English I can illustrate by describing the specific effects on my classes.

One of the most important elements in the change-over was the reduction in the number of subjects the candidate was required to present for examination. In the past, under the so-called New Plan, he was required to take four prescribed subjects which he had pursued through his senior year to an advanced stage. Under the Old Plan, he could present five subjects at the end of his junior year and four twelve months later. Both plans, often called *Comprehensive* and *Restrictive,* respectively, demanded that one of the advanced examinations would have to be English. This provision, by its inflexibility, attached obvious importance to the high school course in grammar, composition, and literature. No boy could possibly be admitted to the freshman class at Harvard or any other reputable college without it. Every one knew, therefore, that the university considered a knowledge of English an absolute essential and that the teacher would feel a great obligation to prepare the candidate to meet the requirement. The student, too, with so much hinging on his being fully equipped to cope with any examination, would feel obliged to pay undivided attention in class, to perform unquestioningly every assignment, and even to ask for extra work.

For the teacher it was a perfect situation. I pointed out at the beginning of the term what my classes could expect: weekly themes; study of prescribed books; collateral reading of three novels, three plays, one volume of verse by a poet of each pupil's own choice, and one biography; and a full written report for each work read. While outlining this course, I made clear to my students that I was not piling on unnecessary burdens just to keep them busy; I was merely treating the examination coming in mid-June as a coach would his big game of the season. And they should welcome each assignment as a vital practice session to condition them for the supreme effort. After all, even as it was, they would have only about thirty themes, about eighteen reports on books, and ten trial questions on the works studied in class. Nobody whimpered, wailed, or gnashed his teeth.

Since the abolition of the examination, every possible obstacle to arousing interest or attaching importance to preparation has been placed in the path of the teacher of English. All incentives to stimulate learning by the student have been removed. In the first place, English (in any of the three aspects of the subject—grammar, composition, and literature) is no longer a prerequisite for admission to Harvard. The candidate has complete freedom as to which three subjects he will elect for his one-hour achievement tests. A boy with even a grain of common sense will choose the trio in which he can achieve the highest grades; and a sympathetic teacher will advise him to do so, although it may mean that he takes tests in Latin, French, and German or any other unbalanced combination. In view of the nature of the objective tests, subjects which depend merely on memory are obviously the most popular choices.

Where does that situation leave the teacher of senior English? Completely out of the running. For obvious reasons, most boys would prefer to prepare for tests in almost any other subject. The only students in my class preparing for Harvard who might present English as a choice would be a talented few, at most six or seven of thirty-five members. Obviously, in such a class, whenever the work became specific preparation for the test, four-fifths of the group was not interested; for all that we could do was the most elementary hackwork in composition, such as drills in the mechanics or exercises in the correction of faulty sentences—the kind of thing we used to do and still do in the first and second years of high school. What alternative was there? From a practical point of view, none. Those who were headed for the test wished to do nothing else; the others were concentrating on the three subjects in which they were to be tested. Beyond the dilemma created by these circumstances, came an even greater problem.

No course in English worthy of the name can omit the writing of at least one composition per week and the reading of good books in the four major types of literature—drama, fiction, verse, and nonfiction. Yet even the boys preparing for the examination balked at the inescapable assignment. After all, *the objective test for which they were being groomed in English composition did not call for the writing of one complete sentence,* let alone a series of connected paragraphs. *Nor were they asked to name even a single book read in the secondary school, to say nothing of discussing their reading.* Therefore, however eloquent my plea or insistent my demand, they refused to consider the work seriously or to put time and effort into carrying out the assignments that I had always believed the backbone of any English course. Why should I insist on this procedure while other masters were spending all their time on specific preparation for the coming tests—due in January or March? Finally, did I not realize that by reason of my assignments their grades were bound to be lower, their standing in the class would then go down, and their chances for prizes and scholarship aid would be jeopardized.

I was thus placed in a position that was not only vulnerable, but impossible to defend. Their claims were factual and valid. My way out is indefensible from the standpoint of educational principles and ideals but unavoidable under present conditions. To teach my classes, according to sound philosophical theory and practice, had become impossible. The school year had been shortened by at least three months; for after the final round of tests had been given in March, it was a losing battle to get any serious work done. Therefore, I had two choices, both of which made my position humiliating: either I give up my proven methods of teaching English by eliminating reading and writing assignments; or I sacrifice my integrity as an honest man by raising grades in order to place boys in my sections on a par with those in others. I took the latter alternative as the lesser evil, but I was frustrated and unhappy. For at least the last ten years of my tenure, I was prevented from performing my function as a teacher in the way that I knew I could and should; and I was miserable in the realization that I was an unwilling party to the tragedy that was taking place.

Meanwhile the school was being adjusted to the new conditions. The late Lee Dunn, nominally and officially the librarian, had ceased long before to serve as custodian of the books except in a perfunctory way. His duties had become manifold and far-reaching. After serving as right-hand man to Headmaster Joe Powers, he continued to take on more and more of the advisory functions of the headmaster in connection with the boys in the graduating class. Under George McKim and Jack Doyle, he became adviser to the seniors and liaison officer between the school and the college admissions offices. Ubiquitous, energetic, and able, he made preparation of the boys for the new tests (especially the Scholastic Aptitude) his particular business and conducted special classes during the noon hour and after school. Although highly appreciated by the boys and their parents, his activities helped further to destroy the importance to students of their classroom and subject masters. For teachers of English, his supplementary aid was helpful—particularly in preparing candidates for the verbal part of the scholastic aptitude test—in that he prepared reams of mimeographed sheets containing hundreds of sample questions. A typical batch, taken from the Thorndike series, demonstrates the idea underlying them:

Synonyms (210 alphabetically arranged)

From the four or five choices the one closest to the meaning of the given word should be selected:

(1) apathy....1. emotion 2. attitude 3. fury 4. insensibility

(3) arrogant....1. insulting 2. haughty 3. impervious 4. turbulent

(13) bland....1. roguish 2. gentle 3. involuntarily 4. slimy 5. perfume

(46) commiserate....1. pity 2. praise 3. neglect 4. misery 5. company

(91) oscillate....1. kiss 2. waver 3. harden 4. set apart

(121) surreptitious....1. careful 2. destructive 3. distrustful 4. clandestine

(149) trenchant....1. salient 2. incisive 3. abysmal 4. fortuitous 5. erratic

Antonyms

From the four or five choices select the word opposite in meaning to the word given

(163) credulous....1. debit 2. ritual 3. belief 4. swindling 5. skepticism

(166) commiserate....1. debonair 2. disconsolate 3. pitiless 4. pleasurable

(171) temerity. . . . 1. reticent 2. cautious 3. soothing 4. agitated 5. dangerous

(179) adulation. . . . 1. placate 2. refine 3. corrupt 4. flatter 5. disparage

Analogies

(1) Water is to fluid as iron is to 1. metal 2. rusty 3. solid 4. rails 5. mines

(2) Poetry is to words as music is to 1. rhythm 2. motor 3. notes 4. melody 5. subject

(20) Physician is to patient as attorney is to 1. judge 2. client 3. politician 4. doctor

(27) Untrue is to disloyal as mendacious is to 1. frivolous 2. steadfast 3. scandalous 4. dishonest 5. placid

(28) Complaint is to charge as ruction is to 1. arrest 2. acquittal 3. row 4. apprehension 5. accusation

Undoubtedly these elaborate briefings helped boys with good memories to obtain higher grades at the expense of true learning and real education. But the hours spent were taken from the time that used to be devoted to reading good books and writing compositions. This memory work, upon which great emphasis was placed by the senior adviser, convinced the boys in my classes taking the English test that I should plan my course with only this type of preparation in mind. If confronted with the outrage committed on the proper teaching of composition and literature by such methods, the College Board officials or defenders of the present tests would point self-righteously to their booklets with their admonitions.

For instance, in the one called *College Board Tests* (1953-54) a paragraph on Page 3 headed "Is special preparation necessary?" contains these statements: "No special preparation is necessary, because the tests are made up by college and school teachers who insure that the questions are fair to all candidates, whether they are students at public or independent schools, at traditional or progressive schools, or at schools located in different sections of the country. . . . The tests should be taken in stride, without cramming, because they are designed to minimize the effect of last-minute studying. . . ."

Regardless of these helpful hints and self-serving statements, no school in the Greater Boston area with large numbers taking the tests failed to engage in herculean labors in preparation. Tutoring schools in Cambridge and Boston have been doing a land-office business; and one of them, Manter Hall, has sold thousands of copies of its handbook "Senior English Review Exercises" to frantic boys and girls. This practical volume of ninety-four pages contains every type of test likely to be given. Its table of contents includes the following topics: synonyms, antonyms, analogies, vocabulary, common errors, scrambled paragraphs, and poetry. The type of question asked on poetry may be of interest; for it, too, must be answered by figures, symbols, or letters so that it may be graded by the calculating robots. One question deals with two poems—Robert Frost's "Stopping by Woods on a Snowy Evening" and Oliver Goldsmith's "An Elegy on the Death of a Mad Dog." The candidate is merely asked to rearrange stanzas placed out of their original order by numbering them properly. What a far cry from the paraphrasing or summarizing of the past! Another type is just as simple. This test was given at Latin School as a fair sample of what the boys might expect:

I

Opportunity

They do me wrong who say I come no more,
  When once I knock and fail to find you in;
For every day I stand outside your door
. . . .

Question: Which one of the following lines is wrong
(A) Because of meter?
(B) Because of tone?
(C) Because of meaning?
(D) Which is the correct line?

	Answer
Waiting and hoping and attempting to get in.	. . . .
I often wonder where the deuce you've been.	. . . .
And bid you wake, and rise to fight and win.	. . . .
A solid door, all made of wood and tin.	. . . .

II

Ah, these the woods, the woods I love,
The woods that I'd make home,
Over whose boundless, wondrous groves
. . . .

Question: Which one of the following lines is wrong
(A) Because of meter?
(B) Because of tone?
(C) Because of meaning?
(D) Which is the correct line?

	Answer
Unlike the soft sea foam.	. . . .
Forever I would roam.	. . . .
Oh gee, I'd love to roam.	. . . .
I often think how nice it would be to roam.	. . . .

III

Across the fields of yesterday
He sometimes comes to me,
A little lad just back from play—
. . . .

Question: Which one of the following lines is wrong
(A) Because of meter?
(B) Because of tone?
(C) Because of meaning?
(D) Which is the correct line?

	Answer
I'm glad I didn't stay a wee.	. . . .
I am not filled with glee.	. . . .
I imagine I could have been he.	. . . .
The lad I used to be.	. . . .

It should not be necessary to do more than compare these questions and a few from the past to show how crippling the new requirements have become to a teacher of English. Aside from the fact that not a scrap of connected writing is demanded or a single inquiry made as to what the candidate has read, little attempt is made to evaluate the quality of his mind, his imagination, his organizing ability, his reasoning skill, and his common sense. No question calls for ability to tackle a new problem or to construct a theme, or to discuss ideas connected with his reading, as was formerly the case in such challenging questions as these:

I

(Interpretation of Prose and Verse,
Comprehensive Examination, 1938)

Directions: State fully, clearly, and simply in your own words the meaning of the following passages. Translate such figures of speech as are used by the authors, as indicated in the model below.

Model: The people here, a beast of burden slow,
Toiled onward, prick'd with goads and stings;
Here play'd a tiger, rolling to and fro
The heads and crowns of kings.

Here rose an athlete, strong to break or bind
All force in bonds that might endure,
And here once more like some sick man declined,
And trusted any cure.

Restated: This passage describes several typical conditions of the common people. In the first two lines they are shown in the state of patient submission to servitude. The next two picture them in savage revolutions, such as the French or Russian, when their former rulers are dethroned and killed. The first two lines of the second stanza depict, perhaps, the ideal condition of people in a free democracy—powerful, but with an athlete's restraint. The last two lines show the people weak and ignorant, easily persuaded by any demagogue who has a plausible solution for their troubles.

(a) Since the engineer is also a citizen and a man of family, and since he has a conscious self with which he must always commune and from which he cannot escape, his education should make his mind a library and a drawing room as well as a workshop.

(b) The cynic breaks stained windows
In churches he must pass,
But he will never cast a stone
Into the looking-glass.
—A. M. Sullivan (By permission of the author.)

(c) We're too unseparate out among each other. . . .
Don't join too many gangs. Join few if any.
Join the United States and join a family—
But not much in between unless a college.
—Robert Frost, *A Further Range* (By permission of Henry Holt & Co.)

(d) Even in his most explicit moments a courteous writer will stop short of rubbing into your mind the last item of all he means. He will lead you right up to the verge of a full comprehension of what he is at; he will edge you into the right corner and put the pie within reach of your hand, and then he will withdraw gently and leave you to put in your thumb and pull out a plum and think what a bright boy or girl you are.
—C. E. Montague, *A Writer's Notes on His Trade* (adapted) (By permission of the author)

(e) They call the towns for the kings that bear no scars:
They keep the names of the great for time to stare at . . .
And we fought here; that with heavy toil
Earthed up the powerful cities of this land—
What are we? When will our fame come?
An old man in a hill town
a handful of
Dust under the dry grass at Otumba.
—Archibald MacLeish, *Conquistador* (By permission of Houghton Mifflin Co.)

(f) Only that day dawns to which we are awake.

Is it not obvious that such a question would challenge, interest, and provoke the mind of the student? Would it not awaken the teacher to the need of providing his pupils with the necessary amount and quality of reading in preparation? Would it not involve the candidate's learning to write as well as to read? The contrast between such searching questions and the pitifully inadequate ones of the present tests is shattering. It indicates to what depths we have fallen in the past twenty years. But there is still more evidence. Let us see what was demanded before 1940 by way of the candidate's discussion of books that he had read during his secondary school course.

II (Questions on Shakespeare)

A. (1926) Ruskin said about Shakespeare's plays, "The catastrophe is caused always by the folly or fault of a man; the redemption, if there be any, is by the virtue and wisdom of a woman, and failing that, there is none." Apply this statement to the hero and heroine in either *Hamlet* or *Macbeth* and show whether you believe it to be true or false.

B. (1932) Show the conflict of impulse and reason in certain actions of either Hamlet or Macbeth.

III (Questions on Milton)

A. (1931) Why should any one today be interested in Milton's minor poems? Cite or quote lines or passages in support of your answer.

B. (1933) From your knowledge of Milton as revealed in his minor poems explain, with specific references, what you think would be his attitude toward (a) the social pleasures or (b) the personal ideals of today?

IV (Questions on Essays)

A. (1924) "To the ill-starred Burns was given the power of making man's life more venerable, but that of wisely guiding his own life was not given." Illustrate this statement by means of specific events in his life. Mention some of his poems and show exactly how they make life more venerable.

B. (1933) In the light of Johnson's experience, comment on the proposition: No man becomes truly educated until he takes his education into his own hands.

V (Comprehensive Questions on Drama and Fiction)

A. (1928) The course of a person's life may be influenced by various agencies, such as his own nature, prevailing customs, personal ambition, regard for other people, patriotic feeling, events beyond his control. From each of three novels select a character, and show in each case how some one of these agencies has influenced him and others associated with him.

B. (1934) "The novelist or dramatist cannot forego the charm of plot without losing a great and legitimate source of interest, but his plot ought not to be governed merely by external circumstances imposed upon the characters from without. It is rather determined by the characters themselves; the outcome of those inner impulses of human nature which it is the chief purpose of the novelist or dramatist to portray."

—C. T. Winchester

(1) Illustrate the truth of this statement by the discussion of one novel and two dramas (one comedy and one tragedy). Answer as fully as your time permits. (50 minutes for both parts)
(2) Give titles and authors of two other novels or dramas in which you think external circumstances have an unusually important part. Give brief reasons for your choice.

These questions gave all candidates an opportunity to show how much and how intelligently they had read and how effectively they could express their ideas. The teacher had in these questions a priceless pedagogical lever with which to lift the thinking of his pupils. Surely he would not be confronted with boys like those in the senior classes of the past fifteen years or so who saw no point in spending valuable time reading and writing when they were not going to be called to account by the college authorities. Why the universities have not admitted, after the experiences of the past two decades, the obvious reason for their need to establish remedial classes in both reading and writing, is not understandable. Any veteran teacher of English at the secondary level could point out the cause of the present illiteracy. The colleges have not defined or insisted upon basic knowledge of the language when screening candidates for admission. If they wish to make an immediate start in the restoration of learning, they should revive at once the old essay examinations.

In addition, they must restore honest grading and absolute standards of academic excellence. Although this factor did not affect my own teaching as much as the elimination of literature and composition as examination subjects, it too had importance. The mystery of present relative scores and curve grading is not solved by the statement of the Board itself. It is eloquent enough to make any further comment superfluous:

The scores are used by colleges as only one measure of the student's ability and academic preparation. Admissions officers also consider school grades, recommendations, interviews, and other indications of the candidate's readiness for college. Each college makes up its own mind about each candidate for admission.

The tests do not have passing or failing grades. They are scored according to a scale on which it is possible to score as low as 200 or as high as 800. Since admission depends upon many factors, including the number and quality of applicants, a score of 500, for example, may be satisfactory at the same college at one time and not at another time. It may be acceptable for one applicant and not for another when taken together with all the other information weighed by admissions officers.

Surely such relative mumbo-jumbo can serve only to confuse rather than clarify any judgment of what the teacher has taught or the pupil has learned. When, under the old scheme, we were given absolute percentage figures for the individuals in a class on a particular examination (with the questions published by Ginn and Company later each year), we had a reasonably accurate idea of how much of the required subject matter had been mastered. On the basis of that valuable information, we were able to gauge how thoroughly we had covered the ground and how effective our teaching had been. Now we know nothing about the student's scholastic fitness for college as a result of the tests. That Latin School boys have continued to capture highest honors gives little satisfaction to any of the old-timers; for we know that our boys have covered much less ground and have performed their work on a much lower level of quality. None of the statistics produced by the apologists for the present state of affairs can convince us that they are anything but relative hogwash to hide the truth. In fact, whenever the senior adviser, Lee Dunn, revealed to some of us the startling results achieved by our boys (usually about 90-95 per cent above the 500 mark, with over 65 per cent in the honors or high honors category), my only reaction was, "If we get those results on the basis of what is being done in our classes, then God help the United States!"

10. RESOLUTION

UNTIL THE RETIREMENT OF HEADMASTER JOSEPH POWERS IN 1948, the practices of the past were continued at Boston Latin School with unbending rigor, a disregard for the winds of controversial theory, and an unconcern toward the actions of the admissions offices.

The routine of weekly tests and monthly grades and insistence on high standards of scholarship were continued by a hard core of veteran teachers. It was not before 1950 that the staff and then the student body began to show serious effects of the new order. With the advent of George McKim, who was appointed headmaster in 1948, after long service in a comprehensive high school for girls, changes were brought about to conform to the unfolding pattern of contemporary American education. With the shift in college entrance requirements away from the predominantly academic, Harvard ceased to be the primary target of our boys or the measuring rod of teaching efficiency for our masters. In contrast to the days when almost half of our graduates became freshmen at Harvard, we were sending only 20 per cent to the college across the Charles. More and more boys were going to colleges with even less stringent academic requirements than those which still demanded three achievement tests. (At the 1958 Fall Alumni Dinner, the present headmaster announced that the 244 graduates of the preceding class had been admitted to 66 different colleges.) As a consequence, Messrs. McKim and Dunn were vitally interested in raising the school grades of our boys. Much greater emphasis was thus placed on marking in accordance with the current practice of basing grades on relative scores and conforming to the curve.

When at a memorable faculty meeting I vigorously protested against this procedure from a standpoint of continuing our honesty in grading and of sustaining our traditional levels of performance, I was informed that the order came from Headquarters and must be carried out. I replied by illustrating the inconsistency of applying a statistical generalization based on thousands of cases to a class of thirty-five boys. For instance, in that year's senior division, an unusually bright one, I should in justice have to award at least ten A's and could fail no one; therefore, I found it impossible to conform to the curve. The answer from the headmaster came fast: "Oh, we don't mind that at all. It's only when too many boys are receiving low grades that the curve should be regarded." When such a method began to be employed throughout the school, grades went up and achievement went down.

Almost without exception, when less is demanded of students, less is done. The impossibility of holding the line became apparent to the entire faculty. Some men, near retirement age, decided to quit. Three outstanding heads of department who might have stayed on for several years as well as several other staunch old-timers resigned. When this happened, those of us who remained knew that we were beaten. As educational conditions, both external and internal, continued to grow worse, retirement became increasingly a temptation.

Before reaching my sixty-fifth birthday in 1957, I resolved the conflict that plagued me. Although my senior divisions had become a source of irritation rather than the stimulus that they had been in the past, I continued to find teaching my other classes a full and rewarding occupation. While they came to me with noticeably less knowledge and inadequate training, I could still interest them sufficiently, by employing my well-tried methods, to lure them into doing considerable reading and writing. My enthusiasm had not been deadened, nor had my energy flagged. My classes continued to be lively, productive, and satisfying. The work itself was, as always, worthwhile.

Beyond the classroom, too, I found life in the school pleasant enough. Congenial colleagues had never been lacking and were not now. The faculty room was, as ever, an escape-hatch as well as a haven of peace and amusement. It was also a spot for unrestrained freedom of expression. A never-ending series of discussions—some serious, many serio-comic, and still others violent in protest against grievances—kept everybody awake, if not alert. Hundreds of stories, occasionally clean and scholarly but more often earthy and ribald, were told and retold. It was a smoke-filled room where teachers talked like men and scorned the politicians and apple-polishers among them. Hilarity and easy small talk usually prevailed. After school, smaller groups of close friends often gathered in neighboring or downtown eating places for coffee and conversation. If I left the school, I should certainly miss this companionship as well as the give-and-take of the classroom.

One other deterrent to resignation was a firm attachment to the school and an unflagging interest in the welfare of its boys. Thirty-one years of pleasant association cannot be shaken off without conflicts and regrets. On the one hand, I knew that in spite of my feelings of futility and hopelessness whenever I viewed the general educational scene, I could not dispel a consciousness of guilt as I thought specifically of the boys I faced each day. I felt a little like a man who was leaving a sinking ship.

I might have remained at my post for five years longer; but the more I considered the circumstances, the more I realized that only one reasonable course lay open to me. During the previous seven or eight years I had withdrawn ever more and more from the educational arena and confined my efforts to the little four-walled world of the classroom. At the same time I was well aware that teaching ideals and principles had suffered destructive damage not only in my own case but in that of every other teacher of integrity, and not a voice was being raised in protest. We bemoaned our fate and tried to comfort one another by saying that little could be done. Finally I decided that if the plight of the classroom teacher—particularly the teacher of two of the three R's—was to be made known to the public, I must devote myself to telling his story. Recognizing that I should need much more time than my job would permit and that if I waited five years I might not have either the strength or the desire to succeed in my purpose, I retired from the Latin School in June, 1957.

My timing was almost perfect. In the fall of 1957 the Russians shattered our complacency by launching their satellites—the Brothers Sputnik. Not the least important result of their startling impact was a sudden realization by the American public that something might be seriously wrong with their schools. By the time widespread confusion and fear had become evident, I was already in England, where I had gone to observe at first hand the workings of their well-co-ordinated school system. I had chosen that country for several reasons: its close resemblance to our own in outlook and democratic attitude; the elimination of problems connected with language; and, above all, the influence of its examinations as a unifying factor for its schools and universities. After having corresponded during the summer with the Ministry of Education, I landed in England in September, ready to begin my study. By the time I returned home two months later, the air was charged with powerful currents of controversy about our schools and our educational ideology. It was not long before I was in the thick of the battle.

In Britain I found a well-integrated system of education, based primarily on the assumption that after pupils had been taught, their knowledge should be thoroughly tested before they were permitted to proceed to a higher institution of learning. To avoid entering into the controversy (which had become a political football between Laborites and Conservatives) as to whether or not a child is too young at eleven and a half to be channeled, by virtue of examinations, into either a college preparatory or a comprehensive secondary school and thus determine the course of his adult life, I limited myself to a study of college entrance examinations and their effects on the general education of boys and girls. For that reason, too,

I confined my visits to the public grammar schools—almost exact replicas of our own Latin School—and to classes in English, so that I could observe what I considered my especial concern and province.

At the office of the Ministry of Education, I had a long interview with Mr. J. O. Roach (in charge of external relations), a former professor of foreign languages. An obviously cultured and highly articulate gentleman, he stated that he had begun his study of Latin at six, Greek at seven, and Oriental languages a little later. For many years prior to his joining the government, he had taught French and Egyptology at the university in Cambridge; and he still lived there, commuting each day to London. He made several interesting observations: that British university students should not be compared with ours, for only 5 per cent of their secondary school pupils matriculate as against 30 per cent of ours; that the English have overemphasized the humanities and minimized technical studies; and that they separate their students into two groups (college preparatory and general) by means of examinations usually before the age of twelve. More important than his comment was his service to me. First, he arranged for my use of the Ministry's well-stocked library; and then he called the chief official at the London County Council, so that he would arrange for my visiting whatever schools might interest me. That gentleman, a Mr. Boyle, proved to be equally gracious and obliging. A young and hard-working head of a very busy office, from which the administration of 1350 schools of the area was conducted, he took time to make the necessary appointments with headmasters; introduced me to the chief of their big educational library on the fourth floor and granted permission for its use at any time; and made a suggestion, which proved very valuable indeed, that I get in touch with Mr. Bruce, the Chief Examiner, with offices at the University of London, who is responsible for the conduct and grading of all school and university entrance examinations.

Mr. Bruce—a communicative, frank, and pleasant man—has complete charge of the Ordinary and Advanced Examinations, which are taken by 300,000 candidates at the end of the academic year and 100,000 at the end of the summer. Passing these examinations admits the candidates to any university in the United Kingdom. He gave some interesting statistics. [*Note:* The ordinary Level Examinations correspond to our old Preliminaries, which used to be given at the end of the junior year of high school; the Advanced, to the old Finals at the end of the senior year; and the Scholarship (for determining recipients of financial aid), to none that has ever been conducted in the United States.] In a London district, 80 examiners are appointed to read at home 500 examinations each in English Composition during a period of three weeks while they are still teaching. These figures are rather startling to a former reader for the College Board, who during the seven or eight days devoted to the reading of examinations at Columbia was expected to do justice to not more than about one hundred papers. In view of the present American claim that the expense of marking essay examinations is one of the reasons for their abolition, how can the impoverished Britishers afford this luxury? According to Bruce's estimate, between 60 and 65 per cent of the candidates taking the English Ordinary Level Examinations pass; and about 70 per cent taking the Advanced (about one fifth of the candidates) pass. The passing grade is now 47 per cent, which sounded low until I saw the examinations and read the directions to readers for grading them.

Their difficulty is apparent in the description of the papers in English Literature, as given in the University of London pamphlet for 1958–59. The syllabus in this subject contains these data:

Ordinary Level

One paper (2½ hours) on prescribed books for 1958:

Section A. Shakespeare (1) *Merchant of Venice;* (2) *Macbeth*

Section B. (1) *A Book of Narrative Verse: The Ancient Mariner, Morte d'Arthur, Sohrab and Rustum, The Glove.* (2) *An Anthology of Modern Verse:* poems by Belloc, Blunden, Booth, Bottomley, Davidson, de la Mare, Drinkwater, Flecker, Gibson, Masefield, Munro, Owen, Sassoon, Stevenson. (3) Dryden: *Absalom and Achitopel,* Part I and *MacFlecknoe.* (4) Keats:

The Eve of St. Agnes, Ode to a Nightingale, To Autumn, Lamia, Chapman's Homer, Bright Star, When I Have Fears.

Section C. Dickens: *Great Expectations.* Conrad: *Four Tales.* Scott: *Redgauntlet.* W. H. Hudson: *A Shepherd's Life.*

Candidates will be required to answer five questions, at least one being chosen from each of the Sections A, B, and C.

Advanced Level

The examination will consist of the following papers:

Paper I: Chaucer and Shakespeare (3 hours)

Paper II: Set Books (3 hours)—selected from a list representative of English literature from Chaucer to the present day. Candidates will be expected to have a special knowledge of the books selected and such general knowledge of the history of literature as is illustrated by them. (Five questions)

Paper III: (3 hours) Passages in verse and prose designed to test ability to elucidate meaning and to show appreciation of literary form and content.

Scholarship Level

Papers I, II, and III, as set for the Advanced Level.

Paper IV: (3 hours) Questions on a wide choice of subjects. The candidate will be required to attempt three questions.

The quality of the papers is shown in these samples taken from a recent examination on *Set Books* (Paper III), in which there were forty questions. The candidate chose five for discussion.

More: *Utopia*

3. An ex-Cabinet minister dated his political career from the accidental purchase of a copy of *Utopia* at a second-hand bookstall. Does your reading of the book help you to understand why this might be so?

or

4. "The ideal of Utopia is discipline, not liberty." Do you agree with this statement about More's *Utopia?* Give reasons.

Spenser: *Faerie Queene*

5. "We cannot go halfway with Spenser; he either bores or enchants us." By reference to Book I of the *Faerie Queen,* explain this point of view.

or

6. "Whether or not it be true, as Ben Jonson said, that Spenser 'writ no language,' it is in fact the perfect language of romance." Amplify this statement by reference to Book I of the *Faerie Queene.*

Masefield: *Reynard the Fox* and Housman: *A Shropshire Lad*

37. By quotation or close reference, compare and contrast the metrical resources of Masefield and Housman in *Reynard the Fox* and *A Shropshire Lad.*

or

38. Both Masefield and Housman love the countryside, but for different reasons. Amplify this statement by reference to *Reynard the Fox* and *A Shropshire Lad.*

A candidate for matriculation at any university in the United Kingdom (and eligibility for one is identical for all) must "obtain passes in (a) the English Language; (b) a language other than English; (c) either Mathematics or an approved Science; and (d) three other subjects, *provided at least two are at the Advanced Level.*" A boy or girl expecting to concentrate in Arts (humanities) leading to B.A. or Ll.B. degrees would take—according to a pamphlet issued by one of the grammar schools—three or four of the following subjects during his final two years: Mathematics, Latin, Greek, English, History, Geography, French, German. "A wide variety of other subjects may also be taken, but the ones mentioned above are the most common. . . . A qualifying standard is required in at least one classical language. Latin is most frequently offered, but Greek may be taken."

(NOTE: That "wide variety" includes such unfamiliar subjects—for an American, at least—as Indian History, English Economic History, Logic, Religious Knowledge, Greek Literature in Translation, Geology, Human Anatomy, Art, Music, and languages of almost infinite variety—Classical Hebrew, Modern Hebrew, Afrikaans, Albanian, Amharic, Classical Arabic, Armenian, and concluding with Ukrainian, Urdu, Vietnamese, Welsh, White Russian, Xosa, Yoruba, and Zulu.)

A teacher of English must, to prepare his pupils for the examinations, have in mind both the Ordinary level in *Language* and the Advanced level in *Literature*. The first requirement applies to all students, regardless of which one of the three major fields of concentration they may have selected for study at the university: (a) Science, leading to the degree of B.Sc. in engineering, medicine, dentistry, or veterinary science; (b) Economics, leading to the degree of B.Sc. (Econ.) or Ll.B.; or (c) Arts, leading to the degree of B.A., or Ll.B. The examination in English Language tests the candidate's knowledge of grammar, composition, and reading comprehension with such questions as the following:

1. Do two of the following exercises, *one* from Group A and *one* from Group B, allowing about half-an-hour for each:

A

(1) Describe one item in a television or sound broadcast programme that has particularly interested you. The item should *not* be a play, and should have lasted thirty to forty-five minutes.

(2) Write a letter to a friend describing a game or sporting event which you have recently seen or taken part in.

(3) Explain to a beginner what he would need to know to use a camera . . . or to embark on a day's fishing or to play chess or to drive a motor-cycle.

(4) Write an account of a train journey or a sea trip you have taken on which something unusual occurred.

B

(5) Give your views on the value of a holiday abroad.

(6) Which do you prefer: competitive games or non-competitive recreations; and why?

(7) Write a composition on "Bargain-hunting."

(8) What are the virtues and dangers of ambition?

2. Summarize, in your own words as far as possible, the argument of the following passage (which contains about 500 words) reducing it to about 170 words.

(Then follows a passage consisting of three substantial paragraphs discussing the attractive and unfavorable characteristics of a British country fair.)

. . . .

5. (a) Analyze the following sentence into clauses, writing out each clause in full. Give the grammatical description of each clause, and state its grammatical function:

   After *telling* us that unless we kept strictly to the instructions he had given *us* throughout the climb we might well risk our lives in this *most* difficult ascent, our guide made it plain that we must wait a day or two before we set out as the weather conditions at that moment were not what we had hoped for.

   (b) Name the part of speech and state the grammatical function of each of the three italicized words in (a).

Considering the preparation necessary for such an examination and, even more, for the three or four Advanced level literature examinations (lasting nine or twelve hours), I concluded that the life of a British teacher of English is not an easy one. Visits to classrooms verified this conclusion. The schoolmasters have to work much harder than their American counterparts. Their work has to be much more intensive and thorough. They must provide their pupils with an incomparably better cultural background. And all because they are compelled to meet the much greater demands of the examinations.

My first visit was to St. Clement Dane's Grammar School, which is attended by some eight hundred boys and staffed by about eighty men. These masters, who earn from six hundred to fifteen hundred pounds per year (fixed salaries in all schools under the jurisdiction of the Ministry of Education), have a working day which lasts from nine o'clock in the morning until four in the afternoon, although a number of them stay for extracurricular activities until five thirty without extra compensation. Each man has six teaching periods and one unassigned period during the school day, interrupted only by a ten-minute coffee break in the faculty room and luncheon in the big dining hall, where he presides at a long table over his boys.

NOTE: The size of the schools and of the individual classes interested me. Compared with ours, they were so small that I hunted down national statistics to make sure that I was not being guided into unusual schools. I was not; for the figures gave proof of what was to me a startling general condition. In the Ministry Report for 1956 on Statistics of Public Education for England and Wales in a table headed *Pupils Per Teacher Ratios* are those for Grammar Schools:

Number of Pupils in Schools in Which the Ratio Is

Under 20	*20-24*	*25-29*	*30-34*	*35 up*	*Ave. No. Pupils per Teacher*
487,010	56,546	563	(none)	(none)	18.1

The first class was composed of a group of lads in the graduating class who were terminating their schooling and were not preparing for the examination in literature. It was presided over by the head of the English Department, who devoted the period to a discussion of the novel as a form, with particular emphasis on Thomas Hardy. The master, in academic gown—as were all members of the faculty—lectured most of the time to the small class of eleven boys (six were absent as a result of the Spanish flu epidemic at that time raging in England). All sixth-form (final year) sections were equally small, because the authorities and the teachers are convinced that they must be to assure proper preparation for the examinations. The boys, as well as the masters, were formally dressed, wearing in many schools uniform blazers and in the others dark jackets. Perfect decorum and close attention were obviously taken for granted. The master concluded the period with a comparison of two pairs of writers whom he termed *complementary novelists:* Meredith and Hardy; Wells and Galsworthy. After he had suggested the collateral reading of three or four novels by Hardy, the period came to a close. The classroom, while small and untidy and lacking pictures or decoration of any sort, had a well-stacked bookcase and a completely filled magazine rack.

From that class, I went to others. One on *Hamlet,* in preparation for the Advanced level examination, was conducted for twelve boys in a small portable hut next to the large and beautifully kept playing fields. Another on *Macbeth* was taught by an eager, enthusiastic, and well-informed young man for a group of some twenty-five fifth-formers, who appeared to be unusually intelligent and interested. Still another class for boys about thirteen years old was engaged in the study of *Richard II* in a sunny room well supplied with pictures. After a very lively review of the preceding day's recitation, they proceeded to act out Scene 2 of Act V in a variety of British accents after the master had moved his desk out of the way of the performers.

During lunch with the headmaster, Mr. J. McGill Glouston, and for some time thereafter, we discussed British education in general and his school in particular, of which he was understandably proud. Although under the general jurisdiction of the London County Council and of the Ministry, the school was originally and continues to be partially supported by an ancient Foundation—a fact which, Mr. Glouston emphasized, gave him a certain independence in running it and selecting his personnel. Almost all members of his faculty have been, consequently, hand-picked honors graduates of the universities; but he, like headmasters in our own country, complained that it was becoming increasingly difficult to get the type of young men needed as teachers with the low salaries offered them. Incomes must be raised to attract them to the profession, which, after all, competes with others for their services.

A few days later I visited another school which helped to strengthen my belief that the British system is far superior to ours. The Bec Grammar School, located on Beechcroft Road, was housed in a very substantial building with beautifully maintained soccer fields on both sides of it. On entering, I was struck by its controlled tone—a low hum of activity in the midst of a quiet calm. Clearly audible sounds came only from the sun-lighted assembly hall opposite the office. There a master was rehearsing two boys at the piano.

After the usual preliminaries I had learned to anticipate when visiting a British school—admittance by a porter, introduction by card to the secretary, and a conversation with the headmaster, who turned me over for the day to the senior master—I was ushered into a succession of English classes. As at St. Clement Dane's, I found in all of them the same close and respectful attention paid to whatever the master said, mature discussion of books prescribed on the examination lists and other related works, and assignment of many written exercises to be done at home. Throughout my stay at the Bec School, I remained in the classroom of Mr. Mulhern, youthful and vigorous head of the English department. One side of the room was entirely covered by a huge, brightly colored mural —done by pupils with unusual artistic skill—representing Chaucer's pilgrims on the road to Canterbury. At first I had assumed that it was merely an appropriate decoration, but I discovered that it served a useful purpose as well when a sixth-form class referred to it from time to time as the boys read orally from the text or discussed incidents and characters. The recitation was most interesting; for constant allusions to the development of our language and to matters of ecclesiastical history punctuated the translation of the verse, and intermittent comments and questions came from the master. Almost as intelligent and scholarly were the periods when the lower forms met. For instance, in a class considering Browning's *The Glove,* attention was directed to peculiarities of the rhyming, to certain sophisticated turns of phrase, and to unusual metrical patterns.

The customary problems connected with schoolboys were still in evidence; for one boy who was not well prepared was told to report for detention, and another who was shaky about the meaning of a classical quotation was told by Mr. Mulhern that his Latin master would be requested to give him extra work. I was interested by another recitation, this time a sixth-form section engaged in a final discussion of Milton's early poems. The informality of tone as well as the quality of the discussion was impressive. The boys were led skillfully into consideration of Puritanism and the poet's personality, his politics, and his religion. At the end, when asked about their enjoyment of the study of Milton, the boys were frank to say that they had enjoyed to a greater degree their previous study of the works of Keats and Shelley. After they had left, the master informed me that this was a relatively poor division; but I was able to comfort him by assuring him that they equalled the best that I had had at Latin School.

At the end of one of my visits, I asked my host how, seemingly without conscious effort, masters in all classes were able to maintain a serious tone, a perfect decorum, and a respectful attitude. This behavior was obviously habitual. Rather taken aback by my question, he turned to me and said quietly, "Well, you know, it has never really occurred to me that our lads are well behaved and mannerly. We rather take for granted that boys are going to conduct themselves as they should. Of course, now and again we get unruly ones, who are punished by means of extra study, demerits, and so forth. And if a bounder really gets out of hand or impudent, off he goes to the headmaster, who will probably thrash him. This extreme is very rare, I assure you; but the main point is that the boys know that the ultimate whipping is there; and they avoid it."

I went to only three private schools—for I was not concerned with them—but I was interested in the comments of the Headmaster Halévy of Wittingehame College in Brighton. Mr. Halévy, a highly communicative gentleman with positive views, operates a unique school, which aims to provide a background of both British and Hebrew culture for 200 boys from twenty countries. His most provocative observation, the accuracy of which I did not challenge and the sincerity of which I had no reason to doubt, was that he dreaded the enrollment of any American students; for his experience with a considerable number of them had led him to believe that, by English standards, they had learned next to nothing in mathematics or any other basic subject. These experiences had ended in his complete contempt for United States educational methods. Not only had entering students created this impression, but it had been deepened by numerous experiences with his graduates: for when some were unable to meet the requirements for admission to British universities, they had been accepted by good colleges in America (among them, M.I.T.) and subsequently had done very well.

To ascribe the success of British secondary education wholly to one cause or set of circumstances would be as inaccurate as it would be unsubstantiated. The long history of their schools, the traditional respect for their schoolmasters, and the intellectual and social climate all contribute. These are peculiarly theirs and cannot be transplanted. But many facts gathered from their pedagogical literature and many elements in their educational apparatus are applicable to our own situation. Three specific items are most important for us: (1) the quality of their teachers; (2) the size of their classes; and (3) their examination system. As the first two can be changed for the better in this country only by the expenditure of vast sums of money, our citizens must be taxed far beyond our present high limits. This problem is obviously beyond solution by any one individual and can be solved only by political agitation and mass action. The other element, their examination system is the answer to many of our difficulties and is the most easily instituted.

11. CRUSADE

AS WE SAILED HOMEWARD FROM SOUTHAMPTON, MY IMMEDIATE plans began to take shape. For the first time in my life, I was not returning to school. During fifty-nine successive terms (eighteen while learning and forty-one while teaching) I had established what seemed to be an unalterable rhythm of routine: June closing, summer interlude, fall opening. The pattern was as constant as the ebb and flow of the tides and as unending as the sea before me. Unnaturally and unbelievably, this design was now—in the autumn of 1957—being destroyed.

Most men look upon freedom from obligation and release from the tyranny of schedules as a blessing beyond hope. I did not. In fact, I feared the removal of duties and deadlines. My doubts about easy adjustment to new-found liberty were not without cause. The only interruption in an unbroken stretch of teaching had come in the form of a sabbatical ten years before. After a two-month Grand Tour of the United States and another sixty days in which I indulged in a long-contemplated reading jag, I found myself one morning sitting on a bench near the pond in the Public Garden. I read the *New York Times* from the left-hand column of the first page to the right-hand column of the last. I yawned and looked up. A few inches away was a seedy fellow-bum. Immediately my current uselessness became unbearable. I got up, strode across Charles Street, took the diagonal path through the Common, and headed for the School Department office at 15 Beacon Street. When I informed the Superintendent that I should like to terminate my leave-of-absence, he looked at me doubtfully as he told me the rules did not permit my return to service before mid-year (February). Although sorry that I could not get back to my classroom immediately, I was happy to end the emptiness of a vegetative existence.

This incident alone was warning enough that contentment for me could come only with action and purposeful work. Without regular employment and some goal, I am lost. Therefore, when retirement had loomed, I knew that I had to provide for full-time employment with a fixed routine. After considerable mental wrestling I decided against teaching at the college level, although sorely tempted when offers came. A lifetime in secondary education had cut deep; and before departure from it, I wished to make a final contribution to it. Twenty years of satisfying labor as a teacher had been followed by an equal number of years of increasing frustration. The sad story of the struggles of a typical twentieth-century schoolmaster to maintain his integrity and his balance had to be told. I owed it to myself, to my colleagues, and to the profession. Before doing anything else, I would record the facts of the revolution which had taken place and how the classroom teacher had reacted to them.

Within a few days of our arrival at home, I had begun to work on a fixed schedule: during the hours usually spent in school (from eight to two-thirty) I wrote; after that, I did the usual work connected with camp. In a matter of weeks I had completed two long articles suitable for such publications as the *Atlantic, Harper's,* or *The Reporter.* This would be a start. I contemplated no difficulty in marketing them; for although there had been a tremendous outcry about our schools from professional writers, enraged parents, agitated professors, and apologists, no teachers had been asked to express an opinion or had volunteered one. As usual, the people who knew most about the situation in the schools—those in direct contact with the victims—were not consulted. At such a moment I should have no difficulty placing my articles. I was badly mistaken.

As often as I submitted my manuscripts, just as often were they returned with polite notes of rejection. Usually editors or readers admitted that what I had to say was pertinent, authoritative, and forceful; but unfortunately they had full inventories, had already accepted material too close to mine in content, or were sorry, etc., etc. . . . By February, I was so disheartened that I was almost ready to give up—in fact, so much so that I applied for work in several colleges for the second semester. Before anything could develop from that source, a rapid sequence of events suddenly changed the even tenor of my life.

These events made me realize that publishing is as erratic as show business, and that a writer's success is as unpredictable as an actor's. One circumstance is accountable for everything that followed during the next two or three months: my son-in-law, Dr. Walter Guralnick, engaged in conversation two patients of his. His interest in the great debate on education is almost as intense as mine; and when he told these men, two important local editors, of my futile attempts to be heard, they became interested enough to suggest that I get in touch with them. After reading my articles, one of them said that he would like to print a piece on the subject of current examination practices if I could simplify the presentation of the topic to the point where his mother-in-law could understand it. Presumably I produced what he wanted; for on the first page and occupying the left-hand double-column—with by-line and photograph—in the *Boston Evening Globe* of February 24, 1958, appeared the article, headlined "HAVE COLLEGES RUINED OUR HIGH SCHOOLS?" Below in bold type a short paragraph declared: "Nearly two generations of Bostonians have learned their English from Philip Marson, who quit Boston Latin School last June because he felt too upset about the way things have been going. . . . Here is what he believes is wrong with education in this country and in Boston particularly."

From that day on I ceased to be an obscure protestant and became a national battler. The spotlight was on me; for within a week, a *Time* magazine reporter, accompanied by a staff photographer, came to talk with me. On March 10, 1958, the interview was published and almost literally brought the world to my door. Telephone calls, telegrams, and letters arrived from the far corners of the earth; and I felt like Chicken Little in the fable. In the article itself, the statements that probably caused the cloudburst of correspondence were no doubt provocative:

"The American school system, from first grade through college has become a huge kindergarten. . . . The colleges had so diluted their entrance requirements that they ceased to function as incentives to scholarship. . . . The experts may come up with figures which say that students are better scholars now than they were. But I don't believe them. These figures are based on percentiles—on the student's relative standing."

The day after the article appeared, I was called by a Cambridge publisher, Ruth Noble of the Berkshire Publishing Company; and in June, a paperback which I completed in two months—*The American Tragedy—Our Schools*—was being sold. I had no sooner agreed to write this polemic, than four national concerns offered to publish the book I am now writing. They were joined shortly thereafter by two others.

Concurrently, I had contributed to the *Thirty-Second Discussion and Debate Manual* an article called "We Can Learn from the British"; had appeared on Chet Huntley's television program *Outlook* in a nation-wide hook-up; and spoken on two radio broadcasts —one national, the other local. Speaking engagements kept me hopping all over New England—from Concord, New Hampshire, to Greenwich, Connecticut. Several speeches were given first-page coverage, and one evoked a flattering editorial in the Manchester *Union-Leader,* put out by a stormy petrel among journalists, William Loeb. It said, in part:

"[The Russians] have shattered our complacency and awakened us to the fact that we have a woefully weak educational system."

These words . . . give us a clear insight into the speaker's character. Here is a man who is not afraid to buck the professional "educationists," who realizes that the American people deserve an accurate analysis of the education for which they are paying. . . . For that reason it is particularly encouraging to see that we still produce men . . . able to analyze critically the work they are doing. Mr. Marson is not proposing anything radical. He is simply saying that we should make intellectual training the prime purpose of education. . . . He is saying that school is a place for work, not play, and that accomplishment should be rewarded, promotions . . . should be earned, and scholastic standards raised. . . . But, even acknowledging that it is true, many will resent Marson's saying it. He may be accused of "attacking our schools."

The truth is that those who seek to maintain mediocrity in education, because of pride in profession, are the real enemies of education. . . .

Such encouragement helped; but even more stimulating and revealing were the letters from parents, teachers, and other troubled people from all over the world. The one coming from the remotest point was written by a member of Parliament in New South Wales, the representative from Wollongeng-Kembla. Their significance may be deduced from the following excerpts from a few of them:

Former Head of the English Department in Brookline:

"As one retired English teacher to another, greetings and salaams. At last the voice of the classroom teacher who really knows the problems has been heard. . . . While administrators may squirm, teachers will bless you heartily for calling attention so authoritatively to what they all know and from which many suffer."

A former colleague:

"I want to tell you how happy you have made us all here at Latin School and even all of my friends because of your wonderful articles. . . . Keep it up, old boy! Let them have it—both barrels! *Mille grazie!* Many thanks from the *profession.*"

Retired Head of English Department, Gloucester (Massachusetts):

"I agree in *toto,* but I didn't know Latin School had gone modern. That I thought was the last stronghold."

Former Head of History Department, Brockton:

"May your words travel far! . . . Those of us who have inveighed against the 'Progressive Movement' will no longer be prophets without honor in our own profession. I just couldn't take it, so I retired four years before the mandatory age; and although I have missed teaching terribly, particularly association with young people, I have been leading a pleasant and I hope not a useless life. . . ."

Teacher, Cheyenne, Wyoming:

"It was with great pleasure that I read your article. My Boston Latin days ended in 1942 when I enlisted in the service. . . . This is my eighth year of teaching, and I have been an advocate of Latin School's mental discipline. . . . My colleagues scoffed at me until Sputnik #1 was launched. . . . The training I had at Latin School has been invaluable to me. I certainly hope it has not fallen by the wayside and forgotten its glorious past. . . . Good luck on your crusade; and if ever you want a staunch supporter in the West, call on me."

Teacher, Santa Fé, New Mexico:

"As a Wellesley graduate raising four sons, I want to congratulate you on your firm stand. I am teaching in so-called junior high, and everything is a 'ball'—as they say. Grammar and spelling are incredible. What kind of people are Americans who can't speak and write their native tongue correctly? . . . . Three cheers for your Honesty!"

Retired teacher and professor, New York:

"The Berkshire Publishing Company has sent me your little concentrated package of educational dynamite. I feel it 'lays it on the line,' as some of our boys would say. Remember I spent some thirty-five years in the secondary classroom before I was 'translated' as a professor of education. . . . Practically all curriculum changes and methodological reforms have not been made by teachers and not even in consultation with them, but by 'professors' of education, many of whom have never been in a classroom. Many others did not like teaching but escaped as soon as they could into realms of greater monetary and prestige rewards to be found in superintendencies and similar rarefied, theoretical spheres of pedagogical fantasy. . . ."

The passages quoted were typical of those received from fellow teachers, but those from other people were fully as interesting as samples of national thinking.

A physician, Lansing, Michigan:

"I was very glad to see you opposing present-day education and hope you keep up the good work . . . I hope you will stress the point that schools are primarily convenient parking places for children, where they are kept out of their parents' way and kept amused . . ."

A father, Los Angeles:

"It was with great delight I read about your efforts on behalf of American schools. As a parent and citizen, I am terribly concerned about the present state of schooling and attitude towards education here, having had the benefits of a Swedish education, in which country scholastic standards are kept high and discipline is not yet a forgotten word. . . . May I express my admiration for your courage?"

A mother and alumna of Radcliffe, Cambridge:

"Congratulations! It is warming that at last some one has pointed at the colleges. They complain of the inadequacy of preparation; but they never concede that they are ultimately responsible for the deficiencies of their freshmen. This situation is why some of us have kept our children in private schools whose standards bear no relation to the minimum requirements of the colleges."

A service wife overseas (letter postmarked F.P.O., San Francisco):

"May I thank you for having the courage to say and the precision of language to express just what our American school system is . . . Long have I wondered when America would wake up to its pitiful and tragic educational inadequacies . . . I have four children of my own. I am worried. It is only men like you who can bring about a true change in our educational system. Try to get our teachers to throw away the crayons, the pretty pictures for coloring, the parties, the two and three 'resting' periods plus two recesses—oh, I could go on and on. . . . Thank God for Sputnik and, may I say, thank God for a few scholarly Americans."

An attorney, Miami:

"Apropos of the *Time* coverage of your views upon secondary education, may I express my heartiest endorsement. . . . As father of three sons, I am quite concerned with their preparatory education, which is yet upcoming. I believe implicitly in a classical education as the only satisfactory training to inculcate proper mental discipline. Since my own schooling was obtained in Europe, as the son of a foreign service careerist, I am woefully unacquainted with secondary schools in the United States. . . . At the risk of imposing on your time, I would like . . . your advice as to a proper school for my boys in preparation for university work; specifically, those schools which emphasize English syntax and rhetoric, literature, Latin and Greek or Hebrew, mathematics, and history. . . . Should you be inclined to answer, . . . please do so with the knowledge that you will have earned the gratitude of two parents who are deeply concerned with the education of their children, distressed over the lack of study discipline and the playfulness which seems to characterize the educator's approach contemporarily, and who earnestly desire to become apostles of the return to a classical education as being the best way of preparing young men for their entrance into a university and for their adulthood."

A radiologist, Plainfield, New Jersey:

"Reading your solid rugged individualistic ideas about how to up the standards of education in this country, I felt like yelling loud enough for you to hear across our New England separation. Bravo, and encouraging you to blast off the other barrel also."

A mother, Scottsdale, Arizona:

"The article about your crusade gives me a new lift. How encouraging it is to weary parents to find champions doing battle. We singly get nowhere. Can we organize to help? . . . Is there any chance that you would be available to speak to a parents' group? We are considering the organization of a *large* committee here in Arizona, since individually we are only smiled upon by the teachers, as though we were children speaking out of turn. . . ."

A resident of Palisades Park, New Jersey:

"It was my pleasure to tune in, for the first time, to the TV program called Outlook on March 30th. . . . I was so interested in what you had to say that I wrote Chet Huntley and got a transcript of the broadcast . . ."

These manifestations of interest, approval, and concern were not only a tonic; they became a mandate. I now had no choice; I had to go on. As similar evidence of national dissatisfaction with the educational *status quo* continued to pour in and still does, I knew I had to analyze the enthusiasm and almost unanimous approval which had been expressed before continuing to act.

After much thought I am convinced that rank-and-file citizens, as well as teachers, have a deep conviction that they have been duped by fast-talking professorial salesmen, have been given a false sense of security by their elected officials, and have been lulled into inaction and conformity by obedient but ambitious authorities. Thus, when a straightforward evaluation by a classroom teacher is followed by the suggestion of a possible solution and a restoration of order, people listen and hope. But before acting, I had to ignore the cheers and the shouting, avoid the haste and pressure which came after the sensational publicity, and yet take full advantage of an incredible opportunity. When, therefore, I began this book, I felt the need of putting down specific articles of faith. Here they are:

A PROGRAM FOR THE RESTORATION OF LEARNING

Credo

Our republic cannot survive and our way of life will disappear unless we can educate our young. In a nation dedicated to democratic processes and rule, we must have informed citizens and wise leaders. The only effective instrument we have for producing such people is our public school system. Unless this system is based on sound philosophical principles and a workable program, it cannot function.

ARTICLE ONE

WE MUST TEACH ALL OF OUR CHILDREN

Every child—white, black, yellow, or red—must be given the opportunity to learn. Whatever his intelligence, he must be afforded the chance to realize his full possibilities. This dictum means equal opportunity—not identical schooling at uniform speed—for all. Individual differences are revealed by children as early as the first grade, and these differences must be taken into account if our educational aims are to be realized. By the time they have reached Grade VII and certainly by the time they have entered Grade IX, three major types of learners will have been differentiated—slow, normal, and fast. For them, as well as their teachers, the happiest arrangement will be to group them accordingly so that they may absorb knowledge at a pace neither too rapid nor too sluggish. As a result of such an arrangement, their entrance into an appropriate college may also be determined. On the basis of their capacities, their appplication of energy, and their desires, they will at the end of Grade XII be channeled respectively into colleges with the highest academic objectives, with moderate scholarly aims, and with greater emphasis on social and vocational adjustment than on studies. The thought of the opening statement in this paragraph bears repetition: EVERY HIGH SCHOOL GRADUATE MUST BE GIVEN THE OPPORTUNITY TO MEET THE REQUIREMENTS FOR ADMISSION TO ANY COLLEGE. Thus, we meet the dubious charge that separating the sheep from the goats runs counter to the American dogma that "all men are created equal." More important, by giving every potential leader—in fine arts, pure science, government, technology, education, or any other field—the education best suited to his needs and capacities, we assure our nation the number and quality of men essential to the effective functioning of democracy.

ARTICLE TWO

WE MUST HAVE ABLE TEACHERS.

A teacher in Utopia would have the qualities and practice the ways of a sage, a saint, and a psychologist. In our workaday world, however, we must settle realistically for a man (or woman) with sufficient knowledge of his subject matter; with a sympathy for and understanding of the learners; and with the ability to present what is to be learned in such a way as to make it interesting and important. In short, he must be informed, patient, kind, and intelligent. These qualifications will be found only among good students who are socially responsible and relatively selfless. They must be disinterested in regard to financial rewards and public acclaim, and they must disregard hours of work. They must be dedicated to their pupils as a pastor is to his flock. Otherwise, the "hungry sheep look up and are not fed."

Such men and women are not all dead and can be found in sufficient numbers. We must, however, make their lives bearable and their labors feasible. They must be honored, respected, and morally supported by parents if they are to educate our children. They must be paid sufficiently well to raise their own children under circumstances as good as ours. In selecting their work, they have forsworn wealth; but they must be able to devote themselves to teaching as a full-time occupation. They must not be called upon, as at present, to exhaust their energies in part-time work as tutors, evening school instructors, and camp directors; or, what is even worse, in completely unrelated work—too often menial and sometimes disgraceful. They must earn enough to avoid all of these—relevant or not—so that they can devote themselves exclusively and unstintingly to what should be a full-time profession and can also find ample time for self-improvement and recreation.

ARTICLE THREE

WE MUST PAY THE BILL FOR THE RIGHT KIND OF EDUCATION.

We cannot get the kind of public education that we must have for survival as a democracy without paying for it. So far we have been unwilling to foot the bill. The billions for physical plant—buildings, grounds, and other facilities—are always forthcoming; but the money for the only inescapable essential—the right people—has never been supplied. If education is to attract the only kind of men and women equal to the task—namely, the best—it must compete for their services with commerce and industry as well as with the other professions. To come anywhere near this objective, salaries must be raised to unprecedented heights, but not beyond the point sufficient to assure reasonable living standards. Teachers do not need to be paid as are movie stars, tycoons, or even doctors; but they must receive compensation adequate to their position in our society. The money may come from local, state, or federal sources; from great foundations; or from fund-raising organizations. The wealth of this country is almost limitless; and enough of it must be made available for what is probably the greatest need of our times—the best possible education for our children.

ARTICLE FOUR

BASIC SUBJECTS MUST BE TAUGHT.

Children will learn whatever adults teach them. Parents have in the past assumed that school officials are educational authorities and have therefore left curricular matters to the experts. Until the appearance in the heavens of the Russian satellites, most of them were unaware that a revolution had taken place in American education which was almost as radical in its effect on our schools as the Communist overturn had been on the czarist economy. After the establishment of Progressive principles and practices, old curricula and courses of study disappeared; and in their place came hugely reduced requirements both quantitatively and qualitatively. Less and less substantial material was taught in the elementary grades, and social promotion based on chronological age replaced advancement determined by scholastic achievement. More and more electives with fewer and fewer prescribed subjects made life in the high schools easier, gayer, and happier. And less and less emphasis was placed on academic success by college admissions offices. The disastrous consequences on our entire educational system—from elementary to university levels—can be met only by a wide, drastic, and deep counter-offensive. Curricular changes of a sweeping character to conform to the best practices of the past in this country and of the present in Europe must be instituted at once.

(a) Reforms must begin at the top by means of greatly increased academic requirements for admission to college. At least four prescribed subjects must be offered by the candidate: English, one foreign language (studied at least three years), history, and either mathematics or science. If he is a candidate for admission to an engineering school or intends to concentrate in the sciences, he must qualify in both of the last-named subjects.

(b) A high school diploma in the college preparatory course will be granted only when the minimum requirements for admission, as stated above, are met. Electives are to be permitted only after these demands have been fulfilled. To earn a diploma, other students must include in their programs English, history, and mathematics as basic studies before being allowed a free choice of electives.

(c) Elementary schools must return to thorough training in fundamental subjects: reading (with emphasis on phonics and on selectivity in the choice of books); writing (with stress on the mechanics, including spelling); grammar (from the fourth grade on); arithmetic (mastery of—not mere exposure to—the four fundamental operations, fractions, percentages, and mensuration); geography; and history.

To train youngsters for citizenship in a democracy, the schools must necessarily consider their most important function and their most sacred duty the successful teaching of reading, writing, speech, and history as the most essential subjects in the curriculum; for upon them hinges the ability of the adult to understand issues, to vote intelligently, and to lead the nation. As for the concept of the "whole child" and his adjustment to society, the school must do what it can; but it cannot be expected to take the place of the home, the church, and the community.

ARTICLE FIVE

QUANTITATIVE AND QUALITATIVE STANDARDS MUST BE ESTABLISHED.

As in England and all over Europe, the highest academic authorities —that is, the faculties of the several fields of concentration in our universities in collaboration with representative secondary and elementary teachers—should determine the stage to which the subjects to be presented by candidates for college admission should be pursued. Thus, not only will boys and girls be properly prepared for study in any college in the country (whatever its scholastic requirements), but will be ready to do satisfactory work on the collegiate level. By this means, too, the educational whims of a particular administrator or the politics of a local school board cannot unduly affect proper preparation of the children of the community. It is, of course, one way to prevent the traditional local jurisdiction over schools from subverting national aims and ideals. If the important matter of standards of achievement is left to each one of the thousands of communities instead of to competent authorities, the current chaos will continue and order cannot be restored.

ARTICLE SIX

WE MUST MEASURE ACCURATELY AND HONESTLY WHAT HAS BEEN TAUGHT AND WHAT HAS BEEN LEARNED. . . .

If we are to evaluate the work done in our schools, we must establish comprehensive tests and restore absolute standards of measurement. We must re-establish the emphasis once placed on connected writing in complete sentences and well-organized paragraphs. Without the return of essay examinations—at least in English and history (possibly in foreign languages, too)—we shall continue the present descent into illiteracy. We are, as I have said elsewhere, the only nation in the Western world which relies solely on the objective test for evaluation of a student's knowledge from the elementary to the university level.

The second step that must be taken is to return to honest grading. Relative scores, percentiles, and "curved" grades do not tell the truth about our students or our teachers. These statistics reveal only how they stand in relation to others, not how much they know or how much they have been taught.

ARTICLE SEVEN

WE MUST ACT BEFORE IT IS TOO LATE.

The present international impasse will be resolved not by bullets, but by brains. If the Russians and Chinese are given credit for reasonable intelligence and strategic sense, we can be sure that they will not resort to the ultimate insanity of atomic warfare. Why should they if they can gain their ends by continuing the stalemate or accepting coexistence as long as necessary? They need do nothing to hasten our destruction. Unless we change our present direction, we shall within twenty-five years prove the old Marxist axiom that the contradictions in our own system will ruin us. One of the chief causes of our present sorry state is the education of our youth. If we teach what should be taught, if they are to learn what should be learned, and if Western individualism and freedom are to prevail as a way of life, our public schools must be improved at once. The essential improvement can come in time only if the leaders of our nation can induce our great universities to act. A specific plan follows:

(a) To educate properly our most gifted youngsters, fifty colleges—at least one in each center of population—must establish highest standards of admission. To assure democratic equality of opportunity, examinations modeled on those of Great Britain should be required of all candidates.
(b) To raise and maintain secondary school standards, all other colleges granting bachelor's degrees must admit only by examination in prescribed subjects, with at least the tests in English and history to be written in essay form.
(c) Grading must be absolute instead of relative in all tests—whether objective or essay.
(d) With ever-increasing numbers of students ambitious to enter college, high and elementary schools would be forced—as they are in England and other countries—to meet the requirements established by the universities.

These are my articles of faith, which must guide my future course as speaker, writer, and advocate. I believe that my plan is the surest and most direct way to stop the present deterioration and to start rebuilding. Whenever Admiral Rickover, Professor Bestor, or any one else suggests a return to first principles, he is greeted by howls of disapproval from the educational wolf-pack. He is immediately accused, as I shall be, of advocating an un-American method of creating an aristocracy of brains and thus creating an intellectual élite. Why Dr. Conant and others immediately sniff a foreign scent in what is a typically American way of determining leadership in any competitive field, I cannot understand. We apply it to almost every other aspect of our lives—to sports, to the arts, to business, and to the sciences. Surely a man, to qualify for a responsible job, must compete with others for acceptance. When a football coach has 150 candidates report for the first practice, he is not denounced as a foreigner when he cuts his squad to workable size; and he is not declared an undesirable alien when he selects the final eleven for purposes of producing a winning team. We do not consider the conductor of a symphony orchestra undemocratic because from the musicians available he chooses the one hundred who, in his judgment, will create the most beautiful music.

By the same token, for the very best of reasons, we must search out the ablest brains in the nation, provide them with effective teachers and adequate facilities, and then train them for leadership. At present, outside of a very few isolated exceptions, our public schools are not staffed or organized to provide the best education for potential leaders. The only institutions equipped for such training are the great independent preparatory schools, which can accommodate pitifully few of our best intellects—and only then if their fathers are wealthy enough or scholarships are available. This limitation of educational opportunity to the rich and well-born is truly undemocratic; and those critics who worry about the establishment of an aristocracy of intellect should face the realities rather than shout down every attempt to raise the academic standards of our public schools.

As for the training of the average citizen, it is fully as important as the training of leaders. If we hope to make democracy work, all of us must be sufficiently schooled to read with comprehension, to listen with understanding, to write clearly enough to let others know what we think, and to know enough about mathematics to be able to make change and to figure out our income taxes, which will undoubtedly be staggering.

12. APPRAISAL

AS I END THIS AUTOBIOGRAPHICAL PHILIPPIC, TWO STANZAS FROM Browning's *Rabbi Ben Ezra* become pertinent:

the first: Grow old along with me!
The best is yet to be,
The last of life, for which the first was made:
Our times are in His hand
Who saith "A whole I planned,
Youth shows but half; trust God; see all, nor be afraid!"

and the fifteenth: Youth ended, I shall try
My gain or loss thereby;
Leave the ashes, what survives is gold:
And I shall weigh the same,
Give life its praise or blame:
Young, all lay in dispute; I shall know, being old.

According to the great Victorian, I should at this stage of my life be able to evaluate the past. Perhaps. But whether or not such self-appraisal is possible, I shall place on the scales, for purposes of comparison, my previous vocation and my present mission. I do so because I am not yet convinced that writing and speaking—even for a great cause—shall become my major occupation and replace teaching. Public speaking I have never really enjoyed. On the one hand, I feel like a strolling player "strutting his stuff" before an audience that expects to be entertained or to be given a temporary lift. On the other hand, I sometimes feel like a traveling salesman arriving in a strange town, displaying his wares, giving his pitch, and then disappearing into the night. Through the years, I have never been able to rid myself of this feeling; and despite the sincerity of my plea and the importance of my cause, I have these same reactions today.

As for writing, I find the creative side of it absorbing and stimulating, perhaps too much so; for, as James Branch Cabell once remarked in *Beyond Life,* making these crooked little letters take on meaning is in itself a considerable trick, if not a minor miracle. But aside from this aspect of it, I am glad I do not have to write for a living. Whatever the project of the moment may be, it takes demonic possession of the writer for its duration: he can think of nothing else, night or day; and he loses interest in family, friends, events, reading, and recreation. It becomes an obsession. It takes over completely, and I am not enjoying the experience. Furthermore, it is a solitary task which forces me to be monastic—devoted to duty and confined to a cell. Finally, in this particular book, I feel as though I am doing a mental and spiritual strip-tease before a mob on Boston Common. At this moment, in this last chapter, I have not only doubts about my continuing to write on a permanent basis, but have yearnings to return to the classroom.

Why do I wish to go back to the world of callow youth, endless paper work, and dull faculty meetings? It is not nostalgia for the "good old school." It is not the inability to shake off the habits and routines of a work-horse who has been put out to pasture. Nor is it my gregarious self crying out for the society of men—and boys. It is many things much deeper than meet the eye.

If I were asked by my grandson or some other lad why I have found teaching so satisfying, I should have no difficulty in explaining. I could show why (as Browning expresses it in the poem quoted above) a teacher's life succeeds "in that it seems to fail" and why everything which the "world's coarse thumb and finger failed to plumb" has made my work stimulating and gratifying. I could also suggest why, a few short weeks before I wrote these words, I remarked to my wife, "Will you believe me when I say that I used to get a bigger thrill from one good class recitation than from everything that has happened during the past year?"

What are the great and abiding satisfactions that make these comments possible and have contributed largely to the richness, interest, and contentment of my life? To put down in cold print the sources of my attitude toward the profession is certainly difficult for me and possibly incredible to others—especially to those who are acquainted with my attempts to overcome handicaps, obstacles, and disappointments. I hope I can clarify my position. More than any other factor, the one which makes teaching a soul-satisfying experience is the youngsters. Helping them to grow up and find their way in the wilderness called the world is, of course, a great social service; but the individual teacher, as he meets his charges day in and day out, is not aware of his contribution. In the secondary school, he is so busy with bewildered, inhibited, but well-meaning adolescents that he has little time for reflection. Subconsciously, however, he is aware of his power and his influence.

Often enough I have been startled, during a chance meeting with a former student, into a realization of the opportunities and the dangers inherent in the continuous contact with impressionable youth. A chance remark, an insinuation, or an expression of belief or opinion has unmeasurable and unforeseeable influence on boys whose confidence and esteem have been previously gained. But caution, based on such a sense of responsibility, must not prevent open, natural, and honest discussion. The great trick on controversial questions is to present as many valid views as possible without revealing one's own. Thus, the master helps the pupil form a new opinion of his own choosing or strengthen an old conviction. In my own classes (and I confess at once that in helping boys and girls attain intellectual maturity, the teacher of English or history has peculiar advantages) I am sure that any number of students were affected by discussions of manners and morals, crime and punishment, thought and action, war and peace, quality and trash in print, party politics, High Church ritual and Puritan simplicity, etc. Such subjects were not dragged in by the master, but grew out of masterpieces studied, talks given by students, or even a sentence in a textbook. Whatever it was, though the ultimate effects were intangible and immediate results unknown, imprints were made on receptive minds as ideas were introduced to some for the first time and were formulated for others as opinions.

These indirect, subtle, but important aids to growth helped the youngsters and stimulated the teacher. They were incidental by-products, for the main business of the school is to impart information and to assure understanding. Whatever the subject matter and however difficult, the teacher must face the problems of explanation, clarification, and recapitulation. When success comes, the satisfactions of the expert follow. Even a routine lesson in grammar or punctuation can produce them. The wag in our department at Latin School often ridiculed the finer techniques of the specialist by stopping a fellow member in the corridor and seriously asking, "By the way, Mark, how's Operation Dangling Participle going these days?" Yet I have no doubt that he, like everybody else in the work, felt a definite exhilaration when able to impart to a class the nice distinction between restrictive and nonrestrictive modifiers. This feeling is comparable to that of a football coach who has just seen his team execute perfectly an intricate play or that of an orchestra leader who has finally heard his men run through a piece faultlessly.

The joy of the craftsman is felt by all teachers, whatever their subject; but only the teacher of English can get the thrill of introducing a pupil to a new realm—the world of great books. The possibilities of future exploration for the young voyager are, of course, infinite; and the opportunities of the teacher for charting the course, limitless. An exposition of the satisfactions derived from this aspect of an English teacher's life could fill volumes, but I will confine it to a few personal conclusions. The work in literature gives so many satisfactions that most teachers are tempted to overemphasize it at the expense of the less glamorous but no less essential chores connected with composition, rhetoric, and grammar.

Whether trying to develop in students a sympathetic understanding of a great masterpiece or luring them into reading other good books, the teacher has to exercise the skill of a master salesman in approach, presentation, and display of samples. The need for salesmanship is undoubtedly present and provocative. But a still greater opportunity for the use of special techniques exists in this area. It is a kind of paradise for the bibliophile and the "ham." With my gluttonous appetite for books, I was in my element. Like all gluttons, or epicures, I was always eager to talk about delicious foods and to arouse the appetites and raise the taste of those around me. Enthusiasm breeds curiosity, and many students have told me that in my class they were assailed by hunger and were forever after afflicted with an insatiable desire for good food. Whatever success I had in developing a taste for good books was attributable partly to careful planning and partly to accidental, incidental, and unconscious action. Under the heading of premeditated assault I would classify such devices as book lists, the study of prescribed classics, and assigned reports on collateral reading. Incidental and suggestive rather than conscious were alluding to a bargain I had found at Goodspeed's bookshop, referring to an interesting article I had come upon, springing a literary wisecrack or telling a pertinent story lifted from the *Saturday Review* or *The New Yorker,* or reading something that had impressed me as interesting.

Even more important as a piece of indirect teaching was my oral reading. I have always loved to read aloud, and people have liked to listen. Whether I read to my daughter or my grandchildren or my long-suffering wife, to friends on request, to an audience in a public hall, to boys at campfire, or to a captive class made little difference; I got the same thrill. Unusually responsive audiences are, of course, meat and drink to people like me; and schoolboys, particularly when what is read is humorous or in dialect or exciting, are probably the most demonstrative listeners in the world. All-time favorites were Leacock's "Hoodoo McFiggin's Christmas," O. Henry's "Ransom of Red Chief," "Gift of the Magi," and "The Cop and the Anthem"; and Fitch's "Ole Skjarsen's First Touchdown" and "Ole's Initiation." My oral reading was not confined, however, to entertainment *per se*. All assigned poetry was read aloud by the master (very few boys could do it well enough): Milton, much of Shakespeare, Burns (in dialect), Browning, and the rest. Many a boy, after such a recitation, has come to my desk with the comment that not until I had read the verse aloud, did he understand it. But regardless of the value of this particular technique and of the subject taught, a teacher must be, at least in part (and fully as much as an orator or a preacher), an actor. To interest his class, he must either be genuinely enthusiastic about what he is teaching—or at least seem to be. Even *Hamlet* can be rendered insufferably dull by one man; and a lesson on the uses of the semicolon can come alive by virtue of the histrionic skill of another.

Beyond all other satisfactions of the teacher, however, is the knowledge that his students are becoming acquainted with the world of ideas. I have spoken of the part played by books in supplying topics for discussion. Just as valuable in developing the students' ability to marshal and organize their thoughts, are their own experiences and powers of observation. The universe rather than merely the world is the present-day adolescent's oyster; and the longer I have taught, the more deeply have I been impressed by the catholicity of his interests and his eagerness to talk about subjects at the moment of greatest importance to him. Not only do I owe my teenage students a great debt for what they have taught me by means of their talks and their papers; but their desire to learn how to express their ideas more clearly and effectively has made the satisfaction of teaching composition, both oral and written, as great as that of teaching literature.

Each year at almost the same time, I have experienced my greatest pedagogical thrill. It should have been hailed by a great shout approximating the fervor of "Eureka!"—"Banzai!"—or "Excelsior!"; but it has always taken the less dramatic form of a husband-to-wife declaration of faith: "Rose, I've done it again! I had just about given up on that gang; but, by Gar, they've come through." What could have brought that on? Simply, that on a set of themes I had been correcting I saw for the first time in that school year that my teaching had taken root. The boys showed clearly that they had learned to consider the reader as their target, to select material with insight and perspective, to organize paragraphs according to a discernible plan, and to make a conscious effort to develop a personal style. The realization of this type of success is a sensation impossible to describe. The nearest thing to it might be what a golfer feels when he gets a hole-in-one or is at last satisfied with his game, or a ball player when he bangs out a line-drive homer.

The satisfactions I have described above can come in education only to the classroom teacher. For that reason I have never aspired to become an administrator. A true teacher does not forsake his profession for money (or for any other reason) if he can possibly continue to teach. This statement is not theory or rationalization. My own experience as a camp director clearly showed me the vast difference between the life of an administrator and that of a teacher. As a result, I have had no doubts whatever as to where I can find peace of mind and contentment in the educational world.

What I have written may sound to outsiders—and even to many insiders—like self-delusion, nostalgia, or ingenuousness. Are these satisfactions, perhaps, the vagaries of a disappointed man or a failure (according to our present set of values)? I can offer no proof to skeptics of my honesty or of the accuracy of my judgment beyond the facts which I have already presented and the additional evidence which one gala event has produced. At my retirement dinner in 1957, I was presented with a huge binder containing letters from former students. From these I am selecting statements which may help to show why I have concluded that the life of a teacher has compensations and rewards enough to satisfy any one who can look beyond the visual range of a materialist.

Dr. Albert Damon:

"... You'll shudder when you read what scientific writing has done to the prose style you tried to teach, but I'll load you with reprints, anyway. I just happen to have a few hundred lying around! ... I suppose the most satisfactory life one can have is to be able to look back and say that it was worth doing and well-spent ... but if I know you, you'll never allow yourself to grow soft contemplating your good works—or your navel. ... What's the big plan for the next forty years?"

Leonard Bernstein:

"... And what an exciting classroom it was! I remember it as an arena in which I first wrestled with—and really understood—scansion, and where for the first time the significant separation between British and American literature was revealed to me. For these things, and many more, I owe you an everlasting debt, and not least for the warmth and joy that you communicated in your teaching. In fact, you taught me a lot about teaching."

Professor Allen Scher, University of Washington, School of Medicine:

"I can remember the very exciting experience of studying English under you. (It was both absolutely and relatively exciting in the otherwise drab curriculum of the Boston Latin School.) First, you made any subject exciting and understandable. Second, you were willing to treat an idea as an idea. Students learned that they could say whatever they felt without fear of ridicule or fear that their ideas would be rejected merely because they were unconventional. I am sure that many, like myself, used your weekly essays as a means to try their wings, to put forward some thoughts as a practice in the use of imagination and logic, and confident that you would reasonably evaluate the premises and the development of the ideas. . . ."

Reverend Charles F. Donovan, S. J., Boston College of Education:

"No teacher ever got me to work so hard in composition. I remember how we used to look forward to those classes when you returned the papers with their two marks. (*Author's Note: one mark for substance; the other, for form and style.*) I can recall how proud I would be to have my heroic efforts rewarded by a 7-8. Of course, there were lower marks. . . . I think I have developed a highly linguistic or verbal approach to education, and I trace this directly back to Joe Hobbs and yourself. If I have any little contribution to make, I feel—and I say this in all simplicity—that you have a real part in it."

Leonard Burkat, Librarian, Boston Symphony Orchestra:

". . . I learned many things in your class—a good deal more than properly belongs under the rubric *English.* I discovered a whole world of art and the intellect that I'd hardly known to exist, and I entered it. I discovered the difference between thought and learning, the difference between knowledge and information, between morality and legality. . . . I have kept some of my old school friendships with classmates who, like me, have wandered far in the world and have known powerful forces and powerful men. We count you among them."

Will Cloney, writer:

". . . In my era, the normal Latin School boy was a working model of an educated robot. . . . I always remember that you disconnected a few wires and transformed an automaton into a chubby little human being. During my teaching years, I tried to follow your example in treating pupils as flesh and blood, not machines . . . I hope, too, that now and then, after reading one of my newspaper stories, you said to yourself, 'That kid must have learned a little from me, after all!' . . . He sure did."

A former student (at the time in deep trouble):

". . . I credit my ability to read and enjoy a book directly to the time you read an O. Henry story to us. The title escapes me, but I do remember the plot. . . . Anyway, I went out and hunted for more O. Henry stories. That started it. I've been reading ever since, and it's a life-saver here. . . ."

Sigmund Stein, druggist, Las Vegas:

". . . I still have the picture in my mind of Phil Marson, fortyish, exacting but fair, ironic but human, socially conscious but not radical, and, above all, an inspiring teacher . . . You may not be aware of what a profound effect you have had on your students. I shall always be grateful to you for arousing my interest in politics and government by assigning the book Lincoln Steffens' *Autobiography*. I was so disturbed and stimulated at the same time by the work that I have never forgotten certain basic lessons in our history."

The above selections are naturally sources of great satisfaction, and the expressions of gratitude are deeply stirring. But equally affecting are reports flowing in to me from near and far about the work my "boys" are doing. These come in the form of conversation, letters, news items, magazine articles, novels, reprints, broadcasts, plays, concerts, TV shows, or gossip columns. What they are doing with their lives—whether in the obscurity of a teaching job in a small town in Vermont or in full view of the entire world—is what interests me above all else. Obviously the knowledge that constructive work is being done by men whom I shall always think of as lads in my classes is the greatest and most abiding satisfaction of all.

To generalize on the basis of one's personal experience and knowledge may be questionable; but in concluding my account, I must chance it. Under almost perfect conditions I began my labors at Boston Latin School. A teacher at that time could reach the heights of achievement in a school traditionally dedicated to high standards of academic performance. When, however, about 1940, the demands for scholarship decreased radically at Harvard and other colleges of quality, problems became so numerous and so complex that the classroom teacher was powerless to solve them. The authority of Harvard was gone, the concern of our own administrative officials about academic excellence became weaker and weaker, and the students—like human beings the world over—did no more than was called for. With the amount of essential preparation diminished to a ridiculous degree, the task of teaching became dull, burdensome, and unpleasant. Instead of being absorbingly occupied with imparting a body of knowledge, I found myself forced to call upon my resourcefulness as an entertainer and my skill in the presentation of interesting rather than difficult or substantial subject matter. True teaching, as veteran members of the faculty knew it could be done, had become almost impossible in the public schools. The results of ignoring the experience of the American past and that of all European nations of the present has constituted nothing less than a national disaster.

To take a place on the mourners' bench and to weep with others would merely increase the volume and intensity of the expressions of grief. Therefore, I determined to do what I could to help remove the rubble, salvage what was usable, and rebuild the structure that had collapsed. My primary objective, then, in this book has been to explain—on the basis of my own experience, observation, and study—what has happened to reduce the work of the classroom teacher to that of baby-sitter and what can be done to restore learning as his basic concern and thus to renew his self-respect. Unless appropriate action is taken at once, it may come too late. It may well be education's last chance.